W9-DAG-024

DRAMA AND SOCIETY
IN THE AGE OF JONSON

By the same Author
*
EXPLORATIONS
SOME SHAKESPEAREAN THEMES
AN APPROACH TO HAMLET
FURTHER EXPLORATIONS

Drama & Society
in the Age of Jonson

L. C. KNIGHTS

King Edward VII Professor of English Literature
in the University of Cambridge

Chatto & Windus

LONDON : 1968

Published by
Chatto & Windus Ltd
42 William IV Street
London W.C.2
*
Clarke, Irwin & Co. Ltd.
Toronto

First published 1937
Second impression 1951
Third impression 1957
Fourth impression 1962
Fifth impression 1968

SBN 7011 0874 6

Printed in Great Britain by
William Lewis (Printers) Ltd
Cardiff

To
MY FATHER & MOTHER

CONTENTS

vii

FOREWORD

THE undertaking of this piece of research was, perhaps, more hazardous than such things usually are, since at the outset it was impossible to guess how profitable it would be. Most critics of the 'great period' of English drama make some reference to the economic and social background of the time, just as most historians draw on a few of the plays for 'evidence'. But neither critic nor historian has made a study of economic conditions and the drama, *in conjunction*, in order to throw light on one of the more important problems of our own time: the relation between economic activities and general culture.

The purpose of *Drama and Society in the Age of Jonson* is, I think, sufficiently indicated in the Introduction. The questions raised there concerning 'culture', tradition and environment are questions which anyone alive to the present must try to answer; they do not, I have insisted, admit of an easy solution. But a genuine contemporary interest is unavoidably more than an interest in the present, and the first necessity is to investigate the background of culture in a period when there is, by common consent, a healthy national culture to be studied. The late Elizabethan and early Stuart period was a natural choice. In this book I suggest a few of the intercommunications between economic and social conditions and one of the cultural forms of the period.

In Part I, I have assembled some of the more important facts about the economic environment in the late sixteenth century and the early seventeenth century (Chapters I and II); I have tried to present the social significance of those facts (Chapter III); and I have sketched some of the main ideas that were brought to bear on social and economic problems (Chapter IV). Part II consists of a study of plays by Jonson, Dekker, Heywood, Middleton and Massinger, (*a*) to determine whether there is any relationship between the events described in Part I and the bulk of Jacobean comedy; if there is a relationship to suggest its nature; (*b*) to see if there is any relationship between

ix

literary excellence and a given state of society—including the 'popular' ideas and attitudes of that society.

Later I hope to present a fuller account of Elizabethan-Jacobean culture in relation to its environment—an account, that is, of the communal aspects of Elizabethan life in town, village and 'household' on the one hand, and of the agents of transmission—religion, education and literature—on the other; a study of the contemporary reading public will join hands with a more comprehensive account of the non-economic aspects of economic activities than the limits of the present book allow. In this way it may be possible to provide a satisfactory basis for comparison with the present.

The facts used in Chapter I ('The Inherited Economic Order') and in Chapter II ('The Development of Capitalist Enterprise') are drawn almost entirely from the standard works on economic history (particularly from Cunningham, Ashley, Unwin and Lipson), from Scott's *Joint-Stock Companies* and Heckscher's *Mercantilism*, and from a large number of specialist monographs. H. M. Robertson's *Aspects of the Rise of Economic Individualism* was particularly helpful. Chapter III ('New Elements in the National Life') draws on the historians, but embodies also the result of a good deal of personal investigation. In Chapter IV ('Social Theory') my debt to *Religion and the Rise of Capitalism* is great and obvious, but the illustrations, unless otherwise stated, are taken direct from the sources. Part II (Chapters V to X) on 'The Dramatists' is, I think, as original as criticism of this kind can be, but here and throughout I have made due acknowledgements in my footnotes. Appendix A ('Elizabethan Prose'—which together with the present Introduction and Chapter VI appeared first in *Scrutiny*) is included because it contains relevant illustration and suggests some further lines of work; Appendix B ('Seventeenth-Century Melancholy'—reproduced, with the Editor's permission, from the *Criterion*), because it gives an interesting sidelight on the extra-literary relations of literature.

It remains to record some more particular obligations: to

Christ's College, Cambridge, where my tenure of the Adelaide
Stoll Bachelor Research Scholarship in 1930–31 made it possible to begin a piece of work continued since with many inter-
ruptions; to Dr. G. B. Harrison for some valuable information;
to Dr. R. H. Tawney, not only for his published work, but for
personal encouragement and advice, particularly for telling me
to read *The Lives of the Berkeleys*; to my wife, for invaluable
help in preparing the book for publication; and to F. R.
Leavis—but here the debt is altogether too large for public
acknowledgement.

L. C. KNIGHTS
Manchester University, December 1936

ABBREVIATIONS

Ashley, I:

Ashley, W. J., *An Introduction to English Economic History and Theory, Part I, The Middle Ages.*

Ashley, II:

An Introduction to English Economic History and Theory, Part II, The End of the Middle Ages.

Cunningham, I:

Cunningham, W., *The Growth of English Industry and Commerce, The Middle Ages* (4th edn. 1905).

Cunningham, II:

The Growth of English Industry and Commerce, Modern Times (5th edn. 1912).

Lipson, II and III:

Lipson, E., *An Economic History of England*, Vols. II and III, *The Age of Mercantilism.*

Scott, I, II, and III:

Scott, W. R., *The Constitution and Finance of English, Scottish and Irish Joint-Stock Companies to 1720*, Vols. I, II, and III.

T. and P., I, II, III:

Tudor Economic Documents, ed. R. H. Tawney and Eileen Power, Vols. I, II, and III.

Religion and Capitalism

R. H. Tawney, *Religion and the Rise of Capitalism.*

Tawney, Wilson:

Wilson, Thomas, *A Discourse upon Usury*, edited with an Introduction by R. H. Tawney.

Unwin, *Gilds*:

Unwin, George, *The Gilds and Companies of London.*

Unwin, *Industrial Organization*:

Unwin, George, *Industrial Organization in the Sixteenth and Seventeenth Centuries.*

In Part II the figures in brackets following a reference to the scene of a play indicate the volume and page of the standard edition of the dramatist concerned.—See Bibliography.

SHAKESPEARE AND PROFIT INFLATIONS

IN spite of the frequency with which 'the effects of environment', 'cultural superstructure' and similar phrases appear in contemporary discussion we are still largely in the dark concerning the nature of the problem, or problems, that are covered by such terms.   When we discuss the relations between economic conditions and 'culture' what, exactly, are we talking about?

The need for investigation can be indicated by a few quotations.   In the Preface to the *Critique of Political Economy* Marx wrote:

> The methods of production in material life determine the general character of the social, political, and spiritual processes of life.   It is not the consciousness of men that determines their being, but, on the contrary, their social being determines their consciousness.[1]

Later Marxists have not got any further in showing the nature of the influence of 'methods of production' on 'consciousness', on the 'spiritual processes of life'. Thus R. D. Charques:

> It is necessary to bear in mind the simple truth that a people's culture takes form and colour from the economic ordering of society.   It is part of the civilized superstructure

[1] *A Contribution to the Critique of Political Economy*, tr. N. I. Stone, Second Edition, p. 11.

of art, morals, religion, law and the rest which is built up on the basis of the productive relations in society.[1]

This, one would have thought, deserved some application and expansion from those who were intuitively conscious of its significance; but Mr Charques is not alone in failing to elucidate the 'simple truth', and 'form and colour' remain mere counters. A simple relationship is of course constantly assumed. John Strachey, for example, finds that the Catholic Revival of recent years is 'just what we should expect'.

> For life, with the growth of large-scale production, is becoming less and less individual and more and more communal again. Thus, for anyone who can achieve religious belief at all, the Catholic form of Christianity is becoming increasingly appropriate.[2]

Such boldness in grasping the prickly subject of religion prepares us for the facility with which Mr Strachey explains literature in terms of economics; here is his account of the genesis of *Ash Wednesday*:

> Since writing *The Waste Land* Mr Eliot, encouraged no doubt by the 1922–1929 period of capitalist recovery, has left the despair of the Waste Land behind him and taken up the typical position of a highly intellectual reactionary.[3]

And for the Marxist the past presents no more difficulties than the present:

> A tasteless welter of conflicting styles was in the very nature of industrialism. Keats begins his career by re-writing the myth of *Endymion* after a prolonged study of Spenser, and ends it by writing *Hyperion* after a prolonged study of Milton.[4]

[1] 'Literature and the Working-Class Student', *Adult Education*, September 1934, p. 50.
[2] *The Coming Struggle for Power*, p. 61. Is this, one wonders, the kind of 'explanation' that Lenin had in mind when he remarked that 'in explaining our programme we must necessarily explain the actual historical and economic roots of religion'? [3] *Ibid.*, p. 221.
[4] Philip Henderson, *Literature and a Changing Civilisation*, p. 78.

Nor have non-Marxists proved more illuminating; Mr Keynes, for example, has allowed himself to remark:

> We were just in a financial position to afford Shakespeare at the moment when he presented himself. ['Don't you think', one is tempted to ask, 'we might afford just one more now that the slump is over?'] ... I offer it as a thesis for examination by those who like rash generalizations, that by far the larger proportion of the world's great writers and artists have flourished in the atmosphere of buoyancy, exhilaration and the freedom from economic cares felt by the governing class, which is engendered by profit inflations.[1]

It is hard to know what purpose remarks of this kind are meant to serve. Marx was concerned with forging a practical weapon, and some narrowing of vision was, perhaps, necessary;[2] the other writers seem to be engaged in nothing more serious than intellectual flag-waving (Mr Keynes is obviously amusing himself). But what these quotations show—they could be multiplied—is that if we are to avoid the vaguest generalities we have to give a good deal of hard thought to certain fundamental questions. Are the non-economic activities that we call 'culture'—forms of activity that are engaged in as ends, not as means—in any way related to bread-and-butter activities as effect and cause? If so, exactly how are they determined by economic activities? Are there any other factors besides the purely economic

---

[1] *A Treatise on Money*, II, p. 154.

[2] 'Marx and I are ourselves partly to blame for the fact that younger writers sometimes lay more stress on the economic side than is due to it. We had to emphasize this main principle in opposition to our adversaries, who denied it, and we had not always the time, the place or the opportunity to allow the other events involved in the interaction to come into their rights. . . . And I cannot exempt many of the more recent "Marxists" from this reproach, for the most wonderful rubbish has been produced from this quarter too' (Karl Marx and Friedrich Engels, *Correspondence 1846–1895, A Selection* (Martin Lawrence), p. 477).

3

ones that determine the culture of a particular place and time? Is there any essential difference between the popular culture of the present and that of, say, the sixteenth and seventeenth centuries? How has the relationship between earning a living and 'end' activities altered since the Industrial Revolution? What do we mean by 'economic'? And what do we mean by 'culture'? These and many related questions need to be answered (indeed the questions need to be more precisely formulated), not for academic reasons, but in order to help us to achieve a humanly satisfactory attitude towards our most pressing problems of politics, economics and education, to decide what truth—what meaning, even—is in such remarks as, 'With the victory of Socialism is bound up the whole future of art',[1] or, 'A change in society is more imperative . . . than the retention of this or that tradition of literature'.[2]

The exasperating haziness of all those who have attempted to make some correlation between economic activities and culture is not due merely to the lack of a satisfactory definition of the latter term. Perhaps it is due (at any rate one may suggest it provisionally) to the fact that 'the materialist interpretation of history' has not yet been pushed far enough. It is one thing to say that 'in every historical epoch, the prevailing mode of economic production and exchange, and the social organization necessarily following from it, form the basis upon which is built up, *and from which alone can be explained, the* political and *intellectual history of that epoch*',[3] and another to attempt to sub-

[1] Ralph Fox, 'The Relation of Literature to Dialectical Materialism', *Aspects of Dialectical Materialism*, p. 69.

[2] R. D. Charques, *Adult Education*, September 1934, p. 52.

[3] Engels, Preface to the English translation of the *Manifesto of the Communist Party*, p. 6.

4

stantiate the phrase which I have italicized in detail. Methods of production and cultural superstructure may be related in the realm of abstract dialectic, but no one (anthropologists dealing with primitive peoples apart) has yet established the relation in terms of fact and experience.

One reason is that the subject, as usually formulated, is too large and general. It can only be discussed at all in relation to a particular place and time, and then it is seen to split up into a multitude of smaller problems, a bewildering complexity supervening upon the simplicity of the dialectical formulation. The first necessity is to narrow the field. If, for example, we ask ourselves how we should set about determining the relations between dramatic literature (leaving aside religion, lyric poetry, painting, pastimes . . .) and 'the prevailing mode of economic production and exchange' in the Shakespearian period, we are more likely to establish a few useful conclusions than if we continue to discuss the relation of one abstraction to another. It is that question that I propose briefly to consider.

To the economic historian the period covered by the life of Shakespeare is of unusual interest. On the one hand there was the large-scale development of capitalist enterprise, on the other there were the traditional forms of organization of trade and industry, forms which had not yet become anachronistic 'survivals'; the result of the double aspect of the age ('medieval' and 'modern') being that the reign of James I was 'perhaps the period of the greatest economic confusion in our history'. Now the drama, more obviously than any other form of art, is a social product; in the plays produced in the early seventeenth century, if anywhere (it was pre-eminently a period when the theatre was flourishing), we should be able to trace the connection with the economic bases of society.

We may begin with those plays which have a more or less

5   B

overt social reference. None of them, we notice, is a dramatization of an economic problem or consciously intended as propaganda for this or that form of economic organization, and only a few of them—*The Miseries of Enforced Marriage* is an example—are meant to make the audience think about questions of social morality. (There is no dramatization of the Miseries of Monopoly.) What we do find, however, is that the material on which the dramatists work—in comedy and history play—is drawn from—has an immediate reference to—the movements, the significant figures of contemporary life; the satire on usurers, the profiteers and the newly rich, on social ambition and the greed for money, can be abundantly illustrated. And the social interests that are drawn on are not those of one class alone. The narrowing of the range of active interests in Fletcher and in the romances and comedies of the Caroline dramatists, with a corresponding lessening of intensity, is an unmistakable sign of decadence.

Of the dramatists handling social themes Jonson is undoubtedly the greatest, but comparison makes plain that his unique qualities as an artist spring from a common ground that he shares with the majority of his contemporaries. That common ground is represented by certain habits of observation, by certain beliefs or attitudes (the better word) concerning human desires, 'their relative worth and dignity'. In his handling of ambition, greed, lust, acquisitiveness and so on he implicitly, but clearly, refers to a more than personal scheme of values. Jonson in short was working in a tradition. What we have to determine is where that tradition 'came from'.[1]

[1] To the artist the value of a living tradition is that it allows him to concentrate upon his task as a poet; he does not have to do everything for himself. The distance between Jonson's work and Dekker's is the measure of what he actually had to do 'for himself', and proof

The poise and sureness with which Jonson confronts the significant developments of his age, strong in his knowledge of what are, and what are not, fundamental human qualities, will be illustrated in these pages. These significant developments—most of them—were aspects of the growth of capitalism; and company-promoting, 'projecting' and industrial enterprise certainly formed an important part of the world which Jonson and his fellows observed, the world which gave them their knowledge of human nature. It is equally obvious that the standards of judgement that they brought to bear were not formed in that new world of industrial enterprise. They belonged to an older world which was still 'normal', a world of small communities in which, as a recent economic historian has remarked, 'human problems can be truly perceived, which in larger social structures must more or less necessarily be sacrificed'.[1]

Here, I think, is suggested one line of connexion between dramatic literature and the economic ordering of society. If this account is true it is plain that the social dramatists owed a great deal to the traditional economic morality inherited from the Middle Ages. Although that morality was given precise formulation and transmitted by the Church (amongst other agencies), it had been forged in small local units of trade and industry. It was forged because it was useful; in a subsistence economy a community could only exist at all by acting, in the main, as a regulated community. When Dekker damns the 'City doctrine'—

enough of genius. But the point is that Jonson had *something* in common with Dekker, with Heywood, with the journalists and moralists of the common people, whereas the few poets and novelists who count at the present day not only cannot share, they are inevitably hostile to, the attitudes of suitable readers of the *Star*, the *Sunday Express*, or the *Tatler*.

[1] Heckscher, *Mercantilism*, I, p. 42.

Nature sent man into the world, alone,
Without all company, but to care for one—

it is clear that he has inherited a morality which the Middle
Ages had found—shall we say?—expedient.

To say, however, that some of the general attitudes which
Jonson manipulates into art can be traced fairly directly to
certain 'methods of production' does not in the least support the Marxist analysis; it merely suggests a doubt of its
relevance. For the point has been made in saying that the
economic organization from which the bulk of Elizabethan
social morality derived was that of the small, local community *in which 'human problems can be truly perceived'*—
an organization, then, that was not merely 'economic'—not
merely determined by 'economic' motives. But what is
'economic'? Clearly, the sense in which a medieval town-
ship was an 'economic' unit is very different from the sense
in which a large-scale industrial undertaking is 'economic'.
The category, in short, is, here, a misleading abstraction.

An examination of the social themes of the Elizabethan-
Jacobean drama will take us no further than this. But
overt social references form only a small part of that drama;
what we have next to enquire is whether economic conceptions such as 'class' (expressing the productive relationships
of society) can be used to explain more general aspects of
the plays of the period.

At this point a parenthetical return to the 'rash general-
ization' which Mr Keynes based on his analysis of the
economic situation at the end of the sixteenth century, may
be found useful: the remark 'that by far the larger proportion of the world's great writers and artists have flourished
in the atmosphere of buoyancy, exhilaration and the freedom from economic cares felt by the governing class, which
is engendered by profit inflations'. Having noted an important error in fact—few of the Elizabethan governing

8

class actually enjoyed 'freedom from economic cares'—we may ask ourselves a few questions: Who got the bulk of the boom profits? How did the profit-makers spend their money? (In encouraging the arts, or in making further investments? Or did scapegrace heirs direct the new wealth to the notoriously underpaid writers?) More important, why did the profit inflation of 'modern days in the United States'—to which Mr Keynes compares the Elizabethan 'bull' movement—produce what it did instead of a national culture? Of course, Shakespeare's theatre could not have existed if the country had been in the depths of economic misery; but to say this is not to say anything important.

It is, however, true that the Elizabethan drama owed, if not its existence, at least its fortunate development to the persistent patronage of the governing class, a class drawing its wealth mainly from the land and conscious of the encroachment of the 'new men' of commerce and industry. May it not, then, reflect the 'ideology' of that class in more subtle ways than can be explored in the explicit social attitudes ('popular' rather than 'aristocratic') which have been examined? To ask the question is to display its ineptitude. It can only be answered affirmatively by some such formula as that 'Shakespeare's tragic outlook on the world was consequential upon his being the dramatic expression of the feudal aristocracy which in Elizabeth's day had lost their former dominating position' [1]—a remark which, since it

---

[1] 'Shakespeare Through Russian Eyes, A condensation and free translation of two articles, by Lunacharsky and P. S. Kogan', made by Stephen Garry, *The Listener*, 27th December 1934. For another (Marxist) view see 'Marx and Shakespeare', by T. A. Jackson, *International Literature*, No. 2, 1936. Shakespeare, one is glad to learn, was a 'healthy, well-poised, sceptical, melioristic' humanist, 'somewhat to the Left of the centre of advanced bourgeois opinion'. 'To expect from Shakespeare (in between the years 1590–1612) the same appreciation of the revolutionary potentialities of the proletariat as

clearly does not spring from the complexity of full experience of Shakespeare's poetry, does not lead back to anything that can be grasped and discussed.[1]

The influence of 'the governing class' was subtler than
that. It was shown in the way in which Elizabethan dramatic verse reflected their interest in rhetoric, in psychology
and in morals, interests which their economic position
allowed them to cultivate, but which can only be explained
in terms of their education, their religious outlook and
their pastimes (music, we remember, was almost as important as fencing). Education, religion and pastimes, we
are told, can all be related to 'the prevailing mode of
economic production and exchange', but that, at present, is
an article of faith. And the Marxist diagnosis (with the
implication, here, that cultural attributes were *useful* to the
leisured class) seems curiously irrelevant when we realize
that the interests which I have noted permeated the whole
of society: the rhetoric of Shakespeare or Chapman is
paralleled at a lower level by the rhetoric of Kyd; the crude
psychology of the upper-class 'Character' is surpassed by
the shrewd folk observation that was to find its supreme
expression in Bunyan; and if the plays of Chapman or
Tourneur gratified a highly developed taste for moral
casuistry, the pamphlets of Dekker indicate that his popular audience had at least some healthy interest in un-
varnished morals. Above all, there was no barrier of
language between higher and lower such as separates the
different ranges of the contemporary reading public. The
achievement of the great age of English drama (the twenty
or twenty-five years, say, from *Troilus and Cressida* and
was possible to the genius of Marx and Engels *in and after 1844*,
would be to expect an anachronistic miracle.'

[1] I do not see any point in conducting an argument at the level of
Mr Shaw's account of Shakespeare's 'snobbery'. We all know the
passages about 'stinking breath', etc.

Henry IV) was due to the bringing together and the lively interplay of different interests within a fairly homogeneous culture, at a time when 'the art of the people was as closely mingled with the art of the coteries as was the speech of the people that delighted in rhythmical animation, in idiom, in images . . . with the unchanging speech of the poets'.[1] Elizabethan drama, even in its higher ranges, was not the expression of a 'class' culture at all.

So far as I can see there is only one other correlation between Elizabethan drama and the economic ordering of society that it is possible to attempt. It is an essential point that is made by the remark that 'Shakespeare did not create his own language'—his achievement would have been impossible 'if English had not already been there'[2]—and one can work backwards from Shakespeare's English to the community which forged it as a vital medium. The advantage that Shakespeare enjoyed in being able to exploit to the full a popular idiom is paralleled by—is, in fact, part of—corresponding advantages in habits of perception and discrimination, in emotional and intellectual organization—in sensibility. What those advantages were is revealed by comparison with that 'impersonal language that has come, not out of individual life, nor out of life at all, but out of necessities of commerce, of parliament, of board schools, of hurried journeys by rail'.[3] They were the advantages that spring from 'living at first hand', in close touch with 'primary production'.[4] To-day, unless he is exceptionally

[1] W. B. Yeats, 'What is Popular Poetry?' *Essays*, p. 12.

[2] F. R. Leavis, *For Continuity*, pp. 164, 215. The context of both phrases is relevant to this discussion.

[3] W. B. Yeats, *Essays*, p. 373. 'One must not forget that the death of language, the substitution of phrases as nearly impersonal as algebra for words and rhythms varying from man to man, is but a part of the tyranny of impersonal things.' *Ibid.*

[4] For expansion and illustration of this statement see Appendix A, 'Elizabethan Prose'.

11

lucky, the ordinary man has to make a deliberate effort to penetrate a hazy medium which smothers his essential human nature, which interposes between him and things as they are; a medium formed by the lowest common denominator of feelings, perceptions and ideas acceptable to the devitalized products of a machine economy. The luck of the Elizabethan in *not* having such a veil to pierce, in being able to obtain whatever satisfactions were possible at first hand, was of course due to 'the prevailing methods of production and exchange', to the fact that mass-production, standardization and division of labour, although not unknown, were still exceptional and undeveloped. But—we are back to the point that I made earlier—to say that the qualities embodied in Shakespeare's English had an economic base, is to remind ourselves that making a living was not merely a *means*, and that the 'economic' activities which helped to mould that supremely expressive medium fostered qualities (perceptions and general habits of response) that were not 'economic' at all. We remind ourselves, in short, of the dangerous facility with which the word 'economic' tempts us to beg the essential questions. Dramatic poetry of course was only one part of a larger whole, but it seems that only along lines similar to those that I have indicated can we hope to map the social and economic bases of Elizabethan-Jacobean culture and to make some profitable correlations. This book is offered as a start.

THE BACKGROUND

CHAPTER ONE

THE INHERITED ECONOMIC
ORDER UNDER ELIZABETH

THERE is no harm in simplifying so long as we do not mistake our simplifications for more than they are. It is convenient to say, then, that the economic activities of Englishmen in the late Elizabethan and early Stuart period fall into two patterns. The basic pattern was the economic organization directly inherited from the Middle Ages, whilst superimposed on this was the pattern formed by the development of capitalist enterprise. The necessary qualifications are obvious. What we may call the traditional order was not static; since the fourteenth century modification and development had been slow but continuous. Even more obviously the newer organizations (most of them had a medieval ancestry) were changing very rapidly indeed, and, however we define 'capitalist', many forms of capitalist activity existed side by side. Nor were the two patterns, or modes, distinct; they both interacted and merged. And we have to remember too that outward economic forms tend to persist when the functions that they were designed to express have changed, so that, as in the later history of the gilds, it is often difficult to tell whether we are dealing with a survival from another age or with a new development.

All the same the economic life of England under Elizabeth and the first Stuarts can best be understood when we are conscious of its two aspects. It was during this period that modern forms of commercial and industrial enterprise took shape, and my account of Tudor-Stuart economic life will be mainly concerned with these. But it is important to realize that they *were* new, and that men thought of them as new. The basic economic activities were still, very largely, traditional.

For the sake of clarity later it is necessary to give here a brief summary of the main features of economic life in England in the Middle Ages. By far the most important was the organization of agriculture—the system of manor and village and open fields. Except in the wool trade production in each district was carried on at a subsistence level; it supplied the immediate needs of the local population or, at most, of those who were directly connected with the locality. Society was organized to obtain a living from the land. Feudal tenure, for example, was based on service and inheritance; it ensured, that is, a regular succession of those who could be made to work the land or who could be made responsible for its working. The essential function of feudal society may be slightly obscured in the upper ranges; it is clear enough to need no stressing in the manorial communities that formed the base of the pyramid. The bulk of the population were tillers of the soil. Of these the largest class were the villeins, who worked the land of their immediate lord, who subsisted on their share in the arable fields, meadow, woods and common pasture, and who inherited their customary rights and duties from their fathers.

The civilization of medieval England was a local civilization. Churchmen, nobles and administrative officers acted as a unifying and centripetal force; but even the greater landowners, journeying from manor to manor, 'lived on their own', and the opinions and attitudes of the village priest did not differ very much from those of his parishioners. The modern village (most of the farmers live outside it)

16

only gives a feeble suggestion of the extent to which the medieval village was a *community*. Not only was it—except for a very few necessities—economically self-sufficient, it functioned as a unit, and a common way of life was determined by the labour in the open fields, by attendance at the parish church and the manorial courts, by the mere fact of living in a small cluster of houses along the village street.

It is easy to understand why medieval thought was dominated by tradition, the custom of the community. In the towns the organization of the manor was paralleled, in many respects, by the organization of the gilds. They too expressed a strong corporate spirit, and ensured, not 'progress' and a rising 'standard of living', but subsistence at a familiar level. They were based, of course, on local privilege, and in some ways they may have borne hardly on the native non-gildsman as well as on the 'foreigner', though by the end of the Middle Ages there were few who did not belong to some form of professional association.[1] But protection of the rights of members as a body was not their only function; they regulated the relations of individuals of the same trade, and consumers' interests were considered in the provisions for fair dealing and maintaining the quality of the goods sold:[2] in the—comparatively small—towns a sense of community was not confined to the separate crafts.

The structure of society as a whole was determined by the conditions of life in small economic groups. It is usual to speak of medieval society as a fairly rigid class system,

[1] Unwin, *Gilds*, 172.
[2] Described, for example, by Ashley, I, pp. 74-76, 90-91. Compare, Unwin, *Gilds*, p. 172: 'Nor was the corporate spirit by any means a purely selfish one. The jealous spirit of professional honour which is recognized as one of the most important contributions to modern civilization, was an essential part of it.'

with a rough equality prevailing within the different strata. But the conception of class is misleading when applied to the Middle Ages. In the first place, the functional groups often cut across the lines that we recognize as class divisions: even a large landowner had his place, 'belonged', in a community which included men of all ranks, and the villeins on the manors where he resided, as well as his large and miscellaneous 'household',[1] felt a relationship with him rather than with villeins and retainers elsewhere. Secondly, medieval man was conscious of *status*, rather than of class; conscious, that is, of his position and function within a local community, rather than of membership in a nation-wide order of more or less equal wealth. In the country and in the towns producing to meet a regular local demand, status tended to be fixed and traditional—the common analogy for the state was the human body: the various parts were members one of another, but each member had his place and his particular function—and on the whole a man's expectations in life were determined by the position in society in which he happened to be born. 'The ordinary object of ambition was not so much that of rising out of one's grade, but of standing well in that grade; the citizen did not aim at being a knight, but at being warden and master of his gild, or alderman and mayor of his town.'[2] In the few larger towns there must always have been some opportunity for individual acquisition that would lead to change of status,[3] but industrial and commercial enterprise

[1] For the importance of the household and 'housekeeping' see below, p. 112 ff.

[2] Cunningham, I, p. 464. And see Holdsworth, *History of English Law*, II, pp. 464-466, on status.

[3] In London, as early as the fourteenth century, one can see the embryo of a society in which the old distinctions were to become irrelevant; gild membership, for example, meant one thing if you were a leather-seller, another if you were merely a saddlemaker. See Unwin, *Gilds*, chaps. vi and vii.

was not yet—and could not be—sufficiently developed to become a serious disruptive force.

In medieval England, to adapt the summary of an American historian, 'social organization was marked by three general characteristics: the close connexion of the whole population with the soil; the large corporate or coöperative element in the life of the people; and the extent to which the whole structure rested upon custom, not upon either established law or written contract'.[1]   Two other, related, aspects of medieval life remain to be noticed.   In the Middle Ages activities connected with getting a living included a very great deal that cannot be brought under the modern category 'economic'.   The agricultural worker has, of course, left us no 'evidence', but the accepted account of gild life will serve to make the point.   'The brotherhood', says Ashley, 'was unlike a modern society aiming at some particular material advantage, in that it entered into a great part of everyday life.   Sick gildsmen were visited, and wine and food sent to them from the feasts; brethren who had fallen into poverty were relieved; their daughters were dowered for marriage or the convent; and when a member died his funeral was attended by the brethren and the due rites provided for.'[2]   As Unwin reminds us, the daily work carried on in the halls of the Livery companies at the end of the fourteenth century represented 'a combination of the activities of a ducal estate-office with those of a charity organization society, and a department for technical education'.[3]   But it was not merely that the gilds engaged in social and religious activities; their whole functioning can only be understood when we are aware of its extra-economic aspects.

[1] E. P. Cheyney, *Social Changes in England in the Sixteenth Century as reflected in Contemporary Literature*, Part I, Rural Changes, p. 19, and cf. p. 106, *op. cit.*
[2] Ashley, I, p. 76, and cf. pp. 91-92 *op. cit.*
[3] *Gilds and Companies*, p. 192.

The apprenticeship system, for example, regulated competition whilst ensuring a regular succession of skilled craftsmen; it also ensured continuity of a tradition that was more than the tradition of a craft. 'It was an essential feature of the medieval system', says Lipson, 'that the apprentice should reside with the master, whose duty it was to instil social virtues into the boy as well as to teach him knowledge of a craft.' It was not until the eighteenth century that the relations of master and apprentice were 'reconstituted on a basis of wage-contract, a cash nexus supplying the place of the parental bond'.[1]

So too medieval economic activities were not guided by purely economic considerations—as these were understood in the nineteenth century. Theories of the just price, of intrinsic value, of usury, of fair dealing, of the relations of master and servant, were evolved by clerical theorists, embodied in canon law, and enforced by the courts. By the end of the thirteenth century there was a large body of positive law and a still larger body of common opinion concerning the rights and duties of men in their social and economic relationships.[2] Needless to say, the avaricious of all classes prevented common practice from reaching more than its usual approximation to ideal theory. But the point is not that the economic theory of the schoolmen was neglected, but that it was evolved at all, and that its general validity was not questioned even by those who ignored it. Dr Tawney tells us that, 'The first fundamental assumption which is taken over by the sixteenth century [from the Middle Ages] is that the ultimate standard of human institutions and activities is

---

[1] Lipson, II, pp. 42-43. Compare, in a different field: 'The great households were very notable social institutions and schools of manners if not of learning' (Cunningham, I, p. 241).

[2] Described by Ashley, I, chap. iii; II, chap. vi. I am aware of the late medieval qualifications, with regard to usury for example.

religion'.[1]   It is better to say, as he himself points out, that the Middle Ages were not conscious of a division between secular and religious in the way in which we are conscious of it.   The schoolmen who formulated standards for business dealing were not thought of as dictating from one sphere to another, because, to a large extent, they were only making explicit what was implicit in the functioning of a scarcity economy.   It is not to deny the importance or the moral value of the canonist doctrine to say that 'the community could only subsist by acting, in the main, as a regulated community'.[2]

As will be seen, many of the ideas and attitudes springing originally from the medieval economic order were current throughout the sixteenth century and even later.   Their 'hardy vitality' [3] was not merely due to conservative tenacity —a cultural lag; the ideas survived because conditions similar to those in which they emerged were still a widespread and effective part of contemporary life.   When considering Tudor economic life we tend to think mainly of the changes—enclosures, the expansion of industry and overseas trade—which indicate the important developments of the future, and certainly there is no need to minimize their importance.   But a slight redirection of attention is sufficient to bring into focus the traditional order—forms of economic effort and organization that a medieval man would have found it easy to understand—on which the newer elements supervened.

Political history is responsible for many false perspectives,

[1] *Religion and the Rise of Capitalism*, p. 19.
[2] See p. 7, above.
[3] 'The hardy vitality of medieval municipal policy' (Heckscher, *Mercantilism*, II. p. 269).

and one of them is due to the almost exclusive attention that it gives to specifically urban activities. One has to emphasize the commonplace that in the sixteenth century—indeed until the Industrial Revolution—the main business of the country lay in agriculture.[1] This alone was sufficient to ensure a high degree of continuity of tradition from the preceding centuries. Moreover, even after the great enclosure movement under the Tudors the greater part of the countryside was still cultivated on the old open-field system, and—apart from the increase of sheep-farming—there had been no change in agricultural method comparable to that which was to take place in the eighteenth century. Villein right had been transformed into a variety of tenures, and there was an increasingly numerous class of landless labourers. But the copyholders—the bulk of the village population—held their land by customary payments which corresponded to the customary services of the villein; when forced to defend their rights they appealed to 'immemorial custom' and 'times beyond the memory of man'. The manor had decayed as an administrative unit—though for centuries to come the manor-house was to be a dominant factor in village life—but the village itself, even if affected by the growth of the domestic system, was still an isolated and, to a large extent, a self-sufficient community. Not only was English civilization in the sixteenth century still closely in touch with the soil, there is an important sense in which it was still a local rather than a national civilization.

And apart from agriculture economic life contained patterns that are recognizably medieval, even though modified from their original form. Anything approaching exact evidence is, of course, not available, but for many individual craftsmen conditions of work must have been very similar to

[1] For approximate figures see Ashley, *Economic Organization of England*, p. 119.

what they were in the fourteenth century. Writing in the early years of this century, Unwin observed:

> Even at the present day the butcher and the baker, the joiner and the builder, the working shoemaker and tailor of a small town are often little removed from the simplicity of the handicraft system. Capital and labour are both represented in the trading master craftsman who sells the product of both these factors direct to the consumer; and the thrifty journeyman who wishes to start business on his own account does not meet with any insuperable obstacle.[1]

Differentiation of function in industry had, of course, begun in the Middle Ages—between capital and labour, between making and selling, and between the various branches of some forms of manufacture—and it had been carried much further by the sixteenth century. But it was a process that was very far indeed from being highly or uniformly developed. 'Quite a considerable amount of the industry by which the elementary needs of the community were supplied ... continued in the sixteenth and seventeenth centuries to be carried on under the limited but stable conditions of a purely local market.'[2] And in all the 'local' trades—victualling, shoemaking, tailoring, etc.—differentiation, if begun at all, was still in its early stages.[3] If, in the medieval gild system, 'the master craftsman producing work on materials of his own and selling it direct to the consumer' was 'the predominant figure',[4] he still played an important part under Elizabeth. Even the domestic system left room for the semi-independent small master.

If one turns from the individual to the organization of the

---

[1] *Industrial Organization*, p. 61.   [2] *Ibid.*
[3] Unwin, *op. cit.*, pp. 61-69. Cf. Ashley, II, p. 103: 'In the smaller crafts and the smaller centres of industry conditions long remained patriarchal after they had been greatly modified elsewhere'.
[4] *Industrial Organization*, p. 67.

older trades and industries it is the difference between the Tudor-Stuart and the medieval gild system that is most immediately apparent: strictly, it is impossible to speak any longer of '*a* gild system'—the gilds and companies exhibit too many different characteristics. By the sixteenth century few of the gilds were simple, homogeneous bodies each expressing a common interest. In the greater companies at least the larger masters had got control, and the upper ranks of the hierarchy—those who were 'of the livery'—tended more and more to represent a purely mercantile interest, separate from, if not opposed to, the manufacturing interest of the small masters, who now, in each company, composed the yeomanry (in the Tudor period the journeymen's interests seem to have been hardly represented at all).[1] This fundamental opposition between craftsman and trader— often a large middleman or exporter not bred to the craft— explains a good many of the opposing policies that are found in Tudor and early Stuart industrial history. The last effective transformation of the gilds is seen in the incorporated companies of small masters which, in several instances in the early seventeenth century, were formed out of the yeomanry of the greater companies. But any form of gild organization proved, in the long run, incompatible with capitalist expansion. Most of the newer industries had, of course, developed from the first on different lines; but even in the industries organized on a gild basis the class of small masters —who had once made common cause against the merchants —tended to split into a body of larger manufacturing employers on the one hand, and a mass of journeymen on the other.[2] This process was well advanced by the time of the Whig revolution, and the surviving gilds and companies were soon to be little more than dignified relics. The his-

[1] Unwin, *Gilds*, pp. 227–228.
[2] Unwin, *Industrial Organization*, pp. 198-201.

24

tory of Trade Unionism, it is worth noting, begins in the eighteenth century.

This is the crudest outline; the account of gild organization under the Tudors and early Stuarts given in detail by Unwin [1] shows a bewildering variety of changing forms. But beneath the variety, at least until the Civil War, one can trace the lines that run from the medieval system. The gilds, it is true, had been deprived of their religious, though not their social, significance in the early years of the Reformation, but their economic activities increased, if anything, as general conditions became more complex; and throughout the reigns of Elizabeth, James I, and Charles I they continued to give effective expression to the principle that each trade should be regulated as a whole, and—in spite of important exceptions—regulated primarily by those immediately engaged in that trade.[2] The direction and emphasis of regulation varied in each gild as different sets of interests gained control, but there was a lowest common denominator of regulating activity—shared by all the gilds—which had remained fairly constant since the Middle Ages. The courts of the larger London companies, for example, were not only concerned with the general direction of trade policy; in their weekly or fortnightly meetings 'the multifarious questions arising out of the company's regulation of trade and industry, and its maintenance of order and discipline amongst its members, were dealt with as they arose'. Disputes between members, or between master and workman, were settled; apprentices were admonished, punished

[1] The whole of this and the preceding paragraph is drawn from his *Gilds and Companies*, chaps. xiv and xv, and *Industrial Organization*, chaps. iii, iv, v, and *passim*.

[2] 'The principle of the full control of each trade by a single company' was clearly marked in the early Stuart incorporations.—*Gilds and Companies*, p. 264. For a summary account of the survival of the craft gilds into the seventeenth century see Lipson, III, p. 330 ff.

or protected. 'Small debts of various kinds are ordered to be paid by instalments. Unsatisfactory bargains are revised. Ill-executed work is condemned.' [1]

The purpose of all this activity was the protection of gild members and the furtherance of their interests, particularly —as the merchant capitalists drew away from the old organizations—the preservation of the status of the master craftsman. It isn't very helpful, however, to say that the Tudor gilds were motivated by self-interest: it is perfectly true, but it is true of trade associations at all times and in all places. What is important is the way in which self-interest functions. In the Elizabethan gilds it still functioned by means of regulation and adjustment, both between members and between each gild and the rest of the community, so that, as in their earlier history, the gilds did not *merely* protect vested interests. Professor Ashley points to 'the merit of the Gild System that it did for a time, and in large measure, succeed in reconciling the interests of consumers and producers'. [2] Something of that merit can still be found in the Elizabethan period. The requirement of a seven years' apprenticeship kept down the number of master craftsmen; it was also 'a security for good work'. [3] There was at least a likelihood that 'false work' would be detected before it was sold, and although any argument will serve to beat your enemy with, the stress laid on good workmanship by the parties in industrial disputes in the sixteenth century is still

[1] *Gilds*, pp. 220-223.

[2] Ashley, II, p. 168. The quotation continues: 'The tendency of modern competition is to sacrifice the producers; to assume that so long as articles are produced cheaply, it hardly matters what the remuneration of the workmen may be; but the gild legislation kept steadily before itself the ideal of combining good quality and a price that was fair to the consumer, with a fitting remuneration to the workman'. On the consumers' standpoint in medieval municipal policy see Heckscher, *Mercantilism*, I, p. 128 ff.

[3] Ashley, II, p. 166.

26

significant. A commonly accepted sense of gild responsibility towards the public in the Elizabethan-Jacobean period is reflected in the fact that the gilds were used as agents of the state supervision of certain industries.[1] Of course it reflects other things as well, and the supervision was not always either honest or efficient. But I am not concerned to make out a case for or against the gilds. The point is that the mere conception of an ordered trade was not likely to spring from the newer forms of commercial activity; it was a medieval conception, and that it was kept alive into the seventeenth century seems to be largely because the gilds continued as an active part of city life.

The economic history of the Elizabethan and early Stuart period is the history of the increasing dominance of newer forms of activity which look forward to the nineteenth century, and the disintegration of a traditional order with its roots in the Middle Ages; by the time of the Civil War the balance had plainly shifted in favour of the new. Until comparatively recent times it was usual for historians—following Macaulay who was fascinated by 'the brilliant industrial development' and the accumulation of capital—to discuss this process of change in terms of 'progress' (for what progress meant to Macaulay see the essay on Southey): trade and industry advanced as the medieval restrictions on economic freedom broke down; expansion was equated with improvement. Thus a standard monograph on the monopolies concludes: 'Although for a time the efforts to curb the crown in its encroachments upon public liberties seemed to have been in vain, the permanent outcome was the triumph of freedom'.[2] (Freedom for whom and to what ends is what one has to ask.) Even Unwin, whose studies did so

---

[1] Cunningham, II, pp. 295-312; Lipson, III, chap. v, section 5; Unwin, *Gilds*, chap. xvii.

[2] W. H. Price, *The English Patents of Monopoly*, p. 132.

27

much to exhibit the complex functioning of the older forms, could commit himself to easy generalizations of this kind. Describing the development of industry outside the town gilds, he says:

> Throughout almost all the social legislation of the Tudor period we may see the England of the past erecting vain barriers against the England of the future. To a large extent it was a struggle between town and country, but strange as it may seem to us, the country was often on the side of freedom and progress, whilst the towns represented stagnation and privilege.[1]

This is a point of view to which I shall return (it has important political implications). Here it is sufficient to notice that 'freedom' and 'progress' imply a wholesale moral judgement that can only hinder the kind of discrimination and evaluation that is relevant to the study of history. I do not mean of course that one should substitute for the Whig view a nostalgic glorification of the more remote past, picturing the traditional order as an ideal harmony shattered by the assaults of a ruthless 'commercial spirit'. The life of the period cannot be understood in terms of either naïve oversimplification.

Relevant discrimination is not a simple or straightforward process. The traditional economic organization under Elizabeth affected the quality of individual lives inasmuch as it prescribed, or allowed, certain patterns of living, whilst excluding others, and fostered certain ideals or general moral attitudes. Since the abstract formulations of contemporary moralists are only useful as pointers, and since the minute particulars of experience in which the value of individual lives resided are for ever beyond our reach, it is at least arguable that the patterns and the ideals can only be

[1] *Shakespeare's England*, I, p. 325 ('Commerce and Coinage').

judged as they are concretely embodied in what remains to us as literature.

Evaluation of this kind is a main purpose of this book. But first it is necessary to show the economic changes, with the accompanying social changes, which led ultimately to the formation of a new, 'capitalist' order of society, and then to indicate the ideals and theories that were, at the time, more or less consciously opposed to that development.

CHAPTER TWO

THE DEVELOPMENT
OF CAPITALIST ENTERPRISE

WHAT is still the current view of the constitutional developments of the seventeenth century is indicated by these two quotations:

> Elizabeth's strict control had nursed her people through perilous years into a strong nation. She had kept order for them until they were fully able to manage their own affairs. By the time her task was over England was ready to embark upon the adventure of governing herself. . . . The Stuart dynasty never had a chance from the beginning; Elizabeth had served her country's need so effectually, given it peace in which to develop and grow, that by the time her long reign was over she had enabled her people to outgrow their need for her and her kind.[1]

And for the latter part of the century:

> The shaking off of a hated dynasty, the security and peace which followed, the establishment of a government of freedom corresponding to the wishes of the people, which was guaranteed by the conspicuous influence of the acquisitive middle classes—all this must have had an active influence on the spirit of enterprise. The growth of industry was checked by the political disputes during the last years before the Revolution and by the uncertainty of the new conditions during the first years after. But about 1691 it went forward with redoubled strength.[2]

[1] M. St. Clare Byrne, *Elizabethan Life in Town and Country*, pp. 9-10.
[2] Richard Ehrenberg, *Capital and Finance in the Age of the Renaissance* (English translation by H. M. Lucas), p. 365.

30

But, one asks, who were Elizabeth's 'people' who were ready to embark on the adventure of governing themselves? Who hated the Stuart dynasty? and whose wishes were mainly consulted in 'the establishment of a government of freedom' in 1688? The second quotation—which so obviously shares the attitude towards the growth of industry commented on at the end of Chapter I—suggests that the answer in each case is 'the acquisitive middle classes'.

The extent to which the constitutional opposition in the first half of the seventeenth century represented the people of England, the kind of freedom guaranteed by the new governing class in the second half of the century, are perhaps matters for debate. Before long we may expect a thorough revision of the common estimate here; historians are already abandoning the simple Whig view.[1] But if we are not to repeat the mistake of so many nineteenth-century historians in reading history backwards, in the light, this time, of a different set of contemporary political ideas, we have to recognize that a good deal of work remains to be done before a revised estimate is possible. It would be interesting to have, for example, a thorough investigation of the 'eleven years' tyranny' of Charles I, of the business connexions of the parliamentary leaders in 1639–1642, and of the political affiliations of representative *nouveaux riches* in the seventeenth century, made by an historian writing outside the 'Whig' preconceptions. More generally, what is wanted is a history of the Tudor-Stuart period that would take as far as it would go the interpretation of political development in terms of the play of economic interests—a different matter from the discussion of 'the economic interpretation of history' in general terms.

The main point at least is clear: that by the middle of the

[1] Apart from the Marxists, H. Butterfield has stated the general case against *The Whig Interpretation of History*.

seventeenth century a new class had arisen which was strong enough to obtain political representation, and—what is more important in the present connexion—its emergence in the sixteenth and early seventeenth centuries had affected the whole pattern of English life. It was a class that can be loosely described as 'a capitalist middle class'—a phrase that is misleading unless we remember that it included landed proprietors as well as merchant and industrial capitalists (though the new 'landed interest' was, as I shall show, very different from the older landed nobility and gentry); that it included also many who—in terms of wealth, titles and distinction—were considerably above the middle-class status of to-day; and that it was far from representing a solid block of identical persons and families throughout any given period. The purpose of this chapter is to show certain aspects of the development of capitalism, including the emergence of that new class, and to indicate the effect of this development on English life in the later years of Elizabeth and the reign of James I.[1]

The Discoveries and the Development of Capitalism

Since history has not provided a succession of clear-cut types of economic organization it is impossible to point to a decade, or to a generation, when the capitalist era in Europe 'begins'. Fortunately the slicing up of history in this way

[1] G. R. Stirling Taylor's *A Modern History of England, 1485-1932: A Study in Politics, Economics and Ethics* contains the only attempt at a radical reinterpretation of Tudor-Stuart political history that I know of. But the book is mainly valuable in suggestion. Mr Taylor indicates the economic interests of the Puritan leaders, but his remark that 'The more one examines it, the more the Puritan opposition to the Stuarts appears as an endeavour to protect their own middle-class interests against the nation as a whole' needs to be followed up in detail; I don't suppose the case is a simple one. At all events Marvell didn't think it so.

is unnecessary; it is sufficient to say that in the sixteenth century, more particularly in the second half of the sixteenth century, capitalist processes were established.[1] In England, at all events, the change was most plainly marked during the forty or fifty years that preceded the death of James I, and by the end of that period it is clear that modern capitalism had been born.

This account is justified whatever definition of 'capitalism' we adopt. The most obvious characteristic of capitalist organization, we may say, is the division between the employer who owns the instruments of production (tools, materials) and the finished goods, on the one hand, and the hired workman who owns nothing but his labour, on the other. In this sense, since not all medieval journeymen became masters, many gild masters were capitalists. But capitalism implies more than this; it implies the accumulation of 'a store of wealth that can be turned into new and more profitable channels as occasion arises' (something for which there is no opportunity in a local industry supplying a more or less regular demand) and, in its more advanced stages, large-scale production and the division of labour. The emergence of any form of capitalist organization is, therefore, dependent on two factors: the existence of a wider market than the medieval local community—improved methods of communication are involved here—and an adequate supply of money. Further capitalist development presupposes also a permanent class of labourers who have

---

[1] 'The circulation of commodities is the starting-point of capital. Commodity production and that highly developed form of commodity circulation which is known as commerce constitute the historical groundwork upon which it rises. The modern history of capital begins in the sixteenth century with the establishment of a worldwide commercial system and the opening of a world market' (Karl Marx, *Capital* (English translation by Eden and Cedar Paul, Everyman Edition), p. 132).

no choice but to work for hire, and technological advance that facilitates the division of labour.[1]

Some of these conditions were present in the Middle Ages.[2] Commerce is necessarily capitalistic: you can't man your own ship or load the goods you have made on your own mule and lead it over the St. Gotthard. From the time of the Crusades Venice had developed an extensive trade with the East (in the early years a good deal of it was 'one-sided trade', or plunder), and by the thirteenth century the towns of northern Italy and of Flanders were centres of international rather than local commerce. Here, and along the few great overland trade routes such as the Rhine valley, capitalist development was inevitable. Similarly, industries producing for an export market, such as the cloth and brass industries in Flanders, the Florentine woollen and, later, silk industries, were organized on capitalist, or semi-capitalist, lines. And capitalist finance can be traced back to the Middle Ages; to the Papal tax system, to Italian banking in the thirteenth century, to the credit system in use at the great medieval fairs.

But in medieval Europe as a whole, more particularly in countries such as England which lay on the boundaries of European civilization, large-scale commerce and capitalist industry were exceptional. Sixteenth-century capitalism was largely a development of conditions that already existed, but the great stimulus to that development, it is safe to say, was provided by the Discoveries. These not only transformed the geographical perspective of Europe; the opening up of new markets in the far East stimulated industrial as well as commercial activity, and the discovery of treasure in

[1] In turn, of course, the development of capitalism itself stimulates the growth of the market, the circulation of money and mechanical invention, and perpetuates a labouring class; and these again become causes and conditioning factors as the process gathers momentum.

[2] See H. M. Robertson, *op. cit.*, chap. ii.

the Spanish Americas turned what might have been a steady process into a revolution.[1]

It would be difficult to overestimate the importance of the influx of American gold and silver into Europe in hastening the disintegration of the medieval economic order. From the early years of the sixteenth century Spain received a steady supply of gold from her American conquests; her colonial policy was one of immediate and wholesale exploitation. In 1545 came the discovery of the silver mines of Potosi and 'from the middle of the sixteenth century to the 'thirties of the seventeenth the treasure of the Indies poured into the motherland at a rate that exceeded the most fantastic dreams of the *conquistadores*'.[2] From Spain, mainly by trade (Spain was industrially backward) but partly by more direct means (plunder, or the payment of Crown debts), American gold and silver were diffused throughout the world—particularly to England, France and the Low Countries, and from there, in the course of trade in spices and oriental goods, to the far East.[3] Between 1500 and 1600 the stock of precious metals in Europe is estimated to have trebled.[4]

The effect of the Spanish-American treasure in stimulating capitalist enterprise is clearly seen in England. According to Mr Keynes:

> The boom period in England definitely began with the return of Drake's first important expedition (his third voyage) in 1573, and was confirmed by the immense gains of his second expedition which returned home in 1580. . . . Indeed, the booty brought back by Drake in the *Golden Hind* [5]

[1] See Robertson, *op. cit.*, chap. vii; Earl J. Hamilton, 'American Treasure and the Rise of Capitalism', in *Economica*, IX (November 1929); J. M. Keynes, *A Treatise on Money*, II, chap. xxx ('Spanish Treasure'). [2] Hamilton, *op. cit.*, p. 345.

[3] Hamilton, *op. cit.*, p. 346. [4] Robertson, *op. cit.*, pp. 178-179.

[5] About £600,000 in 1580, according to W. R. Scott, *Joint-Stock*

may fairly be considered the fountain and origin of British Foreign Investment. Elizabeth paid off out of the proceeds the whole of her foreign debt and invested a part of the balance (about £42,000) in the Levant Company; largely out of the profits of the Levant Company there was formed the East India Company, the profits of which during the seventeenth and eighteenth centuries were the main foundations of England's foreign connexions, and so on. . . . It was not the absolute value of the bullion brought into the country—perhaps not more than £2,000,000 or £3,000,000 from first to last—which mattered, but the *indirect* effect of this on profit and enterprise, the increment of the country's wealth in buildings and improvements being probably several times the above figures.[1]

But it was not only that there was now more money available for use in commercial, industrial and financial undertakings. The revolution in prices, consequent on the vastly increased supply of gold and silver, undermined the rule of custom in business and, at the same time as the Discoveries 'widened the economic horizon', stimulated the pursuit of gain by promising large profits to the enterprising. In most European countries prices rose continuously throughout the sixteenth century, with accelerated speed from about 1550. Although England, for various reasons, was not immediately affected by the continental price movement, the debasement of the currency by Henry VIII caused a general 'dearth', which the recoinage of 1560–1561 was intended to relieve. By this time, however, the country was beginning to receive a share of the Spanish treasure; the second half of

Companies, I, pp. 81-82, and the adventurers who had invested in the voyage received 4700 per cent. on their money. Drake's expedition of 1587, organized on a joint-stock basis, seems to have made a gross profit of 138 per cent. 'This was not considered great, since Raleigh wrote that 100 per cent. (also gross) was but "a small return", and that he "might have gotten more to have sent his ships fishing" ' (*op. cit.*, I, p. 87).

[1] J. M. Keynes, *A Treatise on Money*, II, pp. 156-157.

the century, to the bewilderment of the common people, was 'a period of revolutionary price changes', and the upward trend did not cease until *c.* 1650, when prices were approximately three times what they had been in 1500.[1] The important point of course is not merely that prices rose but that they were only slowly followed by rents and wages. The process that, in effect, deprived labourers and landlords of a large part of their incomes provided undreamed-of opportunities for the capitalist.

For a period of almost two hundred years English and French capitalists—and presumably those of other economically advanced countries—must have enjoyed incomes analogous to those American profiteers reaped from a similar divergence between prices and wages from 1916 to 1919. . . . [By the end of the sixteenth century] the lag of wages behind prices had quadrupled profits.

The windfalls thus received, along with gains from the East India trade, furnished the means to build up capital equipment, and the stupendous profits obtainable supplied an incentive for the feverish pursuit of capitalistic enterprise. We find, as might be expected, that during the seventeenth and latter part of the sixteenth centuries England, France and the Low Countries were seething with such genuinely capitalistic phenomena as systematic mechanical invention, company promotion, and speculation in the shares of financial and trading concerns.[2]

The greater part of the fruits of the economic progress and capital accumulation of the Elizabethan and Jacobean age accrued to the profiteer rather than to the wage-earner. . . . Never in the annals of the modern world has there existed so prolonged and so rich an opportunity for the business man, the speculator and the profiteer. In these golden years modern capitalism was born.[3]

[1] Keynes, *op. cit.*, pp. 153-154, Earl J. Hamilton, *American Treasure and the Price Revolution in Spain, 1501–1650* (Harvard Economic Studies), p. 207.

[2] Hamilton, 'American Treasure and the Rise of Capitalism', *Economica*, IX, pp. 355-356.   [3] J. M. Keynes, *op. cit.*, pp. 158-159.

Capitalist Finance.   The Growth of a Money Market

I have already commented on the difficulty of distinguishing causes and effects in the development of a complex process. The rise of large-scale finance, which is a characteristic of the sixteenth century, was of course largely due to the increased commercial and industrial activity that has still to be considered.   But the rise of an international money market was itself one of the first causes of economic expansion and, since 'the force of money in determining the course of the world's history meets us at every turn at this period', it is convenient to consider it here.   The flow of capital—particularly the capital released by the Spanish discoveries—that was necessary for that expansion was largely directed by the international financiers.

I have not found a better account of the development of European finance in the sixteenth century than that given by Dr Richard Ehrenberg in *Capital and Finance in the Age of the Renaissance.*[1]   Dr Ehrenberg takes as his text the tag, *Pecunia nervus belli.*   By the time of the Renaissance, he points out, warfare had ceased to be waged by feudal levies and, on the Continent at least, was becoming 'a heavy industry'[2] conducted largely by mercenary troops who would not wait for pay whilst money was collected by the usual expedients;[3] in any case money was often required far from the place where it was raised.[4]   The sixteenth and seventeenth centuries were periods of almost continuous warfare, and the sums spent for military purposes were enormous.[5]

---

[1] English translation by H. M. Lucas.   The quotation in the first paragraph occurs on p. 98.

[2] *Op. cit.*, p. 375.   [3] *Op. cit.*, p. 32.   [4] *Op. cit.*, p. 29.

[5] For example, 'The expenditure of the Spanish Crown in putting down the rebellion in the Netherlands averaged two to three million gold crowns a year, *i.e.* more than the yearly revenue of the Netherlands Government during the most flourishing trade period' (*op. cit.*, p. 28).

The swift mobilization of credit was at once a necessity of state and something which the existing state mechanism could not achieve. Kings and princes therefore were forced to rely on individual financiers; it was not a coincidence that the rise of the house of Fugger took place in the early sixteenth century during the dissensions within the Empire and the long struggle between France and the Hapsburgs.

As early as the fourteenth century there had been Christian capitalists—the Bardi and Peruzzi, for example—whose resources were large enough to supply the financial needs of princes, but none had achieved the international status of the Fugger.

> About 1525 the Fugger were, beyond dispute, the most influential financiers of their time. Their business relations reached from Hungary and Poland to Spain, from Antwerp to Naples. In the words of the contemporary chronicler of Augsburg, Clemens Sender, 'The names of Jakob Fugger and his nephews are known in all kingdoms and lands; yea, among the heathen also. Emperors, Kings, Princes and Lords have sent to treat with him, the Pope has greeted him as his well beloved son and embraced him, and the Cardinals have risen up before him. All the merchants of the world have called him an enlightened man, and all the heathen have wondered because of him. He is the glory of all Germany.' [1]

In the years 1511 to 1527 the Fugger made a profit of '927 per cent., or an average of $54\frac{1}{2}$ per cent. for each year'.[2] They were indispensable to the Emperor, and their financial web covered Europe until the seventeenth century, when the unpaid debts of the Hapsburgs caused their decline.[3]

[1] *Op. cit.*, p. 83. The Fugger also 'formed extensive libraries, and collected at a great expense ancient MSS. of the classics, which they caused to be printed', and were connoisseurs of pictures and antiques. —J. W. Burgon, *The Life and Times of Sir Thomas Gresham*, I, pp. 62-63.
[2] Ehrenberg, *op. cit.*, p. 85.   [3] *Op. cit.*, p. 131.

It was necessary to mention the Fugger not only because they had a place in the popular imagination of the sixteenth century similar to that of the Rothschilds at a later date, but because they, together with the Welser, the Hochstetter, the Strozzi and a few other dynasties, brought about a radical transformation in the European economic scene. In the course of the sixteenth century it became impossible for 'isolated financial magnates . . . to satisfy the growing demands of the princes for capital'.[1]   The leading financiers accordingly began to collect and concentrate whatever free money was available, consciously turning to account 'the inclination already present in many quarters to wish for a high return on their money without any effort'.[2]   This process, together with the increasing volume of trade, caused the growth of the great Bourses or money markets, the greatest of which was at Antwerp.   The situation in the middle years of the sixteenth century is best described in Dr Ehrenberg's own words:

> The trading companies now attracted from every side the free money capital of the small holders of capital, and for this they paid a much lower rate than what they were able to get in financial dealings.   On the Bourses themselves the great financiers borrowed more and more outside capital, which could not else have found employment and was therefore relatively cheap. . . . The ambition to share in the Antwerp and Lyons financial dealings affected an ever-widening circle, until even the most violent increase of the demand did not exhaust the supply, and whole classes of the European peoples were seized by a regular mania or craze for the possession of these magic parchments known on the world Bourses as King's Bonds, Court Bonds, or Bonds of the Receivers General.[3]

From 1552 onwards a real madness or 'mania' for the

[1] *Op. cit.*, p. 376.   [2] *Op. cit.*, p. 332.
[3] *Op. cit.*, pp. 314-315.

Bourse loans of Antwerp and Lyons seized on the masses all over Europe, and the last vestiges of the science which should be at hand in all speculations was discarded, and a fever for profiteering rushed like a runner gone mad through the richest domains of all the old painfully gathered capital to meet the inevitable crisis.[1]

Yet all the same (Dr Ehrenberg continues) these capital transactions in the world markets of the sixteenth century constitute a forward step of enormous importance in civilization. For the first time business in the different markets had brought together capital from every side on such a scale as to satisfy the largest demands of the most important princes, and to reduce by half the rate of interest on their loans. This made it possible to raise large masses of capital at moderate rates for all the modern developments of civilization and for all the national ends of the different peoples.[2]

There is no need to follow Dr Ehrenberg's account to the end, to the decline of the power of the individual financial magnates as states began to raise their own loans directly from the Bourses.[3]   The point is that in the second half of the sixteenth century an international money market had arisen. The capital concentrated at the great financial centres was available for loans and for investment, and modern financial technique—large-scale speculation and credit transactions—dates from this period. 'The essence of the financial organization of the sixteenth century', says Dr Tawney, 'was internationalism, freedom for every capitalist to undertake every transaction within his means, a unity which had as its symptom the movement of all the principal markets in sympathy with each other, and as its

[1] *Op. cit.*, p. 328.
[2] *Op. cit.*, p. 333.
[3] At the time of the French wars of the second half of the seventeenth century, 'It was no longer a single financier, but the whole of the Amsterdam Exchange, which affected the course of history' (*op. cit.*, p. 361).

41

effect the mobilization of immense resources at the strategic points of international finance'.[1]

It was some time before London became a 'strategic point' of the importance of Antwerp or Lyons, but by the second half of the sixteenth century it was closely bound to the European financial system.[2]   In England the same causes were at work as on the Continent, though at first less powerfully.   The French wars of Henry VIII had caused him to borrow large sums from the Fugger, and throughout the century wars or preparation for wars kept the Crown constantly dependent on the power of the financier to mobilize capital.[3]   At first Crown loans were raised abroad, but by the time of the death of Sir Thomas Gresham (1579) English capital was available in sufficient quantity to satisfy the extraordinary credit requirements of the government,[4]—requirements which had combined with the great expansion of foreign trade to call into being a class of financial specialists and to make large-scale credit transactions familiar in London a hundred years before the founding of the Bank of England.[5]

[1] Introduction to *A Discourse upon Usury*, by Thomas Wilson, p. 62.

[2] *Op. cit.*, p. 64.

[3] Dr G. B. Harrison is one of the few writers on the Elizabethan period to stress how constant were Elizabeth's war preparations in the latter part of her reign (see his *Elizabethan Journals, passim*). And before the Armada she had subsidized anti-Spanish forces on the Continent.

[4] Ehrenberg, *op. cit.*, p. 254.

[5] 'By the third quarter of the century the financing of foreign trade had become sufficiently profitable to form the main business of a special group of brokers and discount houses' (Tawney, *op. cit.*, p. 67).   One would like to know more about the native financiers of this period, their antecedents, their social connexions, and the political influence of them and their sons.

42

In English financial history the dominating—one might say, the symbolic—figure of the mid-sixteenth century was Thomas Gresham, the founder (in 1568) of the Royal Exchange.[1]   Gresham was instrumental in carrying out the recoinage of 1560–1561, and it was he who, when Antwerp was sacked during the revolt of the Netherlands, advised the Privy Council to raise its loans from English merchants (using a little compulsion where necessary, but paying 12 per cent. interest instead of the usual 10 per cent., so the merchants were satisfied in the end).   But it is the part he played before then, as the King's agent at Antwerp, that I wish to notice here.   As 'royal merchant' it was Gresham's business to raise loans for the sovereign from the Flemish and German merchants—as well as to supply arms and ammunition, to glean political information and, where opportunity offered, to smuggle bullion from the Continent. When he was appointed in 1551 the interest on the foreign debts incurred by Henry VIII is said to have amounted to £40,000 a year, whilst the exchange stood at 16s. Flemish to the pound sterling.[2]   Within two or three years the pound had gone up to 22s. Flemish, at which rate Gresham was able to discharge all the king's debts.[3]   This, he claimed, was due to his own manipulation of the exchange, and in a letter written to Elizabeth early in her reign, after outlining the reasons for the fall of the pound and the means that he had taken to remedy this, he concluded:

> By this it may plainly appear to your highness, as that the exchange is the thing that eats out all princes, to the whole

[1] J. W. Burgon, *The Life and Times of Sir Thomas Gresham*; H. Hall, *Society in the Elizabethan Age*, chap. v; Scott, I, pp. 25-30; Ehrenberg, *op. cit.*, pp. 252-255.
[2] Burgon, *op. cit.*, I, p. 68.   To secure renewal of the loans Henry had been forced to buy jewels and goods at exorbitant rates—the equivalent of 'taking up on commodity' in humbler spheres.
[3] *Op. cit.*, I, p. 99.

destruction of their commonweal, if it be not substantially looked unto; so likewise the exchange is the chiefest and richest thing only above all other, to restore your Majesty and your realm to fine gold and silver, and is the mean that makes all foreign commodities and your own commodities with all kind of victuals good cheap, and likewise keeps your fine gold and silver within your realm. . . . So consequently the higher the exchange riseth, the more shall your Majesty and your realm and commonweal flourish, which thing is only kept up by art and God's providence.[1]

It doesn't much matter whether Gresham was correct in attributing the improvement to his own 'art' or not; what is important is the recognition of the national importance of fluctuations in the foreign exchange. It was not merely that exchange transactions provided a convenient way of making money for the merchant or financier with capital to spare, the economic welfare of the whole country was becoming dependent on the movement of forces that were beyond the power of any one individual to control.[2]

It is impossible to understand either the industrial development or the economic controversies of the later sixteenth century without some knowledge of this background of international financial dealings. It was international finance that first made capital mobile. It was international finance that prepared the way for the doctrine of complete economic freedom and, 'since problems of currency and

[1] Burgon, I, Appendix XXI.

[2] The exchange rates between two countries are determined by the balance of trade between them, the different values of their currencies, the state of the national credit, and by a variety of complicating factors. Fluctuations in the foreign exchange are caused by the day to day changes in any or all of these. Exchange transactions therefore involve a considerable element of speculation, and as a form of usury they had a good deal of hostile attention in Elizabeth's reign. 'The more risky kinds of these transactions' increased considerably about the middle of the sixteenth century.—See Tawney's Introduction to Wilson's *Discourse*, p. 78 ff., and Sections II, iv, and III, iii.

credit lent themselves more readily than other economic questions to discussions in terms of mechanical causation',[1] for the doctrine of the moral irresponsibility of economics. All that Gresham and the financiers who followed him represented, therefore, would be completely alien to the peasants and small masters who still formed more than three quarters of the population of England.[2]   The ideas of the local community were not those of the Royal Exchange, and a clash was inevitable.[3]

Later there will be occasion to notice the confusion in the economic pronouncements of popular moralists in the Elizabethan period, so it is worth remarking here that in financial matters at least the theory and practice of experts were far from being completely rational and 'scientific'.

> The Public Finance of the sixteenth century is a study which is largely pathological.   There were degrees in the incompetence and immorality of Governments, but the practice of all was bad; and if Elizabeth, with the aid of Gresham, had achieved by the middle of her reign a reputation which stood her in good stead as a borrower, it was due, it may be suspected, less to the virtue of the English Government than to the vices of its neighbours.[4]

No one seems to have realized, for example, that medieval methods of taxation were incompatible with the new demands upon government resources, and English government finance was not established on a sound basis until after

---

[1] Tawney, *op. cit.*, p. 61.   Cf. pp. 134-135, *ibid.*

[2] *Op. cit.*, p. 21.

[3] 'The foreign exchanges confronted the traditional doctrines with an *experimentum crucis*.   Plain men were frankly bewildered by the whole business, and could only murmur helplessly: "There is some mystery in the matter, pray God it may be discovered to the weal of our realm" ' (*op. cit.*, p. 85).

[4] Preface (unsigned) to the English translation of Ehrenberg, *op. cit.*, p. 13.   Cf. Robertson, *Economic Individualism*, p. 183.

the Restoration. The Stuarts, it is well known, had not the financial aptitude of Elizabeth, and their continuous money difficulties culminated in the desperate expedients of Charles I just before the outbreak of civil war. But even the Elizabethan Privy Council did not manage the national income to the best advantage; the commissioners of the subsidy and the assessors were frequently inefficient (and dishonest); [1] at the beginning of the seventeenth century there were no balance sheets of the Crown revenue and expenditure, and 'errors in addition might almost be described as the rule rather than the exception'.[2]

The first quarter of the seventeenth century has been described as 'the period of perhaps the greatest economic confusion in our history'.[3] Throughout Europe it was a period of currency disorder, trade crises were common, and 'monetary confusion prevailed everywhere'.[4] In England, James I's tamperings with the coinage were mischievous and his economic policy was inept, but one has to accept the judgement that 'if James did not understand the difficulties of the time, neither did his ministers, nor could any agreement herein be found among the practical men of the time'.[5] The revolution of prices and the rapid development of international finance had confronted statesmen and theorists with an entirely new and enormously complicated set of problems, which were made more acute by the continuous political disorder on the Continent. I shall try to show the valuable elements in the traditional and popular doctrines

[1] Scott, I, p. 94.

[2] *Ibid.*, I, p. 158. The private companies were not much better. Cf. the account of a balance sheet of an early joint-stock company, *op. cit.*, II, p. 388.

[3] F. H. Durham, 'The Relations of the Crown to Trade under James I' (*Transactions of the Royal Historical Society*, New Series, XIII), p. 199.

[4] Durham, *op. cit.*, pp. 236-240.   [5] *Op. cit.*, p. 200.

that were used in opposition to some of the newer economic developments; but with a knowledge of the general confusion we shall not be surprised if the economics of honest moralists are sometimes shaky, or if plain men attribute dearth not to the movement of European markets but entirely to 'the subtle invention and craft of divers covetous persons'.[1]

Overseas Trade

It is impossible to give an adequate short account of the development of English trade and industry under Elizabeth and James I, and I shall select only those elements that seem to have a special significance. Commerce, in fact, will be treated even more summarily than industry, not because it is less important, but because its direct effects can be described more simply. For most Englishmen of the time, moreover, such matters as the debate on privileged companies for overseas trade seemed less immediate than, say, the usury controversy or the question of internal monopolies. In the long run, of course, the commercial expansion of the period played as great a part as the internal changes in the transformation of medieval into modern England, and one has to be conscious of it as a background to most Elizabethan-Jacobean activities. Here, however, it is sufficient to notice, first, the enormous increase in the volume and variety of foreign trade in the sixteenth century, and secondly the significant development of joint-stock companies.

In the Middle Ages overseas trade had been largely in the hands of foreign merchants, and the destruction of the Steelyard in 1598 is an important date in English commercial history. The medieval rivals of the Hanseatic merchants, the English Merchant Adventurers, had steadily increased in

[1] Cunningham, I, pp. 543-544. Cf. Robertson, *Economic Individualism*, p. 181.

power with the growth of the native cloth industry, and early in the seventeenth century they were the greatest trading company in England.[1] Their trade, however, continued to be mainly with Germany and the Low Countries, and by this time other companies had been formed for trade with the lands opened up by the Discoveries.

The Merchant Adventurers remained throughout their history a regulated company organized on the medieval pattern; some of the newer companies were of the same kind, some traded on a joint stock, and some varied between the two forms. The Eastland Company was incorporated in 1579 as a regulated company; the Russian Company (1553), the Levant Company (1581) and various African companies began as joint-stock companies, though the two former reverted to the older type in the seventeenth century; and the newer principle was most thoroughly developed in the East India Company (1600). The increase in trade is perhaps sufficiently indicated by the names of the companies. The principal export remained English cloth. The Eastland Company, trading to the Baltic, and the Russian Company brought back the all-important naval stores—timber, tar, hemp, wax and cordage; whilst for some time the Russian Company also had an overland trade with Persia. The Levant Company imported silk, drugs and Eastern goods generally from Smyrna and Aleppo, whilst the African companies traded in gold, ivory and spices. (The slave trade was mainly carried on by interlopers.) The East India Company imported from India and the far East, raw silk, saltpetre, pepper and other spices and drugs.[2]

[1] A description of their trade is given by John Wheeler, Secretary to the Company, in *A Treatise of Commerce*, 1601. He estimated that there were then 3500 freemen of the Company, though not all of these were traders (T. and P., III, p. 294).

[2] Cunningham, II, pp. 214-279; Scott, I and II, *passim*; Heckscher, *Mercantilism*, I, p. 375.

Other forms of enterprise—privateering, discovery and colonization—have to be mentioned here, since, in their causes, methods and results, they were all closely related to the commercial development of the period. Not only was foreign trade occasionally allied with freebooting,[1] the various activities of the Elizabethan seamen afford interesting illustrations of contemporary speculation and investment. The raids on Spanish America were all conducted by joint-stock companies, and the enormous profits to the shareholders in Drake's round-the-world voyage of 1577–1580 resulted in a boom in privateering.[2] Similarly the voyages of discovery were largely a form of economic investment. The Russian Company was at first known as 'The mystery and company of the Merchants adventurers for the discovery of regions . . . and places unknown',[3] whilst the expenses of Frobisher's voyages to the North-West (1576–1578) were borne by a syndicate, the members of which either adventured goods or took out shares in money.[4] Several short-lived plantation companies were formed under Elizabeth, but English colonization was unsuccessful until the reign of James I, when the ending of officially sanctioned privateering and, perhaps, a slight increase in scepticism concerning new El Dorados, removed the temptations that

[1] W. Sombart, *The Quintessence of Capitalism* (translated and edited by M. Epstein), chap. vi, section 1. Continuous fighting was a corollary of trade at this period; apart from fights with pirates and the natives of newly discovered lands, there were continuous armed clashes between the traders of different—or even of the same—countries. The Dutch-English feud, for example, ranged from the East Indies (Amboyna, 1623) to the northern whaling grounds, where in 1614 four Dutch warships overcame the thirteen armed whalers of the Russian Company. In the same region fights between the crews of different English ships were 'not infrequent'.—Scott, II, pp. 54, 72-74.   [2] *Op. cit.*, I, pp. 70-87.   [3] *Op. cit.*, II, p. 37.
[4] *Op. cit.*, II, pp. 76-81. The voyages were not merely intended to discover a North-West passage; Frobisher believed that he had discovered gold.

accounted for the failure of Raleigh's ventures in the previous reign. As Cunningham pointed out, 'Religious motives had much to do in shaping the character of particular settlements, but the main impulse in the work of colonization was economic. The plantations offered a field for the profitable investment of capital.'[1] The Virginia Company obtained a royal charter in 1606, whilst the allied Somers Islands Company (1612),[2] after founding its fortunes on ambergris and pearls, continued to thrive on tobacco after the older company had been wound up and Virginia taken under Crown control in 1624. And various companies attempted to colonize other parts of the North American mainland, Nova Scotia and some of the West India Islands.[3]

There is no need to stress the psychological effect of maritime enterprise in the age of Marlowe and of Donne; it is sufficient to recall *Tamburlaine* or the *Songs and Sonets*.[4] The material results of 'all this almost incredible Trade and Traffique'[5] can be briefly summarized. In the first place there was the growth in numbers, wealth and importance of the large merchants. Harrison noticed this in his *Description of England*, and remarked that they 'often change estate with gentlemen, as gentlemen do with them, by a mutual conversion of the one into the other'.[6] The remark made of the members of the Russian Company in the sixteen-twenties

[1] Cunningham, II, p. 342.

[2] Or Bermuda Company. 'It was eventually decided that the title should be the Somers Islands, partly in commemoration of the discoverer, partly in punning allusion to the temperate climate' (Scott, II, p. 260). See Ben Jonson on other advertising devices of the period, p. 215, below. [3] Scott, II, pp. 246-337.

[4] The prevailing geographical enthusiasm is brought out by Miss E. G. R. Taylor, *Late Tudor and Early Stuart Geography, 1583-1650*.

[5] John Wheeler, *op. cit.*, T. and P., III, p. 285.

[6] *Description of England* (1577), Book II, ed. Furnivall ('Shakespeare's England'), p. 131 (1586 addition). Their feasts, he said (p. 148), equalled those of the nobility.

that they 'grew very rich and got great estates'[1] might be applied to many other merchants of the period. The desire of those newly enriched by trade to become landed proprietors accounts for a good deal of the contemporary social dislocation. At the beginning of the seventeenth century it was claimed that merchandise was 'the chiefest and richest of all other [trades] and of greater extent and importance than all the rest',[2] and it is significant that by this time the conception of the 'mere merchant', as opposed to the retail trader, had taken shape. Before this date, the Merchant Adventurers' Company had decreed 'that no brother thereof should occupy over the sea and at home by retail at one time, but using the one he should leave the other',[3] and regulation had become increasingly strict. 'Towards the end of the sixteenth and at the beginning of the seventeenth century, the separation of retail from wholesale, local from foreign trade can be taken as generally recognized.'[4] As one of the lawyers in Wilson's *Discourse upon Usury* remarked: 'Touching retailers at home. . . . I place them in a lower degree, as not worthy the name of merchants. . . . Whereas the merchant adventurer is and may be taken for a lord's fellow in dignity, as well as for his hardy adventuring upon the seas, to carry out our plenty, as for his royal and noble wholesales, that he makes to divers men upon his return, when he bringeth in our want.'[5] The class divisions that we know were clearly taking shape.

But others besides merchants shared in the commercial profits. The formation of joint-stock companies provided an opportunity for anyone with capital to invest,

[1] Quoted by Scott, II, p. 66.
[2] Sir Edwin Sandys (1604), quoted by Scott, I, p. 120.
[3] T. and P., II, p. 53.
[4] Heckscher, *Mercantilism*, I, pp. 377-379. There were, of course, many exceptions to the general rule.
[5] Ed. Tawney, p. 203 (quoted by Heckscher, *loc. cit.*).

and from 1600 the sale of shares became increasingly common.[1] The privateering, discovery and plantation companies were largely composed of courtiers and noblemen. Elizabeth herself invested in Drake's syndicate, and adventured a ship in Frobisher's second voyage.[2] The subscribers to Frobisher's expeditions included Burghley, Howard, the Earls of Warwick, Leicester, and Sussex, Walsingham, Philip Sidney, the Countess of Pembroke and Edward Dyer, as well as Sir Thomas Gresham and the merchant Michael Lok.[3] In the following reign Shakespeare's Earl of Southampton became treasurer of the Virginia Company; and he was one of the principal shareholders in the Somers Islands Company, which included the Countess of Bedford, the Earl of Pembroke, Sir Robert Mansfield, Lord Cavendish (the Earl of Devonshire) and Robert Rich, Earl of Warwick, who afterwards became governor of the Company.[4] Similarly, Sir William Alexander, Earl of Stirling, also an investor in mining enterprises, had a principal interest in the Nova Scotia Company (1621)—intended to 'disburden' Scotland 'of all such younger brothers and mean gentlemen whose means are short of their birth, worth or minds, who otherwise must be troublesome to the houses and friends, from whence they are descended'[5]—whilst the adventurers in the Providence Island Company (1629) included several Puritan aristocrats who were later to become active in opposition to Charles I.[6]

---

[1] Scott, II, p. 161. [2] *Ibid.*, I, pp. 75, 80.

[3] Ralph M. Sargent, *At the Court of Queen Elizabeth. The Life and Lyrics of Sir Edward Dyer*, p. 41.

[4] Scott, II, pp. 263-264, 272, 290.

[5] *Ibid.*, II, pp. 318-320. Alexander was also an adventurer in the Canada Company.

[6] *E.g.* Sir Nathaniel Rich, Lord Holland, Lord Brook and Viscount Saye and Sele, the secretary being John Pym—Scott, II, pp. 327-337. See also G. R. Stirling Taylor, *Oliver Cromwell*, pp. 124-125.

It was natural, of course, that those who could use some political influence should be interested in ventures of this kind, just as they were invoked in the industrial monopolies and projects. The participation of others than 'mere merchants' in the strictly commercial undertakings was limited by the provisions of the regulated companies—and the joint-stock companies tended to revert to that form. Elizabeth, however, had lent four men-of-war to the African Company in 1561 on condition of receiving a third of the profits, whilst she and some of the Privy Council had invested in the joint-stock of the Levant Company in 1581.[1] It is significant also that in 1629 the East India Company decided to pay its dividend in cash rather than in calicoes 'in order to give contentment to the gentry'.[2]

This enumeration of names at least suggests that 'the commercial spirit' was not confined to the strictly commercial classes. Investment was becoming common, and a successful investment in an overseas venture meant a good deal more than 5 per cent. per annum. None of the trading companies managed to approach the 4700 per cent. dividend paid by Drake's syndicate in 1580, but in the following year a Persian expedition of the Russian Company that paid a mere 106 per cent. (on three years) was considered a failure, since previous expeditions had probably yielded as much as

[1] Scott, I, pp. 30, 70; II, p. 84. For the investments of James I and Charles I in trade see Heckscher, *Mercantilism*, I, p. 438.

[2] Scott, II, p. 110. The Earl of Nottingham was interested in the early African trade (*ibid.*, II, p. 10), and in the reign of Charles I the Earl of Portland, Lord Arundel and the fourth Earl of Pembroke were all governors of Fishing Companies.—*Ibid.*, II, pp. 369-371. After the Restoration, Prince Rupert was Governor of the 'Royal Adventurers into Africa' as well as of the Hudson's Bay Company (in the latter he was succeeded by James, Duke of York). Compare the quotation from Sir Josiah Child (1681) on the advantages of 'a mixed assembly of noblemen, gentlemen and merchants' for trade.—Scott, I, p. 444.

E

300 per cent. or 400 per cent., whilst the African trade had certainly made very large profits indeed. Several of the early voyages of the East India Company made a division of over 300 per cent., and about the same time the Russian Company paid 90 per cent. annually for two years (1611 and 1612).[1]

The returns thus made help to account for the spread of luxury that was so often commented on by contemporaries,[2] and at the same time they provided capital for further investment. But if they had been merely a factor in a general advance of material civilization there would have been less need to mention them here. Two other considerations help to bring out the significance of these large commercial profits. In the first place, investments of the kind described were highly speculative. The most obvious example is provided by the privateering companies, of which Scott remarks that they 'demanded a peculiar temperament in the investor, in so far as he must undergo very great risks in the hope of commensurate gains'.[3] But that temperament was far from being 'peculiar', though it was certainly fostered by the buccaneering syndicates. Apart from the industrial schemes to which the Fitzdottrels of the age succumbed, the Frobisher expedition was not the only tempting project that failed to pay a penny to its investors. Raleigh's last voyage is a conspicuous example, whilst an earlier Guiana Company literally 'promised gold mountains', and 'filled the minds of (the) company so full of vain expectations and golden hopes, that their insatiable and covetous minds, being wholly set thereon, could not be satisfied with anything but only

---

[1] Russian Company: Scott, I, p. 70; II, pp. 44-45, 53. African Companies: *ibid.*, I, pp. 22-23; II, pp. 4-5. East India Company: *ibid.*, II, pp. 123-125. A summary of joint-stock profits is given by Scott, *ibid.*, I, pp. 446-447.
[2] See below, pp. 117-121.   [3] Scott, I, p. 444.

gold',[1] so that what might have been a profitable trade was neglected. And even in trade, as the records of the joint-stock companies show, there were, inevitably, very considerable fluctuations. As Scott puts it, 'Trade to remote places, having certain elements of privateering, was subject to sudden vicissitudes'.[2] In the whole period the sum of the gains from commerce was very large indeed, but individual investments might well be unlucky. What the increase of joint-stock activities calls attention to is the spread of the speculative temper, the willingness to gamble in the hope of large returns.[3]

Secondly, not only were large commercial profits confined to a comparatively small section of the population, whilst the habits of mind that they fostered were opposed to all the traditional conceptions of reasonable gain, but those profits —and the financial conditions that made them possible— contributed to form a situation which aggravated poverty at the same time as it made it more conspicuous. This larger —moral—significance of commercial expansion will be discussed later, when the other strands of the complex economic pattern have been gathered together. For the moment it is sufficient to realize that during the years when, under Elizabeth and James I, England was 'economically prosperous', that prosperity was far from being universally shared.

Before ending this section one further point remains to be noticed, namely, that traditional elements were still active

---

[1] *A Relation of a Voyage to Guiana*, by Robert Harcourt, 1613, quoted by Scott, II, p. 323.

> Promise gold mountains, and the covetous
> Are still most prodigal.

(Jonson, *The Devil is an Ass* (1616), I, iii.)
A good account of the gold fever of the later 'seventies is given by Sargent, *At the Court of Queen Elizabeth*, chap. iv.

[2] Scott, II, p. 64.

[3] It is significant that public lotteries in England date from the early seventeenth century, the Virginia Company being the first company to raise considerable funds in this way.—Scott, II, pp. 252-255, 272.

even in the commercial organizations that were causing so great a change. The regulated companies retained into the seventeenth century a strong gild spirit. Not only did they carry on foreign trade in the manner of a local monopoly— aiming to keep up prices as well as quality, and to restrict competition, whilst securing reasonable fair play between members [1]—but they supervised the general conduct of individuals. The Merchant Adventurers claimed that they had built chapels and cared for the poor at home, and maintained 'the exercise of Religion amongst them in all the places of their residence hitherto, yea even among those who could not well away with the same', entertaining 'godly and learned Preachers with liberal stipends, and other benefits'. Moreover their ordinances contained 'all kind of good discipline, instruction and rules to bring up youth in and to keep them in order'.[2]

From an economic point of view (says Dr Heckscher), the meticulous regulation of the lives of the merchants, their agents and apprentices is of minor importance, but it throws light on the spirit of the system and expresses the striving after a supra-personal organization, embracing the whole individuality of its members. The members were never described as anything but 'brethren', their wives were 'sisters'; the 'brethren' were to go together to church, to assist at weddings and burials. A whole chapter in the by-laws of the Merchant Adventurers is given up to punishments for indecent language, quarrels between brethren, fighting, drunkenness, card-playing, immorality, keeping of hunting dogs and so on. . . . Apprentices were the children of the large family and were treated as such.[3]

Medieval elements were naturally more conspicuous in

[1] Cf. Lipson, II, p. 232 ff., on the policy embodied by the Merchant Adventurers.
[2] Wheeler, *op. cit.*; T. and P., III, pp. 285 and 303.
[3] Heckscher, *Mercantilism*, I, pp. 379-381. Cf. pp. 374-375, *ibid.*

the regulated companies than in the joint-stock associations, but even they took over something from the past. The East India Company, for example, levied an admission fine from new members, and favoured apprentices, the sons of members and employees above 'all others' who wished to become 'freemen' of the Company.

Equally typical was an early order issued by the East India Company to its agents. They were to collect their whole 'family', *i.e.* their whole staff, for morning and evening prayers. The expression 'mingled business with piety' . . . neatly characterizes the medieval heritage which English merchants preserved more carefully than did the merchants of other countries, and which was later imbued with new life, first by puritanism and then by the evangelical movement. Even the East India Company's rules for the good behaviour of its members at meetings were entirely in the spirit of the gilds and are reminiscent rather of the treatment of classes of school children.[1]

Other joint-stock companies showed some of the same characteristics, and there were various minor provisions for dinners, processions and mutual help which remind us of the gilds.[2] But although the discipline of the regulated companies may have 'helped to form the high personal character on which the old-fashioned merchants prided themselves',[3] and although the joint-stock companies retained some of the features of a 'ruled and ordered trade', the strongest tendency of the age was towards the free investment of capital; and the medieval ordering of commercial relationships

---

[1] Heckscher, *Mercantilism*, I, pp. 397-398. The instructions for the first voyage of the Company 'were not purely of a business nature. Detailed regulations were laid down for the preservation of health on the expedition and for the performance of religious duties: "for that religious government doth best bind men to perform their duties" ' (Lipson, II, p. 272). This is naïve, but the obvious Marxist retort would be, I think, beside the point.

[2] Scott, I, pp. 4-5, 10.   [3] Cunningham, II, p. 220.

was finally to give way before the increase of competition. At the period that we are considering, however, the old and the new were still blended, even in those forms of commercial enterprise which, in the long run, were the most powerful solvents of the traditional organization.

The Development of Industry

The profits made in commerce might be employed in various ways; they might be reinvested in fresh trading ventures, and they might be used in buying real estate and directed to the building and 'luxury' trades; but a large amount of capital thus accumulated found a fresh use in industry. England in the later years of Elizabeth and the reign of James I was alive with industrial projects. Many of the industries concerned were of comparatively recent origin; cloth-making, however, which the Privy Council described in 1616 as 'the noblest and richest manufacture of this kingdom, in the upholding whereof the commonwealth is as much interested as in any one thing whatsoever',[1] had had a long start of the others, and some of the most important aspects of the development of industrial capitalism are brought out by an examination of that industry.

The large-scale manufacture of cloth in England, begun in the later Middle Ages, was completely established by the reign of Henry VIII. Its development on capitalist, or semi-capitalist, lines was determined not only by the size of the market (about 1500 cloth exports formed 70 per cent. of the total exports of the country [2]), but by the extremely complicated processes which it involved. The wool had to be sheared, cleaned and carded before it was spun into yarn; then came weaving, fulling, and stretching, and then the

[1] *Acts of the Privy Council: James I*, III (1616–1617), p. 20.
[2] Astrid Friis, *Alderman Cockayne's Project and the Cloth Trade*, p. 12.

final stages of dyeing and dressing.[1] It is plain that, even though a very large proportion of English cloth was exported undyed and undressed, the woollen industry could not fit into the gild framework. What happened, of course, was that cloth manufacture developed as a 'domestic' industry, largely outside the towns, the various processes being held together by the capitalist clothier.

The average clothier bought his wool from the staplers or other wool merchants, giving it out successively to the carders, spinners, weavers, fullers, and sometimes to the dyers, rowers, and shearers. These worked in their own homes, almost always with their own tools, and were paid by the clothiers as piece-workers.[2]

By the time of Henry VIII the wealthy clothiers were of considerable social importance. John Winchcombe—Deloney's Jack of Newbury—stands as a symbol of many others, and, although we need not accept Deloney's figures, there is no doubt of the amount of labour that they controlled.[3] Under the impetus of rising prices and an expand-

[1] *Ibid.*, pp. 1-3.   [2] *Ibid.*, p. 23.

[3]   Within one room being large and long,
          There stood two hundred Looms full strong:
          Two hundred men the truth is so,
          Wrought in these Looms all in a row.
          By every one a pretty boy,
          Sate making quills with mickle joy;
          And in another place hard by,
          An hundred women merrily
          Were carding hard with joyfull cheer,
          Who singing sate with voices clear.
          And in a chamber close beside,
          Two hundred maidens did abide. . . .
          These pretty maids did never lin,
          But in that place all day did spin. . . .
In addition there were 150 children picking wool, fifty shearmen, eighty rowers, forty dyers, and twenty fullers.—Deloney, *Jacke of Newberie, Works*, ed. F. O. Mann, pp. 20-21. A letter printed in T. and P., I, p. 176, states that an Oxfordshire clothier 'setteth in

ing market (woollen goods formed the principal export of the great trading companies) the cloth industry developed rapidly. 'At the beginning of the seventeenth century the cloth exports of London alone, which were about 130,000 cloths annually, exceeded the average exported from the whole of England during the last years of the reign of Henry VIII.'[1] In Yorkshire, and elsewhere, the small masters might hold their own, but the dominant figure was plainly the clothier who, in the seventeenth century, might employ as many as a thousand persons,[2] and whose capital could bridge the time that must elapse between the buying of the wool and the selling of the cloth to drapers and merchants— often on a long credit.

Apart from the fact that the domestic system of textile manufacture was incompatible with the gild organization of the towns, the sixteenth-century woollen industry has a further representative significance, in its complexity, the opportunities that it offered to enterprise, and the fluctuations in the amount of employment that it provided.

In the first place, the extraordinarily difficult process of readjustment to new industrial conditions is hidden by the simple phrase 'the domestic system'; the reality was not simple. To start with, there were certain broad local distinctions. In the western counties the majority of those engaged in the different branches of cloth manufacture owned their own instruments, but they worked on material supplied by the clothier, and were paid by him. In Yorkshire, on the other hand, the typical figure was the working clothier, who bought his material, worked on it, and sold it himself;[3] even here, however, there were some 'opulent

occupation daily 500 of the king's subjects of all sorts, and if he might have carding and spinning he will set many more in work than he doth' (1538). [1] Friis, *op. cit.*, p. 61.
[2] Lipson, II, pp. 7, 17-18. [3] *Ibid.*, p. 69 ff.

clothiers' who corresponded to the clothiers of the West Country.[1] There were in addition, throughout the country, various classes of smaller capitalist employers—the 'market-spinners, who "set many spinners on work", and sold the yarn without working it up into cloth'; [2] the master combers (mainly in East Anglia) 'who owned the wool, employed journeymen combers to comb it and spinners to convert it into thread, and then sold the yarn to the master weavers'; [3] and master dressers who employed cloth-finishers in their own workshops.[4] The clothier, moreover, might not be merely an entrepreneur, he might possess a factory (more especially for the later processes),[5] he might be a grazier or even an exporter. Further complications in this complicated series of relationships are revealed when we consider the part played by credit in the industry; it was largely the necessity for credit that reduced many originally independent workers to a condition of 'indirect dependence on capital'.[6]

Secondly, the woollen industry was one of the first in which a mere combination of capital and general business ability, without a special technical training, was sufficient to secure success. The clothiers

> were recruited from nearly all classes of society. . . . We hear of people entering upon this occupation late in life, even of a lawyer turned clothier. Sometimes landowners who possessed sheep farms turned clothiers in order to work their own wool. A few merchants may also have invested capital in the manufacture of cloth. . . . Many, however, sprung from the lower classes. Some were originally dealers in wool, others shearers or cloth finishers, and very often men of very poor origin ended their lives as wealthy clothiers.[7]

[1] *Ibid.*, p. 81.　　　　　　[2] *Ibid.*, pp. 13 (note 4), 45.
[3] *Ibid.*, p. 13 (note 4).　　[4] *Ibid.*, pp. 53-54.　　[5] *Ibid.*, p. 54.
[6] The phrase is Sombart's.　For credit in the woollen industry see Lipson, II, pp. 3, 22, 79.
[7] Friis, *op. cit.*, pp. 24-25. Cf. Lipson, II, pp. 14-17.

Here was a career open to talents that would not find much scope in a purely local trade.

Finally, the organization of the industry on a national scale helped to destroy the comparative stability of the local market, and made the lives of individual workmen increasingly dependent upon nation-wide fluctuations of trade. When trade was slack the clothier gave out less work, and one of the most constant preoccupations of the Privy Council in the sixteenth and early seventeenth centuries was how to induce the clothiers—'on whose prosperity, and ability to give work to the poor, depended the social tranquillity of England'[1]—to maintain production in times of depression. Any large dislocation in the cloth-exporting trade—such as was caused, for example, by the war with Spain from 1588 onwards, the expulsion of the Merchant Adventurers from Germany in 1597, or Dutch competition in the reign of James I—reacted immediately on the clothiers and those whom they employed.[2] But contemporary opinion that fluctuations were due to the machinations of middlemen had, no doubt, some foundation in fact,[3] and uncertainty of employment was made inevitable by the nature of 'the domestic system'. 'There were always times in the year when many weavers were out of work, and probably no clothier could keep his men fully occupied the whole year round.'[4] The general situation in the sixteenth century is well described by Dr Robertson:

> Profits increased, but labour discontent and the growth of the 'class war' was violently stimulated, especially in the woollen industry, where the rise of 'clothierism' had greatly

[1] Friis, *op. cit.*, p. 22.   [2] Scott, I, pp. 97, 100, 168.
[3] An Act of 1593, directed against the yarn jobbers ('Drones, idle members, and evil weeds in a commonwealth') reflects popular opinion on the subject.—T. and P., I, pp. 375-376. The necessary function of the middleman is described by Lipson, II, pp. 21-22.
[4] Lipson, II, p. 64.

enhanced the speculative nature of production, and where so much depended on the freedom of the Continental market from war disturbances and on the course of the foreign exchanges. . . . The most cursory glance through the special legislation for the cloth industry and the records of the dealings of the Privy Council with the clothiers and the chief exporters of cloth, the Merchant Adventurers, is sufficient to establish much social unrest caused by the rapid development of this industry on a peculiarly speculative basis. There must have been many occasions of friction in the woollen industry, when, as Deloney put it, 'the poor hate the rich, because they will not set them on work; and the rich hate the poor, because they seem burdenous; so both are offended for want of gain'. These class conflicts inevitably brought about a lessened feeling of solidarity, a greater prominence for sectional interests, and new conceptions of the place of the individual in society.[1]

Almost all the industries that were considerably developed, or that were established, under Elizabeth and James I—for example, the manufacture of salt, glass, soap, wire and iron, mining for tin, copper and coal—were organized on capitalist lines. That is, they required an initial capital outlay and the possession of capital to finance operations; those who controlled the industry, by owning the material, or the material and the instruments of production, were not as a rule themselves craftsmen, and they engaged in the industry with a view to the profits of a national market. The history of the London companies in the sixteenth century and the first half of the seventeenth shows how far the older industries were subject to a parallel development.

It cannot be insisted too strongly that the rise of capitalist industry was not a simple transition from one clearly defined form of economic organization to another, or the mere

[1] Robertson, *Aspects of the Rise of Economic Individualism*, pp. 183-184.

supersession of one set of processes by another set. It is not only in the clothing industry that our definitions of 'capitalist' and 'semi-capitalist' cover an underlying complexity. Tin-mining in Cornwall and Devon provides another instructive example. There were capitalists in the industry in the Middle Ages, but a large quantity of tin continued to be extracted by the 'free miners'.[1] By the end of the sixteenth century the surface supplies of tin were largely exhausted. Deeper mining involved the use of pumps, and pumps required a capital outlay. Tin, moreover, could only be sold twice a year, and the tinners were in constant need of advances from the tin merchants, whose 'hard dealing' is described by Richard Carew:

> When any Western Gent. or person of accompt, wanteth money to defray his expenses at London, he resorteth to one of the Tin Merchants of his acquaintance, to borrow some; but they shall as soon wrest the club out of Hercules' fist, as one penny out of their fingers, unless they give bond for every twenty pound so taken in loan, to deliver a thousand pound weight of tin at the next coinage, which shall be within two or three months, or at farthest within half a year after. At which time the price of every thousand will not fail to be at least twenty three, perhaps twenty five pound: yea, and after promise made, the party must be driven (with some indignity) to make three or four errands to his house, ere he shall get the money delivered. In this sort, some one Merchant will have five hundred pound out beforehand, reaping thereby a double commodity, both of excessive gain for his loan, and of assurance to be served with tin for his money. This they say is no Usury, forsooth, because the price of tin is not certainly known beforehand. . . . But if to take above fifty in the hundred be extremity, whatsoever name you list to give it, this in truth can be none other than cutthroat and abominable dealing.[2]

[1] Lipson, II, p. 170.
[2] Richard Carew, *The Survey of Cornwall* (1602), p. 14 v. ff. (quoted in T. and P., I, p. 289 ff.). The local owners of tin works

Tin-mining was, therefore, indirectly controlled by the capitalist tin merchants even before the latter took direct control, working their own mines and managing their own smelting-houses (or leasing them to poor smelters), as they tended to do in the seventeenth century.[1] Here, as in the woollen industry, we find the same gradual encroachment of capitalist control, the same opportunities for the business man and entrepreneur, and, in the lower ranges of the industry, a similar loss of independence through the necessity for credit or loans.

Whichever of the larger industries we select in this period we find developments that until quite recently were regarded as peculiar to the late eighteenth and early nineteenth centuries. The earliest examples of industrial joint-stock companies were provided by the associated industries of copper-mining and brass-making. The Society of the Mines Royal, to mine copper, and the Mineral and Battery Works, to mine zinc ore (calamine), make brass and draw wire, were formed

treated the labouring tinners in much the same way, on a smaller scale, and a further passage from Carew, illustrating the nature of petty usury, is worth quoting: 'To these hungry flies [the owners of tin works] the poor labouring tinner resorteth, desiring some money before the time of his pay at the deliverance: the other puts him off at first, answering he hath none to spare: in the end, when the poor man is driven through necessity to renew his suit, he falls to questioning, what he will do with the money. Saith the tinner, I will buy bread and meat for my self and my household, and shoes, hosen, petticoats and such like stuff for my wife and children. Suddenly herein, this owner becomes a petty chapman: I will serve thee, saith he: he delivers him so much ware as shall amount to forty shillings, in which he cuts him half in half for the price, and four nobles of money, for which the poor wretch is bound in Darby's bonds, to deliver him two hundredweight of tin at the next Coinage, which may then be worth five pound or four at the very least. And as mischief still creeps onward, this extreme dealing of the London merchant and country chapman in white tin is imitated (or rather exceeded) by the wealthier sort of tinners themselves in the black.'

[1] Herman Levy, *Monopolies, Cartels and Trusts in British Industry*, p. 8.

early in the reign of Elizabeth, and incorporated in 1568. In the latter, as in the iron industry at a somewhat later date, there was a high degree of industrial 'integration'. The company 'owned "calamine mines" in Somersetshire. Thence the ore was conveyed to Nottingham or London (the company had brass factories at both places), copper was purchased from the Mines Royal society, and brass was made. In Monmouthshire the company was possessed of iron mines, whence it obtained ore to make "Osmond iron", which was drawn into wire. Finally, the wire (whether of iron or brass) was used in the manufacture of wool cards.'[1] Moreover, 'the two companies were closely associated, several persons owning shares in both',[2] although they were not formally united until after the Restoration; and since the right of 'mines royal' was involved, and the state was interested in the manufacture of brass for cannon, each enjoyed a monopoly. Even in the reign of Elizabeth the two industries together were estimated to maintain over 10,000 persons;[3] but it was not merely in the amount of labour employed that they marked an important step in the development away from the medieval economy. Each provided an opportunity for the investment of capital in industry, although at first a large proportion of the capital (as well as the mining skill) was provided by Germans.[4] In this way courtiers and noblemen such as Cecil, Leicester, Pembroke and Mountjoy obtained an interest in industry.[5]

In the iron industry, 'The discovery of a process by which coal could be employed in smelting iron ore engaged the attention of inventors for two centuries; and it serves as a

[1] Scott, I, p. 40.   [2] Ibid., p. 41.
[3] Ibid., p. 44. Cf. Scott, II, pp. 417, 425.
[4] Scott, II, p. 387. The brass and wool-card industries at least made handsome profits, although the Mines Royal seem to have worked at a loss for some years.—Ibid., pp. 394, 418.
[5] Scott, I, p. 46; II, pp. 395, 415.

fresh reminder that the "Industrial Revolution" was only the culmination of a long series of industrial experiments in which the initial stages were necessarily the slowest and most arduous.'[1] The career of Dud Dudley in the early seventeenth century would not seem out of place a hundred and fifty years later. Although in the seventeenth century there were still groups of 'free miners' and small independent, or semi-independent, manufacturers of metal wares,[2] the greater part of the iron industry was organized on a capitalist basis. 'The foundry and the forge were capitalist undertakings in which the raw material and the forge were owned, and the product marketed, by an entrepreneur; while capital was also invested in extracting the mineral as well as in the conversion of the metal into finished products.'[3] That there was money to be made in the industry is shown by Thomas Foley, 'who in the early seventeenth century "from almost nothing did get about five thousand pounds per annum or more by iron works", and endowed a hospital with an estate worth six hundred pounds a year'.[4]

Coal-mining, which in the seventeenth century was commonly ranked next to the woollen industry in importance, showed even more striking signs of being economically 'advanced'. Not only did the sinking and, more especially, the draining, of the deep pits that became necessary towards the end of the sixteenth century, involve a large capital outlay,[5] the industry demanded a temperament in the capitalist similar to that of the investors in the more obviously risky joint-stock ventures. 'Coal-mining was of necessity a speculative industry, since it was impossible to forecast even

---

[1] Lipson, II, p. 159. Between 1620 and 1640, 103 patents for inventions were issued, and of these 23 were for furnaces, ovens, smelting and refining.—W. H. Price, *The English Patents of Monopoly*, p. 110.   [2] Lipson, II, pp. 164, 171.
[3] *Ibid.*, p. 162.   [4] *Ibid.*, p. 164.   [5] *Ibid.*, pp. 118, 121.

approximately the risks and expenses involved; and as a field for the investment of capital it attracted those who were prepared to run a great hazard in the hope of substantial returns.'[1]   If many lost their money some made very considerable fortunes,—as did Sutton, the master of the ordnance at Berwick, who in ten years (1570–1580) was said to have made fifty thousand pounds out of coal-mining.[2] The larger coal-owners, however, did their best to eliminate uncertainty by typically modern methods.   By the end of Elizabeth's reign the Hostmen of Newcastle had not only secured a monopoly of the sale of coal in the most important mining district of the country, they owned most of the mines in the Tyne area.   Dr Lipson says of the Hostmen: 'This body exhibited all the characteristics of a highly developed monopoly.   In form it approximated closely to the modern cartel, and it anticipated the principal devices of a controlled market: restriction of membership, limitation of output, and regulation of prices.'[3]   In the early seventeenth century the society numbered about fifty members (not all of whom were actually engaged in the coal trade [4]), although individuals in the various combinations that were formed might head a group of partners.[5]   Naturally, both the monopoly and the 'Limitation of the Vend' received a good deal of hostile criticism, particularly from the London coal merchants. The Hostmen argued that their policy secured equal trading rights to all their members, so that the trade was not engrossed by a very few, that they supervised the quality of production,[6] that capital charges and wages had alike increased, and that some of the shares were held by widows

[1] Lipson, II, p. 119.
[2] *Ibid.*, p. 130.   Cf. Crowley's epigram on 'The Collier of Croydon' (1550): 'For his riches this collier might have been a knight' (*ibid.*, p. 147; T. and P., III, p. 129).
[3] Lipson, II, p. 128.
[4] *Ibid.*, p. 135.   [5] *Ibid.*, p. 132.   [6] *Ibid.*, p. 131.

and orphans.[1] The common opinion, however, was that the richer inhabitants of Newcastle were not content to use their trade 'for their moderate gain with some respect of the commonwealth, but by evil practice seek to increase and augment their gain, to the hurt of other her Majesty's subjects especially those of the poorer sort'.[2]

All that a rapid survey of this kind can do is to indicate the extent of capitalist development in English industry up to the first decades of the seventeenth century. Leaving the results of that development as they affected the lives of individuals to be discussed in the next chapter, we can now make a brief summary of its main economic aspects. By the reign of James I, then, many of the most important industries were conducted on a large scale for a national, or even an international, market, and sufficient capital was available to finance these undertakings. Although a large element of speculation was involved, large returns were made by successful ventures, and 'the profit motive' was the dominant factor in industrial expansion.[3] At the same time there was increasing scope for new forms of enterprise, in company formation and the general organization of industry by the entrepreneur, whilst the middleman had risen

[1] 'A Reply to the London Complaint against Newcastle' (1595), T. and P., I, pp. 282-284.

[2] 'Complaint of the Lord Mayor of London against the Newcastle Coal Monopoly' (1590), T. and P., I, pp. 267-271.

[3] At the end of the sixteenth century London was badly in need of a proper water supply, but when one, Morice, wished to pump water at London Bridge, he was forced to establish the enterprise at his own cost, 'since it was noted in 1593 that "no great man or magistrate" would open his purse to help him, the invention not being considered "sensible" '.—Scott, III, p. 11. It is more likely that potential investors were not interested in a project that did not promise large returns; there was no difficulty in finding capital for the most hair-brained schemes if the undertakers could hold out hopes of sufficient profit.

above his despised status of the Middle Ages to become an indispensable link in the national economy. There were, moreover, constant calls upon the inventive skill of the technician, and from the time of Burghley the state encouraged the introduction of new processes in the manufacture of articles and commodities of common use—paper, starch, sugar, soap, salt, glass, silks, felt, cloth, metal goods, and so on.

There was, of course, another side to industrial progress. Just as commercial expansion tended to increase the distance between the poor and the rich, so the rise of wealthy captains of industry implied a corresponding loss of scope and status, if not of actual earning capacity, for the manual worker. Even in the capitalist industries the small working masters did not completely disappear until the Industrial Revolution, but by the seventeenth century very many had become hired workers or had become dependent upon the capital of the large undertakers. In the lower ranges there was uncertainty and frequent unemployment, due largely to the reaction of trade depressions upon industry, and 'the divorce of the artisan from the soil' and the creation of an industrial proletariat dates from the sixteenth century. Finally we have to notice that capitalist industry, with its dependence upon money power, increased the national importance of credit and usury.

What one has to realize is that these developments, so obviously 'modern', existed in a setting that was still 'medieval' or, at least, 'traditional'. It was the coexistence of such fundamentally opposed kinds of economic organization, even within a single industry, that raised a mass of new problems, often only dimly understood. For contemporaries these all tended to be subsumed into one major problem—the problem of the monopolies; but that is something that demands separate treatment.

Monopolies and Projects

The word 'monopoly' is usually made to do duty for a good many different kinds of exclusive privilege, and, as Dr Heckscher has pointed out, 'the use of the expression has suffered from the same defect as the term treason in the ironic answer in the epigram "treason doth never prosper. . . ."' It has very seldom been applied to anything acceptable to a writer or speaker.'[1] 'Monopoly' was used pejoratively from its first appearance in the language,[2] and by the end of Elizabeth's reign it had already become a convenient shorthand for a variety of practices, so that it is difficult to get at the truth behind the controversy that engaged so much attention during the first forty years of the seventeenth century.

The word was a coinage of the sixteenth century,[3] but one cannot describe the economic history of the Middle Ages without using it. The policy of the gilds, for example, was directed towards securing a monopoly for those engaged in a particular trade in any district. The monopolies exercised by the gilds, however, were very different from the monopolies of the reigns of Elizabeth and James I. The former were possessed by groups of traders or craftsmen; they were local in scope; and they were directed towards securing the preservation of a recognized social order. The latter were held by individuals as well as by corporations; they were national monopolies that drew the entire trade in certain commodities into a few hands; and as often as not

[1] *Mercantilism*, I, p. 270.

[2] 'The Lord Keeper, Sir Nicholas Bacon, was asked his opinion by Queen Elizabeth of one of these Monopoly Licences. And he answered: Will you have me speak truth, Madam? *Licentia omnes deteriores sumus*: We are all the worse for a licence' (Bacon, *Apophthegms*, *Works*, ed. Ellis and Spedding, VII, p. 125).

[3] The first example in the N.E.D. is dated 1534.

71

their purpose was economic exploitation without regard for the community. The Middle Ages of course were not free from monopolistic exploitation,[1] but the provisions that secured the local monopoly of any gild were part of a larger scheme of regulation which regarded such matters as the quality of goods, fair dealing and personal relationships, whilst the typical monopolist of the later period was entirely free from traditional checks and guided only by the desire for profit. Finally, a monopoly that could be justified on many grounds whilst trade was comparatively static, would inevitably become oppressive as soon as trade began to expand.

The variety of practices that 'the monopolies' of the Elizabethan-Jacobean period were meant to serve is brought out by Unwin:

> The monopolies were, in fact, a crude device for solving at one stroke a great many political, social, and economic problems which are not yet solved, and which could only be put on the way towards solution by being carefully separated from each other and dealt with each on its own merits. They were not only to provide the king with money, but also to furnish salaries, pensions, and rewards to his friends and servants; whilst at the same time they were to encourage native industries, to check the evils of 'dumping', to protect the small manufacturer from the domination of the capitalist, and to guarantee to the consumer a supply of sound and serviceable commodities at reasonable rates.[2]

The patentees and monopolists undertook—for a consideration—to perform the functions now entrusted to the Home

[1] See, for example, Unwin, *Gilds*, p. 40 (on the Fishmongers' monopoly), and p. 78 (on price-raising by the London Grocers). Unwin also quotes a statute of 1437 alleging that the gilds raised prices 'for their own singular profit and to the common hurt and damage of the people' (*ibid.*, p. 161). Heckscher (*Mercantilism*, I, p. 273) discusses the nature of gild monopoly or, as he calls it, 'oligopoly based on a fair standard of living'.

[2] Unwin, *Gilds*, pp. 293-294.

Office, the Board of Trade, the departments of Customs and Inland Revenue. They devised and collected a great variety of new indirect taxation, they inspected and penalized trade abuses, they sold dispensations from impracticable laws, and licensed forbidden pleasures.[1]

As these quotations indicate, the monopolies were of four main kinds. The first group consisted of patents delegating various fiscal rights of the Crown—the collection of indirect taxes on certain goods, or the collection of fines and forfeitures.[2] Secondly, there were licences permitting the patentees to relax statute laws that could not be generally applied.[3] Other patents gave powers of supervision over trades and industries; thus Raleigh had the right to issue tavern licences, and the Duke of Lennox that of supervising and sealing New Draperies.[4] But it was the fourth group— the industrial monopolies—that was of greatest economic importance.

It was generally recognized that not only had an inventor the right to exclusive use of his invention for a period of years, but that it was the duty of the state to foster young industries, particularly those that were of national importance. Most of Elizabeth's industrial patents—for mining, saltpetre, glass, alum and steel—could be justified on these grounds. Plainly, however, the invention of a new process

[1] Unwin, 'Commerce and Coinage', *Shakespeare's England*, I, p. 335.

[2] *E.g.* Raleigh's patent 'Of Tonnage and Poundage for Wines', under Elizabeth; the grant to Lord Danvers (for a fixed sum) of fines and forfeitures above £2800 a year, 'the Green Wax' (Sir Roger Aston) and 'Jurors' (Sir Henry Bronker) patents under James I. On the last three see Scott, I, pp. 131, 138.

[3] The grants to the Merchant Adventurers, and various individuals, to export unfinished cloth (Lipson, III, p. 376); the tanning patent, and the patent for gig-mills, the licence to Thomas Cornwallis 'to keep unlawful games'.

[4] Scott, I, pp. 138, 173; Lipson, III, p. 354; Price, *The English Patents of Monopoly*, p. 27.

could be made the excuse for a monopoly over a settled industry, and in the reigns of James I and Charles I many of the major industries were subject to a monopoly that had originated in this way. The patent granted to Cockayne and the New Merchant Adventurers for finishing cloth was only the most notorious instance of a monopoly which promised additional revenue to the Crown and greater wealth to the country, and only succeeded in throwing the whole industry into confusion. The manufacture of glass, alum, iron, salt, starch and soap were all subject to monopolies in this period.[1]

This is not the place to describe the working of any of the monopolies in detail. Their significance is best brought out by a consideration of the motives and pressures that called them into being. In the first place there was the tradition of economic regulation that the Tudor state took over from the medieval gilds and municipalities, and that combined with the mercantilist policy of industrial protection. The administrative patents[2] and the monopolies due to special needs of the state have already been mentioned. Secondly, the financial needs of the Crown formed a strong inducement to farm out state rights for a guaranteed sum, or to create a monopoly for those who would pay well for it. Elizabeth used patents instead of pensions;[3] her successors also used them in a vain attempt to make the crown income equal its expenditure.

[1] Price, *op. cit.*, *passim*; Lipson, III, pp. 355, 362-386.

[2] State supervision was also exercised directly, by means of an administrative staff—the aulnagers in the woollen industry, for example —and indirectly through the existing mechanism of the gilds or through the trading companies.

[3] 'The queen our sister . . . finding . . . that some things had passed her hands, at the importunity of her servants, whom she was willing to reward with little burden to her estate (otherwise by necessary occasion exhausted). . . .' (Proclamation of James I, 1603: Price, *op. cit.*, Appendix I.)

A single judgement on the different sets of motives that might induce the Crown to issue 'monopolies and patents of privilege' is clearly impossible. In the absence of an organized Civil Service it might well appear that a patent was the only means of securing some control over an expanding industry; and even the sale of monopolies by Charles I for fiscal reasons has to be remembered together with his painstaking supervision of industry on the one hand,[1] and the chronic financial embarrassments that resulted from attempting to meet the needs of a modern state with an antiquated system of finance, on the other. But the creation of monopolies might result from other inducements—the pressure of needy courtiers and projectors.

Much of the work now undertaken by the diplomatic corps and civil service was performed without salary by members of the Tudor aristocracy. Many of them had been paid in advance by the grants of monastic land that Henry VIII made to their fathers, but the expenses of an ambassadorship abroad, or even of organizing work at home, were heavy, and Elizabeth's servants inevitably looked to her for perquisites. There was not anything necessarily dishonourable in this. A decent example is provided by Sir Edward Dyer, who spent his life doing miscellaneous governmental work which left him—like Sidney, Walsingham, Hatton and half the great Elizabethans—constantly in debt. His rewards included the stewardship of

[1] Even Unwin, who believed in *laissez-faire*, admitted that 'there was a real bond of interest between the Stuarts and the bodies of small master craftsmen who constituted the working class of the seventeenth century' (*Gilds*, p. 329). 'The records of the Privy Council during the period when Charles governed without a Parliament leave no doubt as to the sincere desire of the King or of his ministers to promote the interests of the working classes' (*Industrial Organization*, p. 143). Charles regularly attended the frequent meetings of the Privy Council, which spent a large part of its time in considering industrial affairs. See Price, *op. cit.*, pp. 40-43.

Woodstock, an unprofitable patent to search out lands concealed from the Crown, and (1576), a 'Licence to pardon and dispense with tanning of leather contrary to the statute of 5 Eliz., and to license any man to be a tanner'. Concerning the tanning patent his biographer remarks: 'Neither Edward Dyer nor his fellow courtiers questioned the social justice of a system which allowed these monopolistic grants to private persons. To them, the operation of such a patent offered simply a fitting and proper means for maintaining the living expenses of men of their class.'[1]

But patents of this kind were not merely a reward for services rendered. As Sir Egerton Brydges remarked, 'The reign of Queen Elizabeth was a period of difficulty for the individuals whom it excited to fame and distinction, in which was cherished an emulation of great things with insufficient means'.[2] The increase in luxury will be discussed later;[3] here we need only remember that courtly 'magnificence' was not often disassociated from ostentation; that the court of James I demanded even greater expenditure than that of Elizabeth; and that those who carried their birthrights proudly on their backs necessarily lived beyond their incomes. A monopoly offered one of the most tempting means of enrichment, and there was keen competition for the rights that a patent might confer.[4] Grants to courtiers had reached formidable proportions by the end of Eliza-

---

[1] Ralph M. Sargent, *At the Court of Queen Elizabeth, The Life and Lyrics of Sir Edward Dyer*, pp. 35-36.

[2] Preface to Breton's *Melancholic Humours* (ed. 1815), p. 4. For the connexion between economic difficulties and the 'melancholy' of the period see Appendix B, 'Seventeenth-Century Melancholy', below.

[3] See below, p. 117. Sargent, *op. cit.*, gives a good account of the expenses of court life under Elizabeth.

[4] Cf. Scott, I, p. 112, for the competition between Lord Buckhurst and the Earl of Oxford for the royal right of pre-emption of tin in 1593.

beth's reign, and were duly noted by a contemporary satirist.

> Ye Courtiers, so may you in courtly sort
> With manners old, old Courtiers long remain,
> So that some upstart courtiers ye refrain,
> Unworthy of a peerless prince's port.
> As courtier leather, courtier pin, and soap,
> And courtier vinegar, and starch and card;
> And courtier cups, such as were never heard,
> And such as shall not court it long, we hope.[1]

In the industrial monopolies the courtier was usually associated with a business man—a union of capital and enterprise with influence. The courtier's 'countenance' [2] was not given for nothing, and the ramifications of bribery made a weight that had to be borne by the nation at large.[3]

---

[1] Bastard, *Chrestoleros*, Book II, Epigr. 17. Cf. Greene, *Quip for an Upstart Courtier, Works* (ed. Grosart), X, pp. 227, 239.

[2] MEERCRAFT: He shall but be an undertaker with me,
    In a most feasible business. It shall cost him
    Nothing. . . . Except he please, but's countenance,
    (That I will have) to appear in't, to great men,
    For which I'll make him one.
                                    (*The Devil is an Ass* (1616), II, i.)
And see the Projector's speeches in Massinger's *The Emperor of the East* (1631), I, ii.

[3] In the reign of James I, Sir Thomas Bartlett, carver-in-ordinary to the Queen, attempted to obtain a monopoly for the Pinmakers' Company; he offered £4000 to Sir Ralph Winwood if he would use his influence on their behalf, and spent £8000 in buying out another courtier interested in the business.—Unwin, *Industrial Organization*, pp. 164-168. In 1615 the Earl of Montgomery and Sir Robert Mansell were admitted into the partnership that had secured the glass monopoly. 'It is doubtful if they paid anything; their influence at Court being regarded as a contribution to the capital' (Scott, I, p. 174); and they were associated with 'divers others of the prime lords of the Court' (Howell, *Familiar Letters*, ed. Jacobs, p. 19), who expected to make something out of the industry. Scott gives other instances (I, pp. 175-176) which show that 'the sums payable to influential persons at Court by those who sought for grants, constituted a great drain on industry'. Heckscher (*Mercantilism*, I, p. 253) quotes

With the evidence that is available, one has to accept the severe verdict that has been passed on these, 'the titled directors and company promoters of that age': [1]

> In the hands of the corrupt courtiers the system of monopolies, designed originally to foster new arts, became degraded into a system of plunder. Projects of all sorts found advocates and, for a considerable time at least, there was no adequate machinery for investigation into the expediency of suits. The great majority of courtiers holding these privileges acted in the boldest spirit of exploitation. Having no acquaintance with the arts over which they were set, the only mission that they recognized was that of helping themselves in a mercenary and extortionate manner.[2]

The courtiers, however, were rarely the initiators of the industrial projects for which monopoly rights were sought, and it is the projector himself who deserves most attention.

In 1637 John Smyth, steward of the Berkeley estates, was involved in a lawsuit concerning land reclaimed from the Severn. The case was likely to form an important precedent, and Smyth tells us that 'to the hearing came a number of projectors, as they ignominiously by as many of better condition then also present, were styled: of whom I have not since heard, nor hope that hereafter I shall'.[3] The remark suggests that even at that date 'projector' was still regarded as a new word; but it was one which had long been

---

one who 'wrote in 1618 with engaging frankness that "having spent a great part of his means in soliciting and seeking after suits, he had at last hit upon one" in the supervision of English lead'. The courtier, Fitton, in *The Staple of News* (1625) is

> a moth, a rascal, a court rat,
> That gnaws the commonwealth with broking suits.
> (IV, i.)

[1] Unwin, 'Commerce and Coinage', *Shakespeare's England*, I, p. 335.

[2] Price, *op. cit.*, p. 17.

[3] John Smyth of Nibley, *The Berkeley Manuscripts* (ed. Sir John Maclean), III, p. 346.

'ignominious'.[1]   Projecting, or the floating of schemes that might be made profitable by means of a monopoly, was a phenomenon of the early seventeenth century that corresponded in some ways to stock-jobbing at a later date.   In a pamphlet of the latter part of the reign of Charles I the projector is thus described:

> He employs all his time, labour, study and experience only to search out the abuses of every place, profession and mystery whatsoever.   Next his greatest study is to propose the fair outside of a reformation; and this he begins with a petition to his majesty, with such mighty pretences of enriching the kingdom that he dares most impudently to affirm that it shall bring to his majesty, his heirs and successors for ever many thousands yearly—yea, and employment for all the poor people of the realm (which how well all these late projects have effected, I leave to judicious censure).[2]

'Advantageous to the country, not burdensome to those affected, profitable to the queen, and a source of some slight profit to the petitioner' was almost the established formula

[1] Robertson (*op. cit.*, p. 192) points out that King James 'used the word "projector" as a general term of abuse along with "viper" and "pest" in a speech to Parliament in 1604'.   He also quotes the author of a contemporary scheme for reorganizing the fishing industry: 'Let not the foul name of project make you prejudicate in your opinions. . . . There is no burden that the sharpness of lewd brains can invent to vex the commonwealth withal, but they style it by the name of Project, pretending a fair face under a foul vizard.'

[2] Brugis, *The Discovery of a Projector* (1641), quoted by Lipson, III, p. 356.   Cf. 'A Catch-poll is one that doth both catch and poll: who is not content only to have the sheep, but must shear it too; and not shear it but to draw blood.   So then by this etymology of the word, any one that sinisterly wrests and screws Monopolies into his hands, to fill his coffers, (though his own conscience whispers in his ear that he beggars the commonwealth) and his Prince never the better for it, but the poor subjects much the worse, he is a Grand Catchpoll.'   (Dekker, *A Strange Horse-Race* (1613), *Non-Dramatic Works*, ed. Grosart, III, pp. 366-367.)

of the patent hunters,[1] and these seem to have found a sufficient number who believed at least in the last part of the description, and were willing to invest accumulated capital in the hope of sharing the 'slight profit'.

> The floating of projects became a craze. The projectors all touted in support of their flotations . . . painting their own schemes with glowing colours, decrying their rivals, and, if this was insufficient, following the Belgian example of raising funds by a lottery. It was not long before the speculative wave became pathological. The bucket-shop type of speculation was too much in evidence.[2]

'The essence of capitalism' may lie in 'rational speculation',[3] but it took more than a hundred years of capitalist activity for investors to learn what 'rational speculation' was. Unfortunately there is no account of the more hair-brained schemes in which the Fitzdottrels of the age lost their money, but the satire of contemporaries affords some indication of the fantastic nature of innumerable projects.[4]

The projects, however, were not all 'for supplying the realm with toothpicks', and the projectors were not all Meercrafts who lived solely on their dupes. Some were actively engaged in organizing the major industries, and the only objection that can be made against these early captains of

[1] E. P. Cheyney, *A History of England from the Armada to the Death of Elizabeth*, II, p. 289.

[2] Robertson, *op. cit.*, p. 191.

[3] *Ibid.*, p. 46.

[4] See below, pp. 210-218, on *The Devil is an Ass*. The list of projects by which Sir Edmund Verney attempted, unsuccessfully, to solve his financial difficulties in the reign of Charles I is of some interest. They included a patent for 'garbling' tobacco, the hackney coach patent, a patent for sealing woollen yarn, and a lease of some reclaimed fen lands, and Sir Edmund considered sharing in a patent 'for the supply of turf to be taken from the waste places of his Majesty's dominions for 14 years' (*Memoirs of the Verney Family during the Seventeenth Century*, I, pp. 68-70).

industry is that they aimed merely at snatching as large a profit as possible for themselves, and that too often they succeeded in ruining or retarding the industries concerned.

A representative example is Sir Arthur Ingram, who managed the royal alum monopoly in the last half of the reign of James I. The son of a linen draper, he became a successful merchant, and then launched into real estate. 'In buying estates his practice was to pay half the purchase-money down, then, pretending to detect some flaw in the title, he would compel the seller to have recourse to a chancery suit. In this way he ruined many.' He lent money to James I, he became Comptroller of the Customs in the Port of London, a secretary to the Council of the North, and an M.P.; he was knighted in 1613, and he founded a hospital at York.[1]

In 1607 Lord Sheffield had secured a monopoly for working the Yorkshire alum deposits, for himself, Sir Thomas Challoner, Sir David Fowles and Sir John Bourchier, who obtained the necessary capital from London merchants. In 1609 the projectors were bought out by the Crown, and after a period of complete confusion the business was taken over by a group of which Ingram was the most prominent partner. The history of the alum monopoly during the next ten years is one of dishonesty and mismanagement. The partners quarrelled with each other and had law-suits with their agents, and as a result of the frequent complaints of peculation an ineffective commission of enquiry was opened in 1616. In 1619 Bourchier, who also had an eye on the soap monopoly, attempted to supplant Ingram, who, he claimed, 'had wrongfully gained £53,000 in seven years, had not disbursed funds entrusted to him for the works, had not performed his covenants, and had abused his workpeople'.[2]

[1] *Dictionary of National Biography.*
[2] Price, *op. cit.*, p. 94. This account of the alum monopoly is taken entirely from chap. vii of Dr Price's book.

Most of the charges seem to have been true. A second commission was instituted and new bids and new bribes were offered for the monopoly, which, in the reign of Charles I came into the hands of Sir Paul Pindar. Ingram, meanwhile, had been forced to retire from the business, but thanks to his influence with the King he not only escaped punishment, but even received compensation on his withdrawal.

> The alum industry was the most important business venture of King James, and it failed, partly through the business inefficiency of the king and his ministers, partly through the gross and culpable mismanagement of those to whom the work was entrusted. . . . Sir Arthur Ingram, who, more than any other, was responsible for the conditions that prevailed at the works, was allowed to follow this enterprise for the king's glory, because he was too much of a rascal to be tolerated even at court, yet had to be provided for. He was permitted to retain his connexion long after his unscrupulous methods were well understood. The ease with which about £100,000 was drawn from the king in successive instalments, only to melt away imperceptibly with but little advantage to the works, would be incomprehensible if it were not known how easily others secured large amounts from the same source. The most that any one of the several commissions of enquiry could discover as a result of all the outlay were a few inadequate buildings, sadly decayed, and a body of desperate and starving workmen. . . . Prices were raised and the quality of the product deteriorated. There can be no possible doubt as to the commercial failure of the monopoly.[1]

The public outcry against monopolies was not of course always a straightforward outburst of indignation. Scott remarks that, 'All through the seventeenth century, the most powerful arguments against existing privileges were those of the would-be monopolists'.[2] But popular opposition ran

[1] Price, *op. cit.*, pp. 100-101.
[2] Scott, I, p. 121. Cf. *ibid.*, p. 248 (examples of monopolists who opposed other people's monopolies); II, pp. 266-289 (the wranglings

deeper than that. 'Nearly all the monopolists had . . . promised to supply a better quality more cheaply. In no single case was this promise fulfilled.'[1] It is difficult to say how far the rise in price of coal, soap, salt, copper-wire, glass and similar articles was directly due to the monopolies, and how far it was due to more general causes. But the abuses in actual administration were notorious. A speaker in the debate of 1601 declared that the town that he represented was 'pestered and continually vexed with the substitutes, or vicegerents, of these monopolitans',[2] and these 'monstrous and unconscionable substitutes'[3] were a frequent cause of complaint. It was said that the searchers for illegal playing cards under D'Arcy's patent summoned offenders to appear at courts fifty miles away, so that the accused compounded with them for a money payment rather than lose their time.[4] A clause in the Statute of Monopolies suggests how some of the patents had been exercised:

> And be it further enacted . . . that if any person or persons . . . . shall be hindered, grieved, disturbed, or disquieted, or his or their goods or chattels any way seized, attached, distrained, taken, carried away, or detained by occasion or pretext of any monopoly . . . that . . . the same person and persons shall and may have his and their remedy for the same at the common law.[5]

of rival monopolists in the Virginia and Somers Islands Companies). Compare *Commons Journals*, I, p. 253 (quoted by Durham, *op. cit.*, p. 205): 'There was a great concourse of Clothiers and Merchants from all parts, and especially of London, who were so divided as that all clothiers and all merchants of England complained of engrossing of trade and restraint of trade by rich merchants of London, and of the London merchants three parts joined in the same complaint of the fourth part, and of the fourth part some stood stiffly for their own companies yet repined at the other companies'.

[1] Levy, *op. cit.*, p. 46.   [2] T. and P., II, p. 270.
[3] *Ibid.*, p. 274.   [4] Scott, I, p. 115.
[5] 21 Jac. I, cap. 3, section IV—Price, *op. cit.*, Appendix A. Compare the king's proclamation in 1603, which declared that many

The farming system that developed under the patent for licensing inns led the delegates and sub-delegates—who had paid for their offices—to issue licences indiscriminately, whilst they punished severely any who refused to obey their regulations.[1]   The agents of the Duke of Lennox, who held the patent for sealing New Draperies, sold the seals that were supposed to be an official guarantee of quality.[2]   The administration of the industrial patents provided similar instances of profiteering combined with brutality.   When in 1618 the monopoly for manufacturing gold and silver thread came into the king's hands, the commissioners followed the example set by private monopolists.

> The gold-thread industry, as a royal monopoly, was conducted with a reckless disregard of the most rudimentary commercial morality.   The silver and the silk were 'sophisticated' shamelessly.   Lead or quick-silver was mixed with the silver; and a workman was brought from Italy, who could dye silk 'with an advantage of weight', whereby an addition of one-third was made. . . . The artizans were bound to produce a certain amount each week, neither more nor less, and they were forced to pay nearly 60 per cent. of their earnings to the Commissioners, who were appointed to supervise them. . . .
> It was shown that Mompesson threatened wire-workers, who withstood him, that he 'would fill all the prisons of

patents were 'of such a nature as could hardly be put in use without hindrance to multitudes of people, or else committed to inferior persons, who in the execution thereof did so exceedingly abuse the same, as they became intolerable' (Price, *op. cit.*, Appendix I).

[1] Scott, I, pp. 173-174.   In 1621, 1000 persons had been outlawed for refusing to pay the licensing fee.   In 1616 Sir Giles Mompesson became one of the commissioners for licensing inns.   He 'performed his duties with reckless audacity.   He charged exorbitant fees, exacted heavy fines from respectable innkeepers for trifling neglect of the licensing laws, and largely increased the number of inns by granting, on payment of heavy sums, new licences to keepers of houses that had been closed on account of disorderly conduct' (*D.N.B.*).

[2] Scott, I, p. 138; Price, *op. cit.*, p. 27.

London with them and that they would rot there'. Sir Edward Villiers used similar language, and this was surpassed by the brutality of the agents, one of whom, in addition to arresting a workman, threatened 'to pull the flesh from his jaws and to starve his wife and children'. The depositions of the wire-drawers before the House of Lords show that these were no mere empty threats.[1]

It is not surprising that in 1621 the king was forced to promise 'the removal of monopolies, of which there were at this time seven hundred in the kingdom, granted by letters patent under the broad seal, to the enriching of some few projectors, and the impoverishing of all the kingdom beside'.[2]

It has been claimed that the attempts to build up the alum industry as a government monopoly 'furnish interesting illustrations to anyone who believes in the unfitness of government to administer industrial undertakings'.[3] Rather, this and similar undertakings provide a comment on protected private enterprise. In a period of capitalist expansion in which the tradition of state regulation was not implemented by an efficient civil service, protection for the 'public good' was inevitably made to serve the interests of 'private profit'. The history of the alum monopoly shows the characteristic features of early industrial capitalism. There was accumulated capital to be invested, and there was a demand for industrial development; there was neither understanding of the new economy nor control. The situation therefore provided a fair field for men like Ingram, to whom Sir Lionel Cranfield wrote in 1607: 'One rule I desire may be observed between you and me, which is that neither of us seek to advance our estates by the other's loss, but that we may join together faithfully to raise our fortunes by such

[1] Scott, I, p. 177. For the interests concerned in the monopoly see Unwin, *Gilds*, pp. 315-317, and pp. 274-275, below.
[2] D'Ewes, *Autobiography* (ed. Halliwell), I, p. 171.
[3] Price, *op. cit.*, p. 82.

casualties as this stirring age shall afford'.[1]   Not all the projectors were dishonest; the one concern of Dud Dudley, for example, seems to have been to find an efficient method of smelting iron with coal.   But the outstanding figures are the Ingrams, the Mompessons, the Cranfields.

It was against this kind of monopolist, in whose hands a more or less considerable political power lay and who without regard for the interests of the thousands he injured changed the social, industrial, and fiscal conditions of the country and brought his dominating influence to bear on the most diverse fields of economic life, against the capitalist financier of large industrial monopolies who made himself unequivocally a dictator of national industry, that the anger of the people and of Parliament was chiefly directed in the anti-monopoly movement.[2]

Note.—In this section I have been concerned merely to establish the more significant features of the system of monopolies.   A very brief chronological account of public policy towards the patents will provide a framework.

As early as 1571 references had been made in Parliament to the abuses of 'licences and promoters',[3] and the question was raised again in 1597, but it was not until 1601 that the subject was thoroughly debated.   Some forty grants were objected to, and as a result the Queen issued a proclamation revoking the more obnoxious patents, and declaring that the others should be liable to trial at common law.   In D'Arcy's case (1603) the decision was against the patentee.   Early in James's reign a Commission for Suits was instituted,[4] and the king made some public protestations, but he did not discontinue the monopolies.   After 1600 patents generally contained a revocation clause. 'In consequence of the oppor-

[1] Lipson, III, p. 357.
[2] Levy, *op. cit.*, p. 59.   [3] Scott, I, p. 53.
[4] 'A pox upon referring to commissioners!' (Lady Tailbush, *The Devil is an Ass*, IV, i).

86

tunity thus afforded, the government assumed an attitude that was as erratic as it was indulgent. Grants which could be so easily revoked might be all the more readily and safely passed, and, on the other hand, they were recalled whenever this was demanded by expediency.'[1] Patents changed hands with bewildering rapidity, and when in 1614 Parliament withheld supplies the king attempted to meet his needs by a reckless granting of monopolies. This was the period of Cockayne's notorious cloth-finishing scheme which, it was estimated, would increase the wealth of the country by £300,000 a year, a substantial portion going direct to the Crown.[2] In 1616 the more complaisant Bacon replaced Ellesmere as Chancellor. In 1621 Parliament took proceedings against Mompesson and Michell, the agents of the Villiers, but the Duke of Buckingham and his brothers escaped impeachment. A royal proclamation revoking certain of the patents was followed in 1624 by the Statute of Monopolies, which declared all internal monopolies illegal, except for a few specified by name, patents for inventions, and monopolies vested in corporations. Charles I's policy of creating monopolistic corporations lies outside the scope of this study. It was prompted partly by fiscal considerations, partly by a genuine desire to protect the small master craftsman; but the effective power remained in the hands of the capitalist undertakers. The statute 'compelled the would-be monopolist to become a company promoter, and it offered the strongest inducements to the would-be

[1] Price, *op. cit.*, p. 30.
[2] By 1614 the charter of the Merchant Adventurers had been called in, the export of undyed and undressed cloth prohibited, and the New Merchant Adventurers incorporated. By 1616 the whole of the cloth trade was in confusion, and in the following year the older company was restored. The results of the experiment formed one of the main causes of the depression which began in 1620. See Friis, *Alderman Cockayne's Project and the Cloth Trade.*

corporation to assume the form of a monopoly'. But 'the craftsmen were only pawns in the game'.[1] Monopolies formed one of the principal grievances of 1639-1640, and a great number of them were cancelled by the Long Parliament.

The 'New Men'

The intensive economic activity that has been described resulted in the rise of a class of 'new men'—clothiers, financiers, merchants, entrepreneurs. These owed their power not to the possession of land, like the old feudal nobility, nor to political-administrative talents, like the newer members of the Tudor aristocracy, but solely to their business ability. There were 'new men', of course, in the Middle Ages, but from the mid-sixteenth century onwards there were far greater opportunities for a far greater number, and the opportunities were not merely economic; the *nouveaux riches* of the reigns of Elizabeth and James I acquired social and political power, and exercised a dominating influence on the course of English history.

Many of these new men have already been mentioned, and short of a complete study (which they deserve [2]), there is little that can be added here. A brief account of a few other representatives of the class will, however, serve to emphasize their importance in the period under discussion.

[1] Unwin, *Gilds*, p. 319.

[2] 'Si vraiment, à chaque période de l'histoire économique correspond une classe nouvelle de capitalistes, il y aura lieu de rechercher soigneusement quelle influence l'apparition, dans l'histoire d'une société bien connue et facile à étudier, d'une generation de "nouveaux riches" d'un type déterminé, a pu exercer sur l'orientation générale de cette société, sur sa vie intellectuelle et morale' (L. Febvre, 'Les Nouveaux Riches et L'Histoire', *Revue des Cours et Conférences*, 15 juin 1922). That indeed would be an interesting study, though it is unlikely that sufficient material is available for the early, formative period of capitalism in England to do more than give the outlines of their careers.

One of the most enterprising was Sir Bevis Bulmer, whose career has recently been the subject of a careful study.[1] In the reigns of Elizabeth and James I he was concerned in a variety of projects: he obtained a patent for 'cutting and making of iron into small rods', he attempted to organize an elaborate lighthouse scheme, and he was one of the first to pump water from the Thames to supply the houses of the West of London; he obtained the right of levying an impost on sea coals, and he was willing to farm the impost on sweet wines. But the main business of his life was mining. He is first heard of in 1566 in connexion with mining affairs in Scotland, and twenty years later he was one of three partners in a silver mine at Combe Martin in Devonshire, which in two years yielded each of the partners £20,000. He mined lead in the Mendips, and lead and gold in Lanarkshire, and he was said to have collected £100,000 worth of gold in the Ettrick Forest. In 1599 he failed to obtain control of the tin mines of Devon and Cornwall, but with the accession of James I his schemes assumed even greater proportions.

> In the first year of the reign, Bulmer had an audience with the king, in which a 'plott' was hatched for providing capital for a search for gold in Scotland with a thoroughness and on a scale unprecedented. The plan was to secure a contribution of £300 sterling from each of 24 gentlemen . . . and in return each should be knighted, and be known for ever as the 'Knight of the Golden Mynes or the Golden Knight'.[2]

Only one knight was made, but to the end of his life Bulmer (now knighted himself) continued to have the king's backing. In 1606 he was concerned in the West Lothian silver mines, whose discovery caused 'a great sensation'. In 1608

---

[1] H. M. Robertson, 'Sir Bevis Bulmer, A Large-Scale Speculator of Elizabethan and Jacobean Times', *Journal of Economic and Business History*, IV, No. 1, Nov. 1931. All of my information on Bulmer is taken from this article.

[2] *Op. cit.*, pp. 110-111.

he was made master of the silver mines at a salary of £56
(Scots) a week. When in 1613 he ceased to work the mines
(which were taken over by a syndicate that included Sir
William Alexander) he retired to the silver-lead mining area
of Alston Moor in Cumberland, where, in 1615, he died in
debt.

Bulmer seems to have been a generous employer and to
have possessed genuine engineering ability, but his representative significance is that he was the new type of business
man *par excellence*. Most of his transactions show considerable business acumen, he knew the uses of advertise-
ment (he is said to have written an account of his life called
'Bulmer's Skill'),[1] and his general outlook, so far as it can be
discovered, shows the combination of shrewd daring and
prudence that characterizes the typical nineteenth-century
captain of industry. His philosophy was summarized by
his lieutenant, Atkinson:

(1) Whosoever is a mineral man [he said] must of force be
a hazard adventurer, not greatly esteeming whether it hit, or

[1] Dr Robertson quotes a set of verses that he had engraved on a
cup made of silver from Combe Martin which he presented to the
City of London:

When Water-Works in Broken Wharf
   At first erected were;
And Bevis Bulmer, by his Art,
   The Waters 'gan to rear;

Dispersed I in Earth did lie,
   Since all beginning old,
In place call'd Combe, where Martin long
   Had hid me in his Mold.

I did no service on the Earth
   Nor no Man set me free;
Till Bulmer, by his skill and charge
   Did frame me, This to be.

Bulmer's water-works were at Broken Wharf, near Blackfriars
Bridge. *Op. cit.*, p. 104.

miss suddenly, as if he were a gamester playing at dice, or such unlawful games, &c.: (viz.) Thine or mine at all, said he. (2) If once a little be adventured in seeking of minerals or mineral stones, and thereby he happen to win, he must esteem it as nothing, said he. (3) But if he hope to win, and throw at all, so lose all and get nothing, yet must he think he hath got something. (4) And if a man find a rich vein of metal by art or accident, let him not esteem thereof, for it is like a man strong with a little; saith he. And if he do seek in hope to find, albeit thereby no profit nor principal doth come, yet must he think himself a rich man, and believe that he hath or shall have, that he hath not; and if he cannot embrace the lessons he cannot be a right mineral man, saith he.[1]

He was, says Dr Robertson, 'one of those who spent their lives in the pursuit of great gain and introduced as much as they could of capitalistic industry into the land. Though not adverse to making the Crown his partner, he was essentially an individualist. He was one of those who exalted enterprise and profit, helping to erect the practical basis on which the theory of economic individualism rests.'[2]

Bulmer, one feels, would have made a fortune in any age; there were others whose talents were more particularly suited to the times. The opportunities open to industrial projectors in the reign of James I have already been illustrated from the career of Arthur Ingram, and there were other fields for the exercise of business ability besides industry. Sir Lionel Cranfield (1575–1645), the mercer's apprentice who became Lord High Treasurer and Earl of Middlesex, owed his fortune to the financial adroitness that he exhibited in the king's service. Cranfield, who began his career in medieval fashion by marrying his master's daughter, was a successful member of the Merchant Adventurers' Company. On the accession of James I he obtained notice at court, and, as the king told later, 'he made so many

[1] *Op. cit.*, p. 119.   [2] *Op. cit.*, pp. 119-120.

projects for my profit . . . was so studious for my profits' that he obtained a variety of official appointments. He became Surveyor-General of the Customs, Master of the Court of Wards, Master of the Great Wardrobe (effecting an annual saving of £23,000 in the royal household) and Chief Commissioner of the Navy. In 1620 he was made a Privy Councillor, and in 1622 Treasurer, in which office he succeeded in making some economies. Although, on the death of his first wife, he had married one of Buckingham's many poor relations, his impeachment in 1624 was due to the rivalry of the favourite, who engineered the attack in the House of Commons.[1] D'Ewes records that he 'saw no man that pitied his fall, having started up suddenly to such great wealth and honour, from a base and mean original, even from a shop which he had kept in London, and accordingly was now evinced of base corruption and bribery in his places'.[2] The judgement was severe. What distinguished Cranfield in that age was not his peculation, of which he may have been guilty,[3] but his rise from obscurity, and his vigorous attempts to manage the royal and the national treasury on the lines on which the Ingrams were managing industry. As Master of the Wardrobe he was accustomed to say: 'The King shall pay no more than other men do, and he shall pay ready money; and if we cannot have it in one place we will have it in another'.[4] His advice was not always of the best,[5] but he was one of the first to apply commercial standards in the management of the national income, 'being in truth a man of great parts and notable dexterity'.[6]

[1] This is clearly brought out by Clarendon, *History of the Rebellion* (ed. 1826), I, p. 39 ff.

[2] D'Ewes, *Autobiography* (ed. Halliwell), I, p. 245.

[3] See Gardiner, *History of England*, 1603–1642, V, p. 230.

[4] Quoted from the *D.N.B.*, from which all unacknowledged information is taken.

[5] Cf. Unwin, *Gilds*, p. 307. [6] Clarendon, I, p. 39.

Cranfield, of course, has a place in political history, and is remembered on that account; but what one has to realize is that fortunes were being made by that kind of enterprise in iron, in coal, in woollen cloth, in cotton, in commerce, in all those branches of activity that have been described. A special section of the study that has been desiderated would have to be given to the great mercantile and commercial figures, the Crisps, the Cockaynes, the Sandys, the Pindars and Courtens. Sir Thomas Smythe (1558–1625) may stand as an example. His father, Thomas Smythe, was the son of a Wiltshire yeoman who became a haberdasher and clothier. Thomas the elder made money as a haberdasher and customer of the port of London.[1] He bought Osterhanger Manor in Kent from Sir Thomas Sackville and much other property from the Earl of Leicester, so that when he died in 1591 his family was already established amongst the 'gentry'. His eldest son, Sir John Smythe (*d.* 1608), was high sheriff of Kent, and father of the first Viscount Strangford, who was made a Knight of the Bath in 1616, 'being a person of distinguished merit and opulent fortune'.[2] Thomas Smythe, second son of Thomas of Osterhanger, went into the city and engaged in overseas trade, in which he became one of the most important figures of the time. He was treasurer of the Virginia Company, Governor of the Russia Company, of the Levant Company, of the Somers Islands Company, and, for almost twenty years, of the East India Company.[3] 'He

---

[1] He held a lease of the Northern Mines from the Mines Royal Society.—Scott, II, p. 395. [2] *D.N.B.*

[3] Scott, II, pp. 250; 52; 91; 106, 262; 92. In the Virginia and Somers Islands Company Smythe was a member of the Warwick party (Scott, II, pp. 246-298, *passim*). The political importance of the larger shareholders is unintentionally brought out by the *D.N.B.*, under 'Rich, Robert, Second Earl of Warwick': 'Warwick's colonial ventures brought him into constant association with the leading men of the puritan party. . . . Meanwhile, in domestic politics, Warwick

amassed a large fortune, a considerable part of which he devoted to charitable purposes and, among others, to the endowment of a free school at Tonbridge.' The quiet summary of the *D.N.B.* hardly does justice to the enormous commercial power, or the social influence, of this merchant prince.

In all the larger towns of England and, as will be seen, in the country, there were men who knew how to grasp the opportunities offered by rising prices, by an expanding trade and industry, though for the most part details of their careers are not available. Hall has collected some facts about an undistinguished London business man, George Stoddard, who flourished in the first half of Elizabeth's reign, whose 'usurious thrift', exercised in merchandising, money-lending and speculation in land, may be considered as typical of innumerable others.[1] But few of the men of this class have left any memorial, though there is evidence enough of their existence and of their anonymous activity. The more eminent, or the more notorious of the self-made men only differed from these in the scope of their undertakings; and all seem to have shared those qualities which were noted as characteristic of the inhabitants of one of the new textile centres:

> They excel the rest in policy and industry, for the use of their trade and grounds, and after the rude and arrogant

rapidly became more prominent in opposition to the policy of Charles I. The revival of the forest laws touched him closely. . . . The opposition to the payment of ship-money in that county [Essex] was attributed to his influence. . . .'

[1] Hall, *Society in the Elizabethan Age*, chap. iv. Hall gives some interesting examples of Stoddard's usurious transactions; there are 'merry bonds' (pp. 52-53), and there is an instance of 'putting out' on one's travels (pp. 53-54). Compare Puntarvolo, in *Every Man out of his Humour*, who 'dealt upon returns'. Stoddard also entangled a country gentleman who forfeited his estate.

manner of their wild country they surpass the rest in wisdom and wealth. They despise their old fashions if they can hear of a new, more commodious, rather affecting novelties than allied to old ceremonies. . . . It should seem that desire of praise and sweetness of their due commendation hath begun and maintained among the people a natural ardency of new inventions annexed to an unyielding industry.[1]

[1] J. Ryder's *Commendations of Yorkshire* (1588), quoted by Heckscher, *Mercantilism*, I, p. 244.

CHAPTER THREE

NEW ELEMENTS
IN THE NATIONAL LIFE

THE last chapter was intended to indicate the powerful economic forces that were at work in the sixteenth century generally, and in the Elizabethan-Jacobean period in particular. The beginnings of those economic changes that resulted in the creation of 'modern England' have their own interest even as an isolated study, but their main significance —it cannot be too often repeated—lies in their effect on the quality of individual lives. This, I have suggested, raises a problem that does not allow a simple answer, and a solution cannot even be approached directly. What I wish to do in this chapter is to group the main results of those changes under headings that suggest the direction which further exploration may take.

Some cautions are necessary. The first is that here we are still concerned with generalizations and with groups of facts, that the mesh is still too large. 'Facts' are important, and any attempt to interpret the past must take account of more than an arbitrary selection of them; but even the widest collection of verified 'facts about' a given period stands in the same relation to the ideal history as a police court report stands to *Macbeth*.

The second caution concerns the use of the word 'new'. When we are dealing with large general topics—'The rise of the middle classes', for example—we have, as far as possible, to test our evidence against that provided by another period, lest it is only ignorance of other times that gives the appearance of novelty or uniqueness to the features that we have selected. This, in turn, does not mean that we are to come to no conclusions: medieval satires on the power of money should not prevent us from seeing the special significance of Jonson's 'Lady Pecunia'. It merely means that the active exercise of tact, the historic sense, is of first importance for the specialist.

Finally, in discussing historical 'movements', we have to take care not to be misled by the metaphor, with its suggestion of straightforward momentum. Movements in history are not often straightforward; they do not begin, come to a head, decline and close. The new assimilates, or is assimilated by, the old, and the product is rarely something that would have been incomprehensible, or even completely unfamiliar, before the new element appeared. Since the nineteenth century applied science has increased the possibilities of catastrophe, but the greater part of history is not catastrophic.[1] Contemporary accounts of innovations, moreover, must be set against a wide background which no one bothered to comment on because it was changing so slowly.

The aspects of English life in the late sixteenth and early seventeenth centuries that will be presented here are those that I believe to be both 'new' and significant. There are

---

[1] Two of these points are well brought out by Febvre: 'Il n'y a pas à travers l'histoire, de "classe bourgeoise", massive et compacte, et sans nuances, qui naisse lentement au Moyen Age, se constitue petit à petit, se développe à partir du xvie. siècle surtout, grandit lentement au xviie., au xviiie., s'épanouit et s'étale brusquement au seuil du xixe., emplit enfin l'univers de sa puissance et de sa grandeur contemporaine. Le regard d'ensemble que jette Pirenne sur l'évolution sociale du capitalisme nous avertit de nuancer davantage notre esquisse, et de mieux regarder la réalité. . . . C'est introduire la diversité là où trop de constructions massives cherchent à implanter une unité factice' ('Les Nouveaux Riches et L'Histoire', *Revue des Cours et Conférences*, 15 juin 1922, p. 439).

few of them for which parallels could not be found in the early sixteenth century, or even in the Middle Ages, but they all represent factors which assumed disturbing proportions for large numbers of people sometime in the reign of Elizabeth or the early Stuarts.

Enclosures and the Growth of a Land Market.   Merchants buying Land

The story of the complex reorganization of large parts of rural England known as 'the enclosure movement' is too well known to be retold here.   Some of the results of that movement, however, need to be illustrated in some detail in order to bring out their full significance.   The origins of the break-up of the manor go back to the fourteenth century. Throughout the fifteenth century there was a steady increase in sheep-farming, and at the same time a tendency in many parts of England for the peasants to consolidate their scattered holdings, but the formation of the great sheep farms and the snatching of the commons, with consequent eviction, depopulation and unemployment, belong to the Tudor period, when woollen manufacture had become the staple industry of the kingdom.

Apart from rearrangements of land amongst the peasants themselves enclosures might take various forms.   The lord of the manor might enclose his demesne land, or he might lease out to a farmer land taken from the estate.   Although the former course involved some loss to the peasant, and the latter helped to increase the tendency towards competitive, instead of customary, rents, neither of these, by themselves, would have created a major social problem; the real damage was done by the enclosure of the commons and the eviction of tenants.[1]   Government interference is a fair index of the

[1] The form taken by eviction depended on the kind of tenure by which an individual tenant held his lands.   See Tawney, *Agrarian*

size of the evils that had to be remedied. 'The first statute against depopulation was passed in 1489; an abortive bill was introduced into the House of Commons in 1656; and between the two lies a series of seven Royal Commissions, twelve Statutes, and a considerable number of Proclamations dealing with one aspect or another of the enclosing movement, as well as numerous decisions on particular cases by the Privy Council, the Court of Star Chamber, and the Court of Requests.'[1] Most of the Tudor enclosures were made in the period ending with the accession of Elizabeth, and a large proportion of the enclosures made after that date were for the purpose of improved arable farming; but the problems created by the sheep farms had come to stay. Miss Durham remarks that the reports of the Commission appointed as a result of the Midland riots in 1607 'show that enclosures of land for sheep-farming had practically ceased. Large areas of land, however, lay idle, and many villages were depopulated as a result of enclosure in the past.'[2]

What I wish to discuss here—leaving aside, for the time

Problem, Part II, chap. iii. The freeholders were safe and, on the whole, prosperous.   [1] Tawney, *op. cit.*, p. 315.

[2] Durham, *The Relations of the Crown to Trade under James I*, pp. 234-235. In 1597 Burghley (?) noted that 'the inconvenience is now come *ad statum*' (T. and P., I, p. 88). By this time the view was gaining ground that enclosures allowed of more efficient arable farming. See Carew, *The Survey of Cornwall* (1602), pp. 66, 66v. Smyth complains of excessive common waste ground, and justifies enclosures which are for 'the general good of the commonwealth, both in the breed of serviceable men and subjects, and of answerable estates and abilities' (*Berkeley Manuscripts*, III, p. 328). It is important to remember that, although 'the returns collected by the Royal Commissions show that in the counties affected most severely less than one-twentieth of the total area was enclosed . . . what mattered to the peasantry . . . [was] not the proportion which the land enclosed bore to the whole area of the county, but the proportion which it bore to the whole area available for cultivation' (Tawney, *op. cit.*, p. 264).

being, the questions of poverty and unemployment—is the development of a new attitude towards the land, an attitude that accompanied the enclosures, partly as cause, partly as effect. The point to start from is the growth of a land market and of speculation in land.

The commercialization of the land, the attempt to exploit it as a source of wealth, rather than to use it as a means of subsistence or to regard it as a source of man-power, began early. Smyth, the historian of the Berkeley family, records of a fifteenth-century Lord Berkeley that he let out some of his manor houses and demesne land 'at racked improved rents', 'as did all other great lords of manors almost throughout the whole kingdom, in the times of Henry VI and Edward IV and after, yea to this present day'.[1] But it was not only by subletting at 'improved rents' that the great landlords could make their acres profitable. Smyth gives to all the Berkeleys a descriptive title—William the Waste All, Maurice the Lawyer, Maurice the Courtier, and so on; the fifth Thomas, who succeeded to the estates in 1523, is, significantly, 'Thomas the Sheepmaster'. As a younger brother's younger son it is not strange that he had thought it necessary to make his own fortunes, but even after his return to Berkeley Castle he 'was a perfect Cotswold shepherd, living a kind of grazier's life, having his flocks of sheep summering in one place and wintering in other places, as he observed the fields and pastures to be found, and could bargain best cheap'.[2]

As Dr Tawney makes plain, commercial forces had been at work in rural England long before the reign of Henry VIII, keeping pace with the development of the woollen industry,

---

[1] Smyth, *Berkeley Manuscripts* (ed. Maclean), II, p. 6. The predecessor of this Lord Berkeley, in the time of Henry IV, had let out land 'by the acre, as he found chapmen and price to his liking' (*loc. cit.*).   [2] *Ibid.*, pp. 221-222.

but the movement away from subsistence agriculture, and all that it implied, was given an enormous impetus by the dissolution of the monasteries. When Henry VIII, in the course of reformation, redistributed the great monastic estates, much of the land, in large or small quantities, came into the hands of those who wanted it as a permanent possession for their families—members of the new aristocracy, citizens wishing to become 'gentlemen', prosperous yeomen building up small farms.[1] But a very large proportion indeed was secured by land-jobbers who bought to sell again as a business speculation.

> Land-jobbers appear, alone, in couples or companies, buy large estates all over England, and then sell parcels later on. They are in some way set off against the other buyers inasmuch as they do not generally care to purchase property of a piece, but parcels scattered over the whole country. Among the land-jobbers are members of the Court of Augmentations, noblemen, gentry and commoners.[2]

Miss Liljegren's study shows how quickly much of the land changed owners, and the process of redistribution continued throughout the sixteenth century.

> From the reign of Henry VIII down to the last days of James I, by far the better part of English landed estate changed owners, and in most cases went from the old nobility by birth and the clergy into the hands of those who possessed money in the period of the Tudors, *i.e.* principally the merchants and industrialists or the newly created nobility and gentry, which, to a great extent, were allied with the former class of people in England.[3]

[1] S. B. Liljegren, *The Fall of the Monasteries and the Social Changes in England leading up to the Great Revolution*, pp. 124-126.

[2] *Op. cit.*, p. 118.

[3] *Op. cit.*, pp. 130-131. Incidentally this helped to foster the enormous number of lawsuits which, in the Elizabethan-Jacobean period, was commented on by such different writers as Harrison, Dekker, and Misselden. Feudal litigiousness was bad enough, but it was

H

But one cannot trace the process by which the members of the rising middle class acquired land merely to the fall of the monasteries.   On the one hand there was the temptation offered by the profits of sheep-farming, on the other there were the increasing financial difficulties of the older landed families.   The expenses of court life had risen heavily with the lavish display demanded by Henry VIII,[1] and the perplexities of courtiers, and of the landed classes generally, increased as the century advanced and prices took a swift upward rise that could not be immediately counterbalanced by raised rents.   We have seen how the courtiers of Elizabeth and James I schemed for perquisites and patents.   It was at this period, too, that the former 'non-commercial classes' began to engage more freely in commercial ventures.[2]   But

nothing compared with that of the later Tudor period.   Smyth provides innumerable examples.   Of Henry, Lord Berkeley (1534–1613), he says, 'I should make the life of this lord a volume of itself if I should particularize but a fourth part (of his lawsuits)' (*Berkeley Manuscripts*, II, p. 302).   Cf.

> . . . Their vanities
> Would fill more volumes of small hand
> Than all the evidence of church land.
> (Webster, *The Devil's Law Case*, II, iii)

[1] Miss Liljegren (*op. cit.*, pp. 137-138) quotes Shakespeare on the nobles at the Field of the Cloth of Gold:

> O many
> Have broke their backs with laying manors on them
> For this great journey.
> (*Henry VIII*, I, i)

Shakespeare was probably thinking of the nobles of his own day, but the account applies to the earlier period.

[2] Probably there had been no rigid separation between the landowning and the trading classes in England from the later Middle Ages onwards.   Smyth tells of a younger son of a Lord Berkeley who engaged in trade in the fifteenth century (*Berkeley Manuscripts*, II, p. 83), and there was no essential difference between commerce and sheep-farming.   But it seems that the commercial ventures of the nobility increased considerably in the later sixteenth century (see

almost inevitably, for noble and squire alike, the new economic circumstances resulted in accumulated debts and the sale
of land. Tawney has pointed out that the loss of land through
mortgages was not unknown in the Middle Ages, but 'what
supplied an additional impetus in the sixteenth century, and
gave to individual transactions almost the character of an
economic movement, was the great increase in the wealth of
the business classes, combined with the poverty of the gentry,
the long rise in prices, and the conservatism of existing
methods of land tenure. As the outburst of new companies
after 1570 shows, the former had money to lend, and the
latter were at their wits' end to obtain it. In such circumstances nothing could stop the vacuum being filled or stop
Sir Petronel Flash from falling in the hands of Old Security.'[1]

There is ample evidence of the acquisition of land by the
middle classes in the sixteenth century. Chaucer's Man of
Law, we remember, had been 'a greet purchasour', but it was
about the second quarter of the sixteenth century that the
buying up of landed estates by lawyers, goldsmiths, merchants and the like, began to engage so much attention from
contemporary moralists. 'As for example of rich men',
says Lever,

> look at the merchants of London, and ye shall see, when as
> by their honest vocation and trade of merchandise God hath
> endowed them with great abundance of riches, then can they
> not be content with the prosperous wealth of that vocation to
> satisfy themselves, and to help other, but their riches must
> abroad in the country to buy farms out of the hands of

above, pp. 51-53), whilst younger sons naturally took advantage of
the opportunities offered by economic expansion. In the debate on
free trade in 1604 Sandys asked, 'What else shall become of gentlemen's younger sons, who cannot live by arms, when there is no war,
and learning preferments are common to all and mean? so that
nothing remains for them, save only, merchandize' (Scott, I, p. 124).
[1] Tawney, Wilson, pp. 35-36.

worshipful gentlemen, honest yeomen, and poor labouring husbands.[1]

Robert Crowley, whose main theme is that each man should 'walk in his vocation' and not meddle with that of others, has several passages on the subject.

> If Merchants would meddle
> with merchandise only,
> And leave farms to such men
> as must live thereby
> Then were they most worthy.

Instead,

> They take farms
> to let them out again,
> To such men as must have them,
> though it be to their pain:
> And to levy great fines
> Or to over the rent. . . .[2]

Not content with a decent living, their one thought is 'to climb'.

> So soon as they have aught to spare,
> Beside their stock that must remain,
> To purchase lands is all their care
> And all the study of their brain.
>
> There can be none unthrifty heir,
> Whom they will not smell out anon,
> And handle him with words full fair,
> Till all his lands is from him gone.
>
> The farms, the woods, and pasture grounds,
> That do lie round about London,
> Are hedged in within their mounds,
> Or else shall be ere they have done.
>
> They have their spies upon each side
> To see when aught is like to fall;
> And as soon as aught can be spied,
> They are ready at the first call.[3]

[1] Thomas Lever, *Sermons* (1550), Arber Reprint, p. 29.
[2] Robert Crowley, *Select Works* (ed. J. M. Cowper, E.E.T.S.), p. 41 (1550).   [3] *Op. cit.*, pp. 87-88.

It would be easy to illustrate these general descriptions and denunciations with particular examples. The account of sales of land in the sixteenth and early seventeenth centuries given in the Berkeley Manuscripts illustrates the growth of land-jobbing and shows the class of men that were acquiring land. Thomas the Sheepmaster sold away one of his manors to 'Robert ffewrother a goldsmith of London' in 1507,[1] but it is at a considerably later date that the sales become more frequent. The difficulty is to know what to select. As one of several examples of speculation resulting from the religious changes we have the account of a house and land in Stinchcombe held by a chantry priest:

> By the dissolution of which chantry in 1 Ed. 6, it came to the Crown and was by that King's letters patents . . . granted (inter alia) to Sir John Thynne and Lawrence Hide and their heirs, who the same year sold the said Messuage and land to Antony Throgmerton and his heirs: who also the same year sold the same to Simon Ecles and his heirs.[2]

Monastic lands went on changing hands throughout the reign of Elizabeth.

> Also in Southend in Nibley is an ancient messuage with divers lands thereto belonging, now the inheritance of Christopher Purnell aforesaid, younger son of Thomas Purnell . . . which he had purchased of William Curnocke of Southend, son of Thomas Curnocke, who purchased the same of Hambury, one of the Auditors to Queen Elizabeth, and he of the said Queen . . . and was parcel of the possessions

---

[1] *Berkeley Manuscripts*, II, p. 222. Cheyney quotes a petition to Henry VIII in 1514 which cites 'Merchants adventurers, cloth-makers, goldsmiths, bochers [*sic*], tanners, and other artificers, and unreasonable covetous persons' as buyers of land for sheep-farming (*Social Changes in England in the Sixteenth Century*, pp. 54-55).

[2] *Berkeley Manuscripts*, III ('Description of the Hundred of Berkeley'), p. 358. Cf. *ibid.*, p. 116 (lands attached to the Chapel of Bradston); p. 369 (Chantry at Stone); p. 39 (two chantries at Newport). Hide, Thynne, and Throgmerton (or Throkmerton) appear frequently as land-jobbers.

of the Monastery or Abbey of Kingswood, and came to the Crown in 29 H. VIII by the dissolution of that monastery.[1]

The middle-class origin of most of the purchasers is indicated by the following:

> The other part of this village is at this day [in the reign of Charles I] the inheritance of William Baldwin of London, draper, whose father, William Baldwin was by Inquest in 19 Jacobi found to die seized of the manor of Filton.[2]

One, Sir George Huntley, enclosed a park in Nimesfield.

> And the inhabitants, out of a rural reluctation against such enclosures, ascribe to the injustice of that act not only his sudden death forthwith after at that place, but the sale of that and all the rest of his land made by his son a short time after, to Sir Robert Ducy, an Alderman of London, whose son Sir Richard Ducy, now dwelleth thereupon, 1639.[3]

Here we see the founding of a county family, but it is plain also that speculation in land, which began with the dissolution of the monasteries, still formed a useful source of income to the early seventeenth-century projector. Some of the chantry lands belonging to the parish church of Berkeley, for example, were granted to Thynne and Hide; part, however, remained in the hands of the Crown until 1608 when James granted them to Sir William Herrick and Sir Arthur Ingram, who sold them the next year to two other speculators, 'shortly after scattered by them to other men upon their several sales'.[4]

[1] *Berkeley Manuscripts*, III, p. 299. The Hanbury mentioned here seems to have been a London goldsmith. His name appears in connexion with the purchase of land on pp. 121 and 302, *ibid*. Cf. pp. 306-307 for the transmission of another monastic manor which passed finally to an alderman of London.

[2] *Ibid.*, p. 197. The elder Baldwin bought the manor.

[3] *Ibid.*, p. 303. Ducy had also bought land in another parish.— *Ibid.*, p. 161. On p. 376 a sale is recorded when one George Thorpe, whose family had been considerable landowners since the fifteenth century, emigrated to Virginia in 1621. [4] *Ibid.*, p. 92.

The conclusions to be drawn from the sales recorded here could certainly be reinforced by examining the history of any of the great landed estates of the sixteenth century, on the one hand, or the career of any of the more important merchants and industrialists, on the other. And the long process of dislocation and readjustment, which began in the reign of Henry VIII, was still going on in the late sixteenth century and the reigns of the early Stuarts. Most of the examples given above come from the later period, and the early seventeenth century, we remember, was a period when an Ingram (to take one example from many) could afford to buy, and a Verney was forced to sell.[1] Nor was the reshuffling of land confined to the large estates and the higher economic ranges of society. The Elizabethan or Jacobean squire was as likely as not to be in debt. Hall's Sir William Darrell (b. 1540) 'owed money to usurers, to tradesmen, and to many of his neighbours. He anticipated his rents and had pawned much of his plate.'[2] Sale of land was often an irresistible temptation—or a necessity. Tawney, discussing the plight of 'the needy gentleman', cites several instances, one of which may be taken as typical.

> A grocer who did business as a money lender gets a country gentleman into his clutches, discounts his bills at twenty-five per cent., renews them at compound interest, and finally, having sold up the debtor, becomes lord of the manor.[3]

Further illustration is unnecessary. As Jonson's Meercraft remarked:

> We see those changes daily: the fair lands
> That were the client's, are the lawyer's now;
> And those rich manors there of goodman Taylor's

[1] *Memoirs of the Verney Family during the Seventeenth Century*, I, pp. 48, 56-57.
[2] H. Hall, *Society in the Elizabethan Age*, p. 10.
[3] Tawney, Wilson, p. 37.

Had once more wood upon them, than the yard
By which they were measured out for their last purchase.
Nature hath these vicissitudes.[1]

Certainly the transactions of Middleton's citizens, by which
they became possessed of estates to which they could ride 'in
the Whitsun holidays ... with a number of citizens and their
wives, some upon pillows, some upon side-saddles',[2] had a
wide background of fact.

The Dislocation of Social Classes and the Decay of 'Housekeeping'

The economic changes that have been noticed—the new
forms of acquisition, the transfer of land—had, of course,
important social consequences, one of which was the dislocation of the customary class relationships.   I have said
that for a proper understanding of the Middle Ages the conception of 'class' is misleading; but to a conservative observer of about 1600, when our familiar economic class
divisions were taking shape, it appeared a chief merit of the
preceding ages that then every man knew his proper station.
'For nowadays most men live above their callings, and
promiscuously step forth vice-versa into one another's
ranks.   The countryman's eye is upon the citizen: the citizen's upon the gentleman: the gentleman's upon the nobleman'.[3]   The majority of the complaints were directed
against the newly made gentleman.   Henry Peacham, in a

---

[1] *The Devil is an Ass*, II, i.

[2] *Michaelmas Term*, IV, i.   It is worth noting here that, 'English
Mercantilist writers of the seventeenth century attributed the
superiority of Dutch capital to English to the circumstance that
newly acquired wealth there did not regularly seek investment in
land' (Max Weber, *The Protestant Ethic and the Spirit of Capitalism*,
tr. Talcott Parsons, p. 173).

[3] E. Misselden, *Free Trade, or The Means to Make Trade Flourish*
(1622), p. 12.

book designed for the education of the upper classes on the lines of Castiglione's *Courtier*, complains of the modern up-start nobility in all countries: the abuse of nobility 'like a plague, I think, hath infected the whole world, every un-deserving and base peasant aiming at nobility: which miserable ambition hath so furnished both town and country with coats of a new list, that, were Democritus living, he might have laughing matter for his life'.[1]   And the study of heraldry is justified because, without a knowledge of that subject, how should we

> discern and know an intruding upstart, shot up with last night's mushroom, from an ancient descended and deserved gentleman, whose grandsires have had their shares in every foughten field by the English since Edward I? or, myself a gentleman, know mine own rank, there being at this instant the world over, such a medley (I had almost said motley) of coats, such intrusion by adding or diminishing into ancient families and houses, that had there not been within these few years a just and commendable course taken by the right hon-ourable the Earls Marshals for the redress of this general and insufferable abuse, we should, I fear me, within these few years, see yeomen as rare in England as they are in France.[2]

The social confusion that Peacham refers to was then, of course, nothing new.   Forty years previously Sir John Smith had remarked, 'as for gentlemen, they be made good cheap in England'.[3]

It was, however, the economic expansion of the later part of the sixteenth century that made 'the shuffling of the times'

[1] Henry Peacham, *The Compleat Gentleman* (1622) (ed. G. S. Gordon), pp. 14-18.

[2] *Ibid.*, p. 160.   For the prosperity of the yeomen-freeholders, and their ability to send their sons to the universities and make them gentlemen, see Harrison, *Description of England* (1577), Book II (ed. Furnivall), p. 133.

[3] *De Republica Anglorum* (1583) (ed. Alston), pp. 39-40.

so noticeable, whilst the sale of knighthoods by James I, and 'the advancement of unworthy persons' in his reign, made newly acquired titles into a popular joke.[1]

The complaints of moralists that merchants and other newly enriched members of the middle classes were buying land (becoming, as they said, 'Gentlemen of the first head') were not based on mere prejudice, the desire to maintain, at all costs, the status of those already in possession. At first sight it might appear so. No one who is familiar with Langland is likely to idealize the relationship between feudal landowners and their tenants. No one who is aware of the incessant petty warfare between neighbouring landowners that marked the end of the Middle Ages is likely to regret the passing of the feudal order.[2] Moreover, many members of the Elizabethan aristocracy—the Dudleys, Sackvilles, Cavendishes and Cecils—were themselves 'new men', new, that is, compared with the Howards, Berkeleys and Northumberlands. It looks like vulgar prejudice (which no doubt

[1] Cf. Dekker, *Jests to Make You Merry, Non-Dramatic Works*, II, pp. 284-285. Two apprentices are watching a newly-made knight; one says, 'By Jove, methinks it is a brave thing to be a knight. A brave thing, quoth his fellow, what an ass art thou, a man may have anything for money.'

Cf. John Davies of Hereford, *Works* (ed. Grosart), *The Civil Wars of Death and Fortune* (1603), verse 34 (A merchant buys patents of nobility); *The Scourge of Folly* (1611), Epig. 246 (A greedy purchaser desires to make his son a knight).

[2] See, for example, the account of the battle of Nibley Green (1469) between William, Lord Berkeley, and Thomas Talbot, Viscount Lisle.—Smyth, *Berkeley Manuscripts*, II, p. 102 ff.; III, pp. 266-268. The internal peace of the Tudors was not easily imposed. Smyth gives instances of local feuds, forcible possession of lands, etc., throughout the greater part of the sixteenth century (*ibid.*, II, pp. 226, 266-270, 272-273, 313). See also Hall, *op. cit.*, Part i, chap. i; on the feuds of Sir William Darrell in the second half of the sixteenth century. 'Arm'd!' says Truewit, 'did you ever see a fellow set out to take possession', when he wants to impress Daw with La-Foole's fearful preparations (*The Silent Woman*, 1609, IV, ii).

it often was [1]) that they, whose rank was due to the administrative services of themselves or their immediate ancestors, should resent the intrusion of those whose advancement was due to commerce or industry.

The last sentence, however, points to a more fundamental significance of the transfer of land in the late Tudor period. Hitherto the possession of land had been associated with certain duties, recognized explicitly or implicitly, and the Elizabethan aristocracy had traditions of public service and responsibility. The point was made by Cunningham:

> There were plenty of new men, in many parts of the country, in the early part of the seventeenth century; their readiness to break with old traditions gave rise to some of the discordant elements of the times. The class into which they had entered was charged . . . with varied and difficult functions; it served as the very backbone of the social system and supplied administrative organs for every possible purpose.[2]

But it was not merely that the older landowners, from the J.P.s to the Privy Councillors, performed important administrative duties; their tradition was more inclusive, and a full account would notice their relations with peasants and household retainers on the one hand, and with scholars and poets on the other. How far, in particular instances, that tradition was active, cannot be determined offhand, but it is something that we cannot overlook if we wish to understand the civilization of the sixteenth century.[3] It was because

[1] 'Men of noble birth are noted to be envious towards new men when they rise; for the distance is altered; and it is like a deceit of the eye, that when others come on they think themselves go back' (Bacon, *Essays*, 'Of Envy').

[2] Cunningham, II, pp. 111-112.

[3] This is another point that I wish to develop later, with special reference to the education and general culture of the Elizabethan upper classes, and their function as patrons of art and literature.

that tradition was not easily assimilated by the newer commercial classes that their acquisition of land meant so much
more than a mere change of ownership.[1]

It is this that gives significance to the contemporary complaints of the decay of 'housekeeping'. The importance of
'housekeeping' in the life of the sixteenth century is something that we, who live in a less patriarchal society, do not
find easy to understand. The household of a great lord in
the country was an important economic unit, not only because it was the pivot of the agricultural work of the sur-
rounding country.

> A great house provisioned itself with little help from the
> outer world; the inhabitants brewed and baked, churned and
> ground their meal, they bred, fed and slew their beeves and
> sheep, and brought up their pigeons and poultry at their own
> doors. Their horses were shod at home, their planks were
> sawn, their rough ironwork was forged and mended. . . .
> Within doors the activity of the family and household was as
> great and as multifarious as without. The spinning of wool
> and flax . . . the fine and coarse needlework, the embroidery,
> the cooking, the curing, the preserving, the distillery that
> went on, were incessant.[2]

And besides those employed in the work of the household
there were poor relations [3] and a more or less numerous

[1] Compare Cecil's note on 'new men' in the service of the state
(1559), T. and P., I, p. 326.

[2] *Memoirs of the Verney Family during the Seventeenth Century*, I,
pp. 5-7. Of Anne, second wife of Thomas, Lord Berkeley (*d.* 1534),
Smyth tells us: 'Country huswifry seemed to be an essential part of
this lady's constitution; a lady that . . . would betimes in winter and
summer mornings make her walks to visit her stable, barns, day-
house, poultry, swinetroughs and the like; which huswifry her
daughter-in-law . . . seeming to decline, and to betake herself to the
delights of youth and greatness, she would sometimes to those about
her swear, By God's blessed sacrament, this gay girl will beggar my
son Henry' (*Berkeley Manuscripts*, II, p. 254).

[3] *The Verney Memoirs*, I, p. 7, gives some instances from the early
seventeenth century.

body of miscellaneous retainers. Harrison says that in the halls of noblemen forty to sixty persons ate daily,[1] and even the lesser gentry seem to have had their 'gentlemen' at their tables.

Nothing is more alien from our habits (says Saintsbury), and hardly anything is more difficult to conceive in our time, than the status of the 'gentlemen' of a great household then. It has been said, with hardly any exaggeration, that it provided an additional profession for men of gentle or respectable birth but not much fortune in those days; and it may be said without any exaggeration at all, that it was a very usual interim occupation between the university and a regular profession, or a post in the civil and military service. We find, for instance, the poet Donne, long after he was married and had children, and while he was hesitating between the law and the Church, holding this position in the household of a very undistinguished person—a mere Surrey knight. From such men upwards to earls and archbishops, every man of fortune and family, or of fortune and office, in of course increasing numbers, had these 'gentle' dependants. . . . They appeared with him on public occasions; they did his miscellaneous business and errands; they gave him consequence; and occasionally, as in the cases of Wyatt and Essex, they still fought for him. Relatively to the then not very numerous population, their numbers must have been extremely large.[2]

Housekeeping, then, had a more than economic significance; it helped to maintain education and general culture. Thus, John Smyth (*b.* 1567), the historian of the Berkeleys, entered the service of Henry, Lord Berkeley, at the age of fourteen, to attend on Thomas (age nine), the son and heir. William Ligon, of an old family related to the Berkeleys, was admitted at the same time and in the same capacity. The three boys were placed under the same tutor

[1] *Description of England*, Book II (ed. Furnivall), pp. 144-145.
[2] *Social England* (ed. Traill and Mann: illustrated edn.), III, p. 518. See also M. St. Clare Byrne in *A Companion to Shakespeare Studies* (ed. G. B. Harrison and H. Granville-Barker), pp. 203-208, 215-218.

and together proceeded to Oxford, whence Smyth went on to the Middle Temple before returning as Steward of the household.[1] Not only did the nobleman's household provide an educational ladder for poor boys of ability (Smyth had previously been at the free school at Derby), it was often a means of support for the mature scholar. Thomas Hariot, the mathematician, was a pensioner of Henry Percy, ninth Earl of Northumberland, who also provided for three other mathematicians, including Nicholas Torperley.[2] Of Lord Henry Berkeley, Smyth tells us that 'He had many flatterers and sycophants, as well of his own family as out of London, captains, scholars, poets, cast courtiers, and the like'.[3]

When writers of the late sixteenth century, therefore, complained of the decay of housekeeping, they were pointing to a major social phenomenon. The complaints were frequent enough; 'the age of hospitality' seems to have been used as an equivalent for 'the good old times', and the decline of the great households became a matter of popular comment. 'And now may I complain', says a minor moralist of the reign of James I, 'of the decay of hospitality in our land, whereby many poor souls are deprived of that relief which they have had heretofore. The time hath been, that men have hunted after worship and credit by good housekeeping, and therein spent great part of their revenues: but now commonly, the greater part of their livings is too little to maintain us and our children in the pomp of pride: yea, and yet all is well if we may maintain that, though no hospitality be maintained therewithal.' [4]

[1] Preface to *Berkeley Manuscripts*, I, pp. iii-iv.

[2] Henry Percy, *Advice to his Son* (ed. G. B. Harrison), Introduction, p. 10.

[3] *Berkeley Manuscripts*, II, p. 286. The question of literary patronage is dealt with by Miss P. Sheavyn in *The Literary Profession in the Elizabethan Age*, but there is room for a further study.

[4] *Greevous Grones for the Poore* (1622), pp. 13-14. Cf. Greene, *A*

The change, of course, cannot be attributed solely to the newer type of landowner. Many of the older families were beginning to sell or let out their lands, thereby loosening their connexion with the countryside, and to abandon the old, expensive style of housekeeping. In the late sixteenth century the country seat was far enough from being a mere holiday resort, but the attractions of a life 'in Town' were already marked. In a dialogue of *Cyvile and Uncyvile Life* (1579) the upholder of country ways declares:

> You know the ancient custom of this realm of England was, that all noblemen and gentlemen, not called to attendance in our Prince's service, did continually inhabit the country, continuing there, from age to age and from ancestor to ancestor, a continual house and hospitality, which got them great love among their neighbours, relieved many poor wretches, and wrought also divers other good effects.... But I see, that gentlemen begin to take another course, and falling from the use of their ancestors, do now either altogether (or very much) leave to dwell in their country houses, inhabiting cities and great towns, which manner of living I cannot allow.[1]

Thirty years later Carew noted the lack of noblemen in

Quippe for an Upstart Courtier (1592), *Works* (ed. Grosart), X, p. 272: 'The niggardness of the lord or master is the cause no more chimneys do smoke: for would they use ancient hospitality as their forefathers did, and value as lightly of pride, as their great grandfathers, then should you see every chimney in the house smoke'. Dekker, *The Gulls Horn Book* (1609), *Non-Dramatic Works* (ed. Grosart), II, p. 237: The Duke (? of Duke Humphrey's Walk) follows the fashion of great men, 'in keeping no house'. Dekker, *A Strange Horse-Race* (1613), *ibid.*, III, p. 337: Hospitality is 'an old Lord that is now no Courtier; for he keeps a place in the country, and all the chimneys in it smoke'. Marginal note: 'They that uphold hospitality are in these days weak, because few'.

Estimates of the causes varied; thus, Barnabe Rich, *The Excellency of Good Women* (1613), p. 15: 'By the pride of women Hospitality is eaten up and good housekeeping is banished out of the country'.

[1] *Cyvile and Uncyvile Life* (1579), Sig. B i, v.—B iii.

Cornwall, which, he says, was partly due to the increase in female inheritors, 'partly for that their issue male, little affecting so remote a corner, liked better to transplant their possessions nearer to the heart of the Realm. Elder times were not so barren.' [1] From the time of the dissolution of the monasteries the government had been exercised by the problem of absenteeism; and in 1596 the Circuit Judges were instructed that 'all gentlemen who had forsaken their country dwellings to live in cities or towns should go back to their country homes',[2] and one of the first proclamations of James I dealt with the same 'great inconvenience'.[3] Judging from the number of proclamations that continued to be issued on the subject, it does not appear that they were very effective.

The decline of housekeeping was not, of course, an absolute 'decay'. Many landowners continued to live in the old style; the 'county families' that were founded in the Elizabethan and early Stuart period were not incapable of assimilating the traditions of the older stock, with whom they were often allied by marriage; and a sense of responsibility towards their locality was alive in very many eighteenth-century landlords, and survived in some of their successors. There was, however, an important moral aspect of the shift in social power that was noted in our period, and the way was prepared for a major breach with the past, a breach that was clearly marked by the changed administration of the poor law after the Restoration. But by that time the social and economic readjustments had had important political consequences as well.[4]

[1] *The Survey of Cornwall* (1602), 63 v.
[2] Cheyney, *A History of England from the Defeat of the Armada to the Death of Elizabeth*, II, p. 13. For the government's attitude towards absenteeism at an earlier date, see Cunningham, I, p. 531.
[3] Cunningham, II, p. 105.
[4] The further acquisition of land by 'new men'—many of them

The satire that was directed against the citizen-gentlemen of the reign of James I cannot be accounted for merely by the fact that the majority of writers depended upon the older aristocracy for a large part of their precarious livelihood. That satire can only be fully understood in the light of the inherited social theory which made of 'walking in one's vocation' a major virtue; [1] and there were, at all events, some genuine reasons for hostility. It was partly, of course, that the ways leading to enrichment were felt to be dubious. In Elizabeth's reign Mulcaster remarked that those who schemed for wealth, 'that Jack may be a gentleman', impoverished many others, 'and though they do not profess the impoverishing of purpose, yet their kind of dealing doth pierce as it passeth: and a thousand pound gain bowls twenty thousand persons'; [2] and very many of the projects leading to wealth in the next reign were certainly far from reputable. Partly also, ostentation on the part of the new rich is always a matter for derision. But the major cause of complaint was that those who acquired their position through the wealth obtained in trade or industry had not a tradition of responsibility which would justify that position. Economic expansion had provided many *carrières ouvertes aux talents*, but the talents that made a Bevis Bulmer—necessary, and even admirable, as they were—were of a peculiar and a limited kind.

Luxury, and the Importance of Money

Most of the lamentations of minor moralists over the

merchants—was of course a feature of the Commonwealth period. See M. James, *Social Policy during the Puritan Revolution*, pp. 85-90.

[1] See below, pp. 144 ff.

[2] Mulcaster, *Positions* (1581) (ed. R. H. Quick), pp. 193-195. Cf. Donne, *Fifty Sermons* (1649), p. 59: 'If we unite riches to riches, we temper a mortar (for the most part) of our own covetousness, and the loss and oppressing of some other men'. And see below, pp. 152 ff.

manners of their times are only of slight interest to the historian; too often they concentrate on petty foibles or exalt permanent traits of human nature into signs of contemporary degeneracy. The frequent attacks on the spread of 'luxury' that we meet with in the Elizabethan-Jacobean period are, however, of more fundamental importance; they point to something more significant than the symptoms themselves.

The medieval pulpit had denounced sumptuousness of attire, excessive feasting, and so on, and observers in the time of Henry VIII believed that unnecessary expenditure was increasing.

> And now from the Tower to Westminster along, every street is full of [luxuries], and their shops glister and shine of glasses, painted cruses, gay daggers, etc., that is able to make any temperate man to gaze on them and to buy somewhat, though it serve to no purpose necessary.[1]

But the opportunities for expenditure at the end of the century were far greater.

I have already spoken of the expenses of court life under Elizabeth, and a large part of a courtier's income went on 'conspicuous consumption'. 'Luxury', however, was not confined to the court. 'The realm', it was said, 'aboundeth in riches, as may be seen by the general excess of the people in purchasing, in buildings, in meat, drink and feastings, and most notably in apparel.' [2] The 'excess' of course, was largely a healthy increase in material comfort and convenience. Harrison pointed out the prosperity of the yeoman class, the increased variety in the nation's diet as a whole, and the improvement in building and furniture,[3]

---

[1] Traill and Mann, *Social England*, III, p. 226.
[2] 1579. Lipson, III, p. 209.
[3] *Description of England*, Book II (ed. Furnivall), pp. 133, 144-145, and chap. xii.

though to his mind too much was spent on clothes, and 'the furniture of our houses also exceedeth, and is grown in manner even to passing delicacy'.[1]

It was, of course, the great increase in foreign trade that made more, and more varied, goods available, and largely provided the money to buy them. At the mid-century one, William Lane, remarked that he had 'for this six or seven years past, marked and well perceived our common wealth to be grown in to such a costliness and chargeableness of living and expenses of foreign commodities, a great part not needful,'[2] and the opening up of the trade to the East at a later date added silks and spices and China goods to the 'perfumed gloves and wanton presents', the 'caps, pins, points, dice, gilt stirrups, etc.'[3] that were received from the Continent. If we wish to find a date for the great increase in expenditure which occurred in the reign of Elizabeth we can fix it in the period 1575–1587—Scott's 'Eleven years of great prosperity'—which included the Persian expeditions of the Russia Company, the formation of the Levant Company, and Drake's round-the-world voyage which paid his shareholders so handsomely.[4]

'Necessary' and unnecessary expenditure alike increased under James I. The upper-class standard was set by the court, which in such matters as dress and entertainment seems to have been a model of rash extravagance.[5] The expensive masques of Queen Anne were paralleled by the

---

[1] *Ibid.*, chap. vii and p. 238.

[2] T. and P., II, p. 184.   [3] T. and P., I, p. 327.

[4] Scott, I, chap. iv.

[5] Of James I it was said: 'He doth wondrously covet learned discourse . . . he doth admire good fashion in clothes. . . . We have lately had many gallants who failed in their suits for want of due observance of these matters [of fashion]. The King is nicely heedful of such points, and dwelleth on good looks and handsome accoutrements' (Letter of Lord Thomas Howard (1607)—*The Letters and Epigrams of Sir John Harington*, ed. McClure, pp. 32-34).

rather more vulgar pageantry of the City,[1] and old-fashioned moralists were appalled by 'our present riot and luxury in diet and apparel',[2] by 'the vanity, lasciviousness, and intolerable pride of these our days, wherein every skipping Jack and every flirting Jill must not only be ring'd (forsooth) very daintily, but must have some special jewel or favour besides'.[3] 'Witness', said another, 'the superfluity and increase of these our times, of this our kingdom, that hath more people than pastures, more bringing forth than breeding for, that is compelled to empty itself into far distant regions and kingdoms.'[4]

The insistence on luxury was partly, of course, due to the prevailing mercantilist conceptions of state economy. Gold and silver trinkets made money scarce,[5] and, more important, the importation of foreign goods implied a corresponding export of the precious metals which might be used, it was thought, to stimulate industry at home.

The general remote cause of our want of money is the great

[1] 'The reign of James I was the Golden Age of the Lord Mayor's Show' (Unwin, *Gilds*, p. 277). See the account of the Grocers' show, on which they spent £900, at the inauguration of Sir Thomas Middleton as Lord Mayor in 1614.—*Ibid.*, p. 278.

[2] Smyth, *Berkeley Manuscripts*, I, p. 160. 'We see divers wear apparel and colours made of a Lordship, lined with Farms and Granges, embroidered with all the plate, gold, and wealth, their Friends and Fathers left them' ('Ester Sowerman', *Ester Hath Hang'd Haman* (1617), pp. 39-40). This is the common form of the complaint that constantly recurs in the contemporary drama and satire.

[3] Henry Swinburne, *A Treatise of Spousals* (1686—written *c.* 1600), p. 209.

[4] Alex. Niccholes, *A Discourse of Marriage and Wiving* (1620, 1st edn., 1615), p. 22.

[5] Malynes complained of 'the great quantity of silver consumed in the making of silver thread, spangles, purls, oaes, and the like, which upon the late examination of . . . the Lord President are found to amount to £80,000 and upwards, yearly; whereas the plate made in London is only but £50,000 or £60,000 worth' (*The Maintenance of Free Trade*, 1622, p. 19).

excess of this kingdom, in consuming the commodities of foreign countries, which prove to us discommodities, in hindering us of so much treasure which otherwise would be brought in, in lieu of these toys. . . . And by this means we draw unto us, and consume amongst us, that great abundance of the wines of Spain, of France, of the Rhine, of the Levant, and of the Islands: the raisins of Spain, the currants of the Levant, the lawns and cambrics of Hannault and the Netherlands, the silks of Italy, the sugars and tobacco of the West Indies, the spices of the East Indies: all of which are of no necessity unto us, and yet are bought with ready money, which otherwise would be brought over in treasure if these were not.[1]

This attitude was not confined to economists, and when Fuller, in 1642, remarked that 'To export things of necessity, and to bring in foreign needless toys, makes a rich merchant and a poor kingdom',[2] he was only echoing the common opinion of the last hundred years.

But the insistence on luxury has, for us, a far greater significance.   It is, I think, safe to say that it points to the transition from a subsistence economy to the early stages of an economy of plenty, with a corresponding change in men's habits, attitudes and general outlook: and the new economy was based on the purchasing power of money.   There had been medieval satires on Lady Meed; medieval preachers had denounced those who had money for their god, and that 'Pecuniae obediunt omnia' had been a complaint of Erasmus;[3] but, in England at least, it was in the early seven-

---

[1] E. Misselden, *Free Trade, or The Means to Make Trade Flourish*, (1622), pp. 11-12.

[2] *The Holy State*, Book II, chap. xvii.   Cf. T. and P., I, p. 327; II, pp. 124-125.   The sumptuary laws of the sixteenth century, and earlier, were based on a similar desire to encourage native cloth-making and to discourage 'unnecessary' imports.   Heckscher points out that the mercantilist attitude towards luxury had changed by the end of the seventeenth century.—*Mercantilism*, II, pp. 289-293.

[3] See Sombart, *The Quintessence of Capitalism* (tr. M. Epstein), pp. 29-30.

teenth century that the Lady Pecunia became, in a special sense, 'the Venus of the time and state'.[1]   Money and competition were becoming the prime movers of economic life.

> In the Middle Ages, coinage had given a unit for the comparison of one ware with another; but it was not an object which men were likely to seek after, except in so far as they desired to lay by for a rainy day.   If they had large sums at command they could not invest them: and so far as the greater part of the population were concerned, their food and clothing were practically determined by their status in the social system.   So long as prices were arranged by calculation, there must have been comparatively little variation in the real reward which a man got for his labour; and while payments were partly made in kind, attention was not directed forcibly to money as a purchasing power.   But with competition prices all this changed; the amount of comforts that a man could procure no longer depended on the regulations of his gild, but on the purchasing power of the money he obtained by the sale of his wares. . . . Money had come to be a thing for which everyone sought, not exactly for its own sake,[2] but because of its purchasing power; it was a convenient representative of all other objects of wealth, and, as such, a thing of which each man desired to have as much as possible. From this time forward the desire of wealth, as the means of gratifying the desire of social distinction and all else, became a much more important factor in economic affairs than it had been before.[3]

In this passage Cunningham is discussing the transition from medieval to Tudor times, and he is right in tracing the signs of change to the early sixteenth century; but his remarks apply with far greater force to the fifty years that

[1] Jonson, *The Staple of News* (1626), II, i.
[2] Inevitably, in a sense, for its own sake also; old Jakob Fugger refused to retire: 'he wants to accumulate capital as much as is in his power'.   Quoted by M. Kovalevsky, *Originating Phases in the Development of Capitalist Economy*.
[3] Cunningham, I, p. 465.

preceded the death of James I. It was this period that saw the sharpest rise in prices caused by American silver, the formation of overseas trading companies, the rise of large-scale speculation, and an almost feverish pursuit of industrial projects. It was in this period that medieval 'status' was finally superseded by the modern 'class', and the ranks of the class system were determined, in the long run, by the possession of money. National policy was becoming more and more clearly determined by the conflicting claims of different industrial and commercial interests.[1] And the things that money could buy had become far more numerous, and were taking a far greater place in men's thoughts than a century previously. 'No man can be ignorant', said Bacon, 'of the idolatry that is generally committed in these degenerate times to money, as if it could do all things public and private.'[2] By the middle of the seventeenth century it was a commonplace. 'Whosoever wanteth money is ever subject to contempt and scorn in the world, let him be furnished with never so good gifts, either of body or of mind. . . . In these times we may say with the wise man: My son, better it is to die than to be poor, for now money is the world's god, and the card which the devil turns up trump to win the set withall. . . . *Pecuniae omnia obediunt*: hence it is so admired that millions venture both souls and bodies for the possession of it.'[3]

The preceding chapter—the account of profits and pro-

---

[1]   The mouth speaks from the abundance of the heart,
So were we taught: but they have found an art,
Lately at Westminster, which is far worse:
Most mouths speak from the abundance of the purse.
(J[ohn] H[eath], *The House of Correction* (1619), Sig. C 4, v)

[2] *Of the True Greatness of the Kingdom of Britain*, *Works* (ed. Spedding, Ellis and Heath), III, p. 55.

[3] *The Worth of a Penny, or a Caution to Keep Money* (1647), p. 15.

jects, of speculation and stock holding—should have provided sufficient evidence of the vastly increased importance of money in the early seventeenth century, and once the point has been made there is no need to look for illustration. But it is worth noticing that many of the features of popular and dramatic satire in this period that are often spoken of as unrelated 'curiosities of the age', were in fact significant aspects of a single movement, a movement that has resulted to-day in the complete dominance of money in an acquisitive society. Satires on alchemy, for example, were not only inspired by a newly enlightened hostility towards superstition; the alchemist was, in repute, a more accessible El Dorado, and the desires of his clients (some of them very highly placed) had an obvious relation to the gold fever that was liable to sweep large sections of the population at any moment;[1] and 'the prospect, as it seemed, of swift and easy enrichment concurred with the practical urgency of dearer living'.[2]

So too the gulling of young heirs, that never-failing subject of Jacobean comedy, was not merely imitated from Terence or Plautus; it had for setting the same economic factors that have been mentioned—the growing attractions of the town combined with the financial difficulties of the gentry, on the one hand, and a determination to raise one's fortune 'by such casualties as this stirring age shall afford', on the other. 'A great state left to an heir', said Bacon, 'is as a lure to all the birds of prey round about to seize on him, if he be not the better stablished in years and judgement.'[3]

---

[1] See above, pp. 54-55. The connexion is made by Sargent, *At the Court of Queen Elizabeth*, pp. 42-46 and chap. vii.

[2] See Ben Jonson, *Works* (ed. C. H. Herford and Percy Simpson), *The Man and his Work*, II, p. 90.

[3] *Essays*, 'Of Riches'. Sir John Harington remarked that 'there is now so many of that association [of sharpers] as much hinders the gain of the father of that faculty' (*Nugae Antiquae*, 226).

Cony-catching and the habits of the roaring boys are fairly thoroughly illustrated in the drama and satire of the period. It would be interesting to know from what classes the multitude of swaggerers and cheats were drawn. Certainly the increase in their numbers points to a major social problem: Alsatia was not picturesque, it was a symbol of the association of poverty and criminality, and of the rootlessness of a small, but growing, section of the population.

Fortune-hunting, moreover, took various forms, and one of the recognized means of enrichment was 'a good marriage'. Marriages, of course, had been arranged for financial reasons in the Middle Ages, which left a bad legacy in the contracting of infants, besides an unpleasant tangle in that part of the Canon Law which regulated sexual relations. But, so far as can be discovered, the proportion of economic marriages increased in the sixteenth century when the merchant was anxious to be allied to blue blood, and the needy gentleman was anxious to be allied to money. 'Marriages in these days are rather made for fornication than for continency, not so much in hope of issue as for gain of money, more for lucre than for love: neither is there any respect had to the quality, so they can embrace the quantity; for nobleness and virtue, alas it is no portion, when a thousand crowns are rather embraced than two thousand good conditions.'[1] And if a minor satirist is thought untrustworthy—though parallels could be multiplied[2]—there

---

[1] Barnaby Rich, *Faults, Faults, and Nothing Else but Faults* (1606), p. 26. Cf. Rich, *My Lady's Looking Glass* (1616), p. 56.

[2] Latimer had complained of 'joining lands to lands, possessions to possessions, neither the virtuous education nor living being regarded', in the marriage of noblemen's children.—*Sermons* (Parker Society), I, p. 95, and cf. *ibid.*, p. 243. In the later part of the century the complaints seem to be more general. Becon, *Works* (Parker Society), II, p. 372: 'Some parents greatly abuse their authority, while they sell their children to other for to be married for worldly

is Bacon: 'They say', remarked a merchant of the New
Atlantis, 'that ye have put marriage out of office. . . . And
when they do marry, what is marriage to them but a very
bargain; wherein is sought alliance, or portion, or reputation, with some desire (almost indifferent) of issue; and not
the faithful nuptial union of man and wife that was first instituted.' [1]   And the account could be reinforced from the
known history of very many families in the seventeenth
century.[2]   On the stage 'the miseries of enforced marriage'
do not only provide a romantic situation to be exploited,
they point to the increasing dominance of the economic
motive in every sphere of human life'.[3]

gain. . . . If money, if riches, if the muck of the world come, let the
child go. . . . Marriages thus made for the most part have never good
success, as experience daily teacheth.' Dekker, *The Seven Deadly Sins
of London* (1606), *Non-Dramatic Works*, I, p. 70: 'You are cruel in
compelling your children (for wealth) to go into loathed beds', etc.
Niccholes, *A Discourse of Marriage and Wiving* (1615), p. 7: 'It is a
fashion much in use in these times to choose wives as chapmen sell
their wares, with *Quantum dabitis?* What is the most you will give?'
Wye Salstonstall, *Picturae Loquentes* (1631), 'The World': 'To make
love the foundation of marriage is contemn'd as befitting the innocency
of Arcadian shepherds, and therefore now they marry portions and
take wives as things to boot'.   Peacham advises his complete gentleman: 'As soon as ye shall be able, look into your estate, labouring not
only to conserve it entire, but to augment it, either by a wise, fore-
thought marriage, or by some other thrifty means' (*The Compleat
Gentleman*, 1622, ed. G. S. Gordon, p. 225).

   [1] *The New Atlantis* (ed. Morley), in *Ideal Commonwealths*, p. 198.
   [2] See, for example, *Memoirs of the Verney Family in the Seventeenth Century*, I, p. 72; *The Autobiography of Lord Herbert of Cherbury* (ed. Sidney Lee), pp. 21-23; D'Ewes, *Autobiography* (ed.
Halliwell), p. 307 ff., where the proceedings resemble negotiations
for a trade treaty rather than the preparations for the marriage of
two human beings.   It is only fair to add that many of these arranged
marriages turned out very happily.
   [3] Weber pointed out that amongst the puritan classes 'a marriage
entered into for purely economic reasons is preferred (because after
all it is inspired by rational motives) to one with erotic foundations'

Above all, there was the burning question of usury. The stage handling of the topic was, of course, provoked by a variety of motives. At the lowest it provided an opportunity for the courtier

> Who in short time with feasting did confound
> A thousand pound a year of gallant ground[1]

to get his own back on the usurer by laughing at the 'snout able to shadow Paul's, it is so great' [2] of his stage representative. But like most of the recurring themes of dramatic satire the stage usurer was a symbol of far-reaching problems.

The medieval restrictions on usury broke down because the economic expansion of the age demanded fluid capital, and because there were increasing opportunities for profitable investment. Shareholders in commercial and industrial ventures received a profit on their investments, so there was no reason why those who lent money on which the

(*The Protestant Ethic*, tr. Talcott Parsons, p. 263). I had intended to include a chapter on the relations of men and women in the early seventeenth century, but discarded it. The treatment of the theme by dramatists may, however, be mentioned here. At one time I thought that the perpetual recurrence of cuckoldry in comedy could be explained (apart from the opportunity for bawdry) by McDougall's theory of laughter as a defence mechanism: the Elizabethans and Jacobeans laughed at cuckoldry (as the Athenians laughed at fleas) because they could not cure it. Adultery was inevitable because of the large proportion of arranged marriages ('It is to be feared', said Fuller, 'that they that marry where they do not love, will love where they do not marry'). But this is a superficial view. The better-class dramatists—Chapman and Fletcher, for example, and George Wilkins in *The Miseries of Enforced Marriage*—were pleading for a more healthy and a more civilized relationship between the sexes; and they were aware of the general economic implications that I have described above. The subject has a further interest inasmuch as it would include the abandonment of the medieval view—which died hard—of the body as a 'house of corruption'.

[1] John Davies of Hereford, *The Scourge of Folly* (1611). *Works* (ed. Grosart), p. 8.

[2] Haughton, *Englishmen for my Money* (1598); Dodsley, *Old Plays*, X, p. 481.

borrower was likely to get a good return should not demand interest. The larger economic undertakings were all based on credit.[1] 'It is certain', said Bacon, 'that the greatest part of trade is driven by young merchants upon borrowing at interest',[2] and there were few of the industrial projects that could be undertaken without credit, cither in the form of shares or loans. 'It is a vanity', Bacon continued, 'to conceive that there would be ordinary borrowing without profit; and it is impossible to conceive the number of inconveniences that will ensue, if borrowing be cramped: therefore to speak of the abolishing of usury is idle; all states have ever had it in one kind or rate or other; so as that opinion must be sent to Utopia.'[3] ''Tis a vain thing to say, Money begets not Money', said Selden, 'for that no doubt it does.'[4] It was for this reason that the legal prohibition of usury was relaxed by the act of 1571 (reviving an act of Henry VIII, repealed in 1552), which fixed a maximum rate of 10 per cent. and gave the money-lender no legal rights to enforce his claim. An act of 1624 fixed the rate at 8 per cent., 'provided that no words in this law contained shall be construed or expounded to allow the practice of usury in point of religion or conscience'.[5]

Unfortunately a very large proportion of the money borrowed in the reigns of Elizabeth and James I was required, not for lucrative expansion, but for subsistence. There were, for example, the needy gentlemen hit by the price revolution, and there were the typical borrowers of the Middle Ages: apprentices wanting to set up on their own, small masters in difficulty, peasants who had not sufficient capital to tide over the period between harvest and harvest.[6] Borrowers of this kind—and numerically they must have

[1] See Lipson, III, pp. 218-219.   [2] *Essays*, 'Of Usury'.
[3] *Ibid*.   [4] *Table-Talk* (Temple edn.), p. 146.
[5] Lipson, III, pp. 224-225.   [6] See Tawney, Wilson, p. 30 ff.

formed by far the largest class—were caught half-way between two systems. The medieval restrictions on usury had broken down, and the modern, regularized, banking-system had not yet evolved; and at the same time there was a greater need of money than ever before.[1]

The Elizabethan-Jacobean period was the usurer's heyday. His proceedings were perhaps less furtive now, but they had all the advantages of irregularity. For although the legal maximum may have been observed in commercial circles, there is no doubt at all that it represented an almost unobtainable minimum for the majority of borrowers. Security the usurer in *Eastward Ho!* is 'content with moderate profit, thirty or forty in the hundred',[2] and Misselden informs us that there was 'not only 10 per cent. usury, but 20, 30, 40 per cent. or even cento per cento per annum given and taken on pledges and pawns, and that on poor people's labour, in London especially'.[3] It is unlikely that the poor —the class that goes to the pawnshop—got any protection from the law. A statutory ten per cent. meant nothing to those who, then as now, had to borrow a shilling at a penny a month interest.[4] And of course there were other tricks. 'Taking up on commodity'—the equivalent of 'truck' and

---

[1] For the 'indirect dependence' of the small master on capital see above, pp. 61, 64-65.

[2] *Eastward Ho!* (1605), II, iii.   [3] *Free Trade* (1622), p. 30.

[4] See Crowley, *One and Thirty Epigrams* (1550), *Works*, E.E.T.S., pp. 49-50.

> You shall (said this broker)
> lend but for a months day,
> And be sure of
> a sufficient gage alway . . .
> Then must you be sure
> that your interest be
> One penny for a shilling
> and three pence for three.
> So by the year's end,
> Twelve months give twelve pence. . . .

compulsory dealing at a firm's store, in the nineteenth and twentieth centuries—was an expedient to which not only the poor were forced to resort: 'As young Inns of Court gentlemen take up satins and other vanities for themselves and their mistresses at 30, 40, 50 per cent'.[1] This is merely an example of profiteering in a luxury trade; frequently it was a condition of a loan that part of it should be received in commodities—'trash, as fire-shovels, brown paper, motley cloak-bags etc. . . . which scarce yield the third part of the sum for which they take them up.[2] It was no exaggeration to say that usury was 'the city's scourge'.[3] The perplexity that it caused was due to the transitional nature of credit transactions. Its prominence in popular literature was due to the fact that the usurer was a familiar figure whose transactions were not yet disguised under the impersonal mechanism of modern society which he was helping to form.

When Ehrenberg said that 'the force of money in determining the course of the world's history meets us at every turn at this period',[4] he was pointing to the European wars of the sixteenth century and the dependence of princes on the financier; but his remark applies with equal force to the everyday lives of Englishmen in the early seventeenth century.

Poverty, Unemployment and Trade Depressions

The widespread poverty of the Middle Ages was something, as it were, in the nature of things, due above all to

[1] Peter Chamberlen, *The Poor Man's Advocate* (1649), p. 17.

[2] Dekker, *The Seven Deadly Sins of London* (1606), *Non-Dramatic Works*, I, p. 60. Cf. 'hobby-horses, dogs, bells and lutestrings', *News from Hell* (1606), *ibid.*, II, p. 108. See also Tawney, Wilson, pp. 34-35; and p. 65 above ('Commodity' dealings in the Stannaries).

[3] R. Brathwait, *A Strappado for the Divell* (1615, ed. Ebsworth), p. 20. The contemporary attitude towards usury is discussed in Chapter IV.

[4] *Capital and Finance in the Age of the Renaissance*, p. 98.

man's immediate dependence upon the seasons. From the sixteenth century onwards poverty appears more and more clearly as man-made; that is, it can be traced to those forms of economic organization that made possible the enrichment of a small minority, and from its beginning the 'economy of abundance' has had an obverse side; enclosures, that sent the value of land soaring, the price revolution, that made fortunes in the City, the general economic expansion that laid the foundations for the Industrial Revolution, were related to the new poverty as cause and effect.

What we vaguely call the working class is bound to suffer a loss of real income during a period of profit inflation. Such a period, we have seen, was the six or seven decades from about 1570 onwards. In spite of government attempts to adjust wages to prices by means of the machinery provided by the Statute of Artificers (1563) there was inevitably a serious lag.

> It is clear (says Unwin) that wages were not raised in the same proportion as prices. In the closing years of the sixteenth century, when the price of wheat was always at least three or four times as high as the average of the previous century, the wages of the skilled workmen were little more than double, and those of the unskilled labourer considerably less than double those of the earlier period. . . . Even with butter at fivepence a pound, beef at twopence, and bread at a penny, the wage earner would find it hard to keep a house over his head and bring up a family on sixpence a day.[1]

It is only occasionally, as in the cases arising out of the silver thread monopoly, that we get glimpses of the economic helplessness of the industrial workers, but the condition of many can have been little better than that of factory hands

[1] *Shakespeare's England*, I, p. 331. J. E. Symes gives it as his opinion that during the last twenty years of Elizabeth's reign, 'the material condition of the labouring class was actually deteriorating' (*Social England*, III, p. 745).

in the nineteenth century. The government—particularly the government of Elizabeth and Charles I—did its best, but as we have seen the machinery of regulation was captured by the larger capitalists, and the coal, lead, and tin miners, the workers in iron, copper, pewter, glass, alum, the makers of soap, starch, saltpetre . . . rarely had an opportunity of appealing beyond their immediate masters. As for those employed in the domestic industries, their 'independence' was mainly nominal, since their fortunes depended entirely upon the large clothiers.[1]

All the workers just mentioned were 'divorced from the soil'; they could not rely, or could rely only to a small extent, on subsidiary agricultural pursuits. We touch here, of course, upon the enormous complex of problems created by the enclosures. From the first, enclosures for sheep-farming involved not only a subsidiary loss, but, for many, complete deprivation of the means of earning a living. Age and disease had created many beggars in the Middle Ages; the unemployment of the able-bodied, the pauperization of large numbers of the population, became a permanent feature of the national economy in the sixteenth century.

The enclosure movement would, by itself, have been sufficient to create the needs which the Elizabethan Poor Law attempted to meet. But the dislocation caused by the enclosures combined with the rapid expansion of industry to create a situation which called for more radical measures. They were measures, of course, which the most enlightened statesman could not have carried out at that time, and it is foolish to suggest alternatives to the admirable attempts of Burghley. But his solution presupposed a 'normal' state of affairs, which had been disturbed, and to which it was possible to return, whereas the country had now entered on

[1] Unwin describes the poor spinners and weavers as 'semi-paupers' (*op. cit.*, pp. 331-332).

a phase of economic development in which trade fluctuations, the recurrence of 'depressions' and industrial unemployment, were inherent.[1]

It is only recently that this aspect of Elizabethan-Jacobean life has been brought into prominence.[2] Dr Lipson has pointed out that 'commercial crises have been a feature of the economic system at least from the sixteenth century, and the Industrial Revolution only intensified, it did not create, the phenomenon of trade depressions'.[3] 'England's commerce, in becoming world-wide, found itself exposed to the vicissitudes of a world economy',[4] and to the medieval scourges, plague and dearth, was added the uncertainty of employment brought about by the fluctuations of foreign trade.

Elizabeth's economic policy was from the first a brave

[1] The limitations of the Elizabethan Poor Law are brought out by the history of the seventeenth century. In the first place it demanded efficient supervision by the central government, a supervision that was relaxed after the Civil War; and it culminated logically in the Settlement Act of 1662, which in turn was replaced by a number of hand-to-mouth expedients when it was found to conflict with the demand of industry for mobile labour in the eighteenth century.

[2] In a book published forty years ago Professor Cheyney remarked that by the end of the sixteenth century, 'A more satisfactory equilibrium in economic production . . . seems to have been attained, and distress and disorder subsided correspondingly. In the great mass of Elizabethan and Jacobean literature there is far less mention of social discontent than in the scanty pages of the prose and verse of the time of Henry VIII and Edward VI' (*Social Changes in England in the Sixteenth Century*, p. 104). In his *History of England from the Defeat of the Armada to the Death of Elizabeth*, II (1926), p. 35, he describes the 'turbulence' of the years 1596–1597: 'There was . . . the whole miserable mass of distress, crime and vagabondage that crowded the gallows, prisons, streets and highways of the time. Unemployment was frequent, poverty was everywhere, enclosures were depriving the small farmer of his livelihood . . . and the problem of feeding the people and keeping them orderly was, although intensified in these years of scarcity, a constant and largely unsolved problem.'

[3] Lipson, II, p. 64.   [4] Lipson, III, p. 294.

attempt to reach an impossible equilibrium.[1] At the beginning of her reign her ministers had to contend with difficulties caused by a depreciated coinage and the interruption of the trade with Flanders, in addition to those caused by plague and bad harvests. The ten or eleven years from 1575 onwards were generally prosperous, but from 1586 until the end of her reign economic expansion was accompanied by a succession of severe depressions at home, brought about largely by the long war with Spain and the closing of continental markets under her control. In the years 1594–1597 there was a great dearth of corn, tillage was described as being very greatly decayed, and there were frequent bread riots; there was much unemployment in the clothing trade, and 'the whole trade of the city was described as being much impaired and its traffic greatly diminished'.[2] Plague, moreover, had been intermittent throughout the 'nineties, and in 1603 (Dekker's 'Wonderful Year') one of the most virulent outbreaks was accompanied by a commercial crisis.[3]

The troubles of the later part of Elizabeth's reign can be largely ascribed to natural causes on the one hand and to political causes on the other—though the immediate effect of war on the welfare of the whole country is itself significant. The increasing part played by purely economic causes, however, can be illustrated from the great depression of 1620–1624. For the first ten years or so of James I's reign the country was officially 'prosperous'; that

---

[1] The general fluctuations, from 1558 to the end of the seventeenth century, are tabulated by Scott, I, pp. 465-467.

[2] Scott, I, p. 100; cf. Lipson, III, pp. 303-305.

[3] 'During the year December 1602 to December 1603, it was reported that 38,138 persons had died of the pestilence in London, this being close on one-quarter of the estimated population at that time. Merchants, like many of the other inhabitants, had fled to escape the risk of infection, and trade was described as "having utterly ceased" for a period of almost six months' (Scott, I, p. 102).

is to say, more and more persons were finding profitable investment for their money in commerce and industrial projects, though—as the history of the monopolies shows—economic progress was accompanied by waste and profiteering. In 1614 came the cloth-finishing scheme which resulted two years later in the complete disorganization of the cloth trade; although the project was abandoned in 1617 the Dutch cloth merchants had taken the opportunity of capturing English markets, and by 1620, when the export of the Merchant Adventurers was little more than half what it had been seven years previously,[1] a major crisis was developing. Not only was the wool trade slow to recover,[2] the general industry of the country had to bear the burden, first, of increased customs duties and the peculation of the farmers of the customs,[3] and secondly of the whole monopoly system which, in its manipulation for the sake of private profit, was now, it is safe to say, fairly throttling the common good of the country. The economic writers of the period 1620–1624 are unanimous in declaring that there was a 'general decay' of trade.[4] Scott describes the prevailing symptoms:

> Markets and fairs were sparsely attended, prices for cattle and wool were low, weavers and agricultural labourers were out of work. There was necessarily a great increase in pauperism; and, as the crisis developed, there were 'mutinies' of the unemployed. At Bath, for instance, the clothiers were 'much decayed', and many of the weavers were being

---

[1] Scott, I, p. 145. The exports of the Eastland Company had declined to one-third of their former bulk.—*Ibid.*, p. 169.

[2] The members of the old Merchant Adventurers' Company 'had to pay some £70,000 in bribes to secure a new charter; and those who provided the money recouped themselves by a tax or imposition deducted from the price offered to the clothiers' (*ibid.*, p. 169).

[3] *Ibid.*, p. 181.

[4] Misselden, *Free Trade* (1622), Sig. A 3, v. 'For what is at this time more enquired after than the causes of the decay of trade?' (*ibid.*, p. 4).

supported by the city. In Gloucester, by 1622, the trade was
described as 'growing worse and worse'. The local authorities were unable to relieve 'the infinite number' of those out of
work. Many of these 'were in case to starve as their faces
did manifest, and they so far oppressed those parts, wherein
they lived, that the abler sort of people there were not able
longer to maintain the same'. Cloth-makers, who kept their
looms running, only paid the weavers 1s. a week in 1622; and,
even under these conditions, the work was carried on at a
loss, since in some districts cloth was 'almost valueless'.
Bankruptcies were multiplying. . . .[1]

In 1625 trade began to improve, but the depression was
'a phenomenon destined to become a recurring feature of
England's industrial development'.[2] There is no need to
trace the repeated crises of the remainder of the Stuart
period; the only point to be made is that by now England
had entered on the stage of economic development in which
the welfare of thousands was dependent upon the movements of a large national and international market. For the
major depressions were not the only cause of unemployment. 'Even in normal times commercial fluctuations were
apparently a permanent feature of the industrial situation.
. . . There were always times in the year when many weavers
were out of work, and probably no clothier could keep all

[1] Scott, I, p. 167. In 1624, 12,000 weavers were out of work.—
Ibid., p. 180. 'In one Wiltshire town forty-four looms stood idle for
half a year—"by which means eight hundred persons, twenty at the
least for each loom in weaving, spinning, and spooling, are now
miserably distressed for want of employment". The distress was
general throughout the kingdom: "The whole commonwealth
suffereth," said a royal edict. Many thousands of spinners, weavers,
fullers and cloth-workers were affected, and disturbances seemed
likely. . . . The unemployed went in groups to the houses of the rich,
demanding food and money, and seized provisions in the market-
place' (Lipson, III, pp. 305-306). The depression resulted in the
setting-up of the first commission on unemployment.
[2] Lipson, III, p. 309.

his men fully occupied the whole year round.'[1]   And apart from the woollen industry, what happened, one wonders, to the miners whom Sir Bevis Bulmer gathered about him, when the mines in a district were shut down; to the alum workers in the period of disorganization under Ingram; or, more generally, to the unskilled labourers who were already drifting to the larger towns.[2]   The answer can be supplied from our own times, for the symptoms of economic disease that we meet with in the early seventeenth century are similar in kind, though not in extent or intensity, to those of the present day.

[1] Lipson, II, p. 64. 'In the West Country it was not unknown for men to be unemployed for several months; and, speaking generally, the domestic worker was assured of less continuous employment than the modern factory operative' (*ibid.*, p. 65).

[2] The enormous growth of London and its suburbs should be commented on here.   London, 'embracing about one-tenth of the whole population . . . had about eight-tenths of the foreign trade of England' (Lipson, II, p. 249).   It was not only the trading facilities that attracted newcomers.   'A "great concourse of people of all sorts" flocked to London from every part of the kingdom.   "It draweth unto it", wrote John Howes (1587) youths "which spend Michaelmas rent in Midsummer moon", soldiers "wanting wars to employ them", masterless men, lusty rogues and common beggars' (Lipson, III, p. 413). This points to the increasing difficulty of poor relief and the growth of the most miserable slum conditions—described by Cunningham, II, pp. 312-317.   In the second place it emphasizes the increasing impersonality of business relations: for example, Unwin points out that, 'In the year 1619 it was stated that there were not above forty members of the leather trades, and those glovers only, residing within the freedom of London, whilst there were glovers, leather-dressers, vellum and parchment makers outside to the number of 3000.   This migration widened the breach already made between the trader and the craftsman, and made it impossible for both to combine satisfactorily in a single organization.   It placed great difficulties in the way of the exercise of effective authority by the companies over the industries they were supposed to regulate.   It made the nominal share of the handicraft members in the company's freedom less and less of a reality' (*Industrial Organization*, p. 128).
The growth of London was the subject of many proclamations,

In the depression of 1620–1624 the clothiers were exhorted by the Privy Council to keep their men employed, even at a loss to themselves. In some cases the justices bore testimony that the employers recognized their responsibilities. 'The clothiers here do yet continue to keep their poor in work as in former times they have done, although it hath been to their great losses; and so they are contented to do as long as they may occupy their trade without undoing of themselves.'[1] But a sense of responsibility of this kind was already, to a large extent, a relic of the past, and that it was kept alive at all was largely due to the supervision of the central government. There were benevolent employers in the eighteenth century, and later, but by the reign of James I the main driving force in industry was the desire for profit. 'Even as a spider hath the best quality of feeling (said Malynes) sitting with the head downwards in her circular web . . . even so have all men (but most especially worldlings looking downwards with the kite) an action and feeling of their benefit and gain, which ruleth the course of trade in general, by good direction to be observed therein.'[2] It was the 'good direction' that was so often lacking, even when there was the will to find it; for the most part men were

whilst its monopoly of the main share of England's trade was often complained of. *E.g.*:

'Our trades do meet in Companies, our Companies at halls, and our halls become monopolies of freedom, tied to London: where all our Crafts and Mysteries are so laid up together, that outrunning all the wisdom and prudence of the land, men live by trades they never learned, nor seek to understand. By means whereof, all our creeks seek to one river, all our rivers run to one port, all our ports join to one town, all our towns make but one city, and all our cities but suburbs to one vast, unwieldy and disorderly Babel of buildings, which the world calls London' (T. Milles, *The Customer's Alphabet*, 1608, Sig. L 1, v.   [1] Lipson, III, p. 307.

[2] *The Centre of the Circle of Commerce* (1623), chap. iii, 'That gain is the Centre of the Circle of Commerce', p. 44.

employed only so long as their work was immediately profitable to their employers.

Finally, the problems of employment and the attempts to meet them serve to remind us that the period was, peculiarly, a period of transition. The modern forms of social and economic organization that were growing out of the older, local, organization of agriculture, trade and industry, were not yet sufficiently developed to appear 'normal', or indeed to be susceptible to complete analysis. To those who considered the newer problems the norm still appeared to be a stable equilibrium within which each man would 'walk contentedly in his vocation'. But that comparative stability was fast disintegrating.

CHAPTER FOUR

SOCIAL THEORY

THE contemporary accounts used in illustration of the economic and social changes of the sixteenth century have perhaps indicated the way in which men regarded those changes, the attitudes and ideas they brought to bear. But the current conceptions of 'the good life', of man's social relationships, his rights and duties, need a more explicit formulation; we have to explore further in the attempt to discover something of the web of beliefs and prejudices, aversions and sympathies which constituted the social attitudes of, say, a fairly conscious member of the first audience of *Volpone* or *A New Way to Pay Old Debts*.[1] Some things we can take for granted. One is that his opinions were not likely to be very different from those of his grandfather or great-grandfather; and so long as there is no contrary evidence we are justified in illustrating from the records of the previous century.[2] We can assume, too, that it does not much matter

[1] The start, unavoidably, is from Dr Tawney's *Religion and the Rise of Capitalism*. I have assumed that anyone likely to read this chapter will be familiar with it, and have contented myself, where possible, with references instead of quotation or summary.

[2] It is important to remember the part played by unwritten lore which, in the age before books and newspapers were abundant, was handed down from father to son, and which still, perhaps, constitutes a large part of country wisdom. See Fuller on proverbs, *The Holy State*, Book I, chap. vi, 3: The good child 'having practised them himself, entails his parents' precepts on his posterity. Therefore such instructions are by Solomon (Prov. i. 9) compared to frontlets and chains (not to a suit of clothes, which serves but one, and quickly wears out, or out of fashion) which have in them a real lasting worth, and are bequeathed as legacies to another age.' For the continuity

from which rank of society this representative spectator was drawn. National taste was remarkably homogeneous,[1] all ranks spoke, roughly, the same language, and shared the same general sentiments; there was no insuperable bar between 'educated' and 'uneducated'. And, above all, the majority of men still thought in terms of a small locality. In Elizabeth's reign, and earlier, there was certainly in existence something that can only be called a national spirit. But English civilization in the early seventeenth century was still, very largely, a local civilization, based on local pieties, local traditions and knowledge. Even London retained many of the characteristics of a small market town.[2]

The fact that men lived together in small local communities helps to explain the moral emphasis of medieval social thought. Dr Heckscher remarks that 'the history of the Middle Ages certainly proves that people can live in much more restricted units of society, held together and tied to a larger cultural circle by means of one chiefly spiritual bond. Not only is such a life physically possible, but, in it, human problems can be truly perceived which in larger social structures must more or less necessarily be sacrificed.'[3] In a small community in which most of the work that serves everyday needs is carried on, it is impossible to think of economic processes as 'impersonal'. On the contrary,

of sixteenth-century and medieval social theory see Tawney, *op. cit.*, pp. 66, 82, 159 and *passim*.

[1] Even allowing for such things as the taste for euphuistic romances at the top (and they very soon reached the populace) and for broadsheet horrors and platitudes at the bottom of the scale.

[2] See Appendix A, 'Elizabethan Prose'.

[3] *Mercantilism*, I, p. 42. Cf. Whateley, *A Bride Bush* (1623), p. 43: 'Why do we love those of our own family more than others, and those of our own town, and of our own street usually (unless quarrels fall out) more than those that are further removed in habitation? but because we have more occasions of familiar conversing with them'. Contrast the impersonality of modern suburban life.

buying and selling and every economic activity is likely
to be regarded simply as 'a case of neighbourly or unneighbourly conduct'.[1] By the end of Elizabeth's reign
the growing impersonality of business was already creating a new temper. But the old survived; God was still
'the clerk of the market',[2] and the exhortation, 'Do as you
would be done by', which forms the burden of Crowley's
'The Merchant's Lesson',[3] is, a hundred years later, the conclusion of Fuller's chapter on 'The Good Merchant': 'Take
our Saviour's wholesale rule: "whatsoever ye would have
men do unto you, do you unto them; for this is the law and
the prophets"'.[4]

These general moral considerations were, perhaps, all that
served the majority of men in their everyday economic dealings. But behind them, ready, as it were, to be brought into
consciousness when occasion prompted, was a more clearly
articulated body of assumptions. In formal theory the

[1] Tawney, *op. cit.*, p. 55. It was noted against the enclosers that
they split up the old village community. 'This community of dwell-
ing, enclosers do sometimes take away in Christ's Church; for they
will have no man almost dwell near them. We may see many of
their houses built alone, like ravens' nests, no birds building near
them' (Francis Trigge, *Humble Petition of Two Sisters* (1604), quoted
by Cheyney, *Social Changes in the Sixteenth Century*, p. 8).
[2] Robert Crowley, *One and Thirty Epigrams* (1550), *Select Works*
(E.E.T.S.), ed. J. M. Cowper, p. 34.
[3] *The Voice of the Last Trumpet* (1550), *ibid.*, p. 90.
[4] Fuller, *Holy State* (1642), Book II, chap. xvii. The way in
which economic thought in the sixteenth century was shot through
with moral considerations is seen in almost all the formal documents
of the period. Cecil (?) for example, drawing up an industrial programme early in Elizabeth's reign, has: 'so by the heed of the masters,
servants may be reduced to obedience to the Prince and to God also;
by the looseness of the times no other remedy is left but by awe of
law to acquaint men with virtue again, whereby the reformation of
religion may be brought in credit, with the amendment of manners,
the want whereof hath been imputed as a thing grown by the liberty
of the Gospel, etc.' (T. and P., I, p. 325).

underlying conception was one of unity, concord and proportion. 'The body politic' had not yet become a submerged metaphor, and, encouraged by the teaching of the Church, men saw the state as an organism composed of different but not independent members. A passage in 'King Edward's Remains' (almost as well known as Menenius' speech in *Coriolanus* and Ulysses' 'order' speech in *Troilus and Cressida*) illustrates this:

> This is the true ordering of the state of a well-fashioned commonwealth, that every part do obey one head, or governor, one law, as all parts of the body obey the head, agree among themselves, and one not to eat up the other through greediness, but that we see that order, moderation, and reason, bridle the affections.[1]

This thought is persistent, and it is impossible to read far in the literature of the time without meeting it. The ideal was 'concord within the realm amongst the several members of the same', and its overthrow was attributed to the direct influence of the devil.[2] Equality of possessions was impossible, but a kingdom should be like a well-ordered family.[3] Even the writer of a manual for customs officials took care to sprinkle his pages with maxims such as 'The beauty of Nature is Order', and remarked that 'All things in Nature do tend to perfection by the Rules of Order and degrees of Goodness'.[4] The firm government of the Tudors was, we may say, an expression of 'the national will'; the period of feudal dissension was too near in time, the danger of further

---

[1] 'King Edward (VI)'s Remains. A Discourse about the Reformation of Many Abuses', Burnet, *History of the Reformation* (ed. N. Pocock), V, p. 98.

[2] G. de Malynes, Merchant, *Saint George for England* (1601), Epistle Dedicatory, Sig. A 4, v.

[3] Malynes, *A Treatise of the Canker of England's Commonwealth* (1601).

[4] T. Milles, *The Customer's Alphabet and Primer* (1608), Sig. F 1, v, and Sig. F 2.

outbreaks too pressing, for men to ignore the value of internal harmony. The Wars of the Roses, said Hall, should be kept in mind as a perpetual example, 'so that all men, more clearer than the sun, may apparently perceive that as by discord great things decay and fall to ruin, so the same by concord be revived and erected'.

Concord, not equality. Differences of rank and status were accepted as part of the natural order. One of those miscellanies, so popular in the seventeenth century, that combined amusement and instruction for (I should imagine) the lower middle classes, has the following representative little homily:

> Let each be subject to's Superior.
> For it would breed confusion in the land,
> If people did admit of no command,
> But like a Plato's Commonwealth, should be
> Subject to none, but in equality.
> Therefore the Lord who of his grace doth love us
> Hath ranked some below us, some above us.
> Above us that we might be cautioned thence
> To show unto them due obedience.
> Below us, that we might thereby express,
> To them our love, to God our thankfulness,
> Our love, that we might our affection show,
> In love to them that ranked are so low. . . .
> In this same decent comely order then
> Of high and low, great and inferior men,
> Thou ranked art.[1]

[1] Richard Brathwait, *A Strappado for the Devil* (1615, ed. J. W. Ebsworth), p. 231. Brathwait is here addressing 'The Tenant'; the previous rhyme, 'To the Landlord' is a plea that landlords should not oppress their poor tenants. Complaints of extravagance in dress are frequently coupled with complaints that degree, or decorum, is not observed. Cf. Latimer, *Sermons* (Parker Society), I, p. 252; Becon, *Works* (Parker Society), I, p. 346 ('Neither ought any woman to go apparelled otherwise than their degree and estate require', etc.). A representative passage from the Jacobean period is: 'This therefore

The system thus advocated was not, of course, a rigid caste system,[1] but moralists and statesmen were agreed that an ordered system of social classes must be preserved, and the whole of the Elizabethan social and industrial legislation aimed at preserving that gradation of estates that was the foundation of a well-ordered commonwealth. And it was not merely a way of 'keeping the poor in their place'.

No one (says Dr Tawney) who reads the writers by whom the agrarian problem is discussed can fail to notice that the official view of the proper system of agrarian relationships was on the whole favourable to the small man, and was, indeed, not very different from that expressed in the demands of the peasants themselves. Not, of course, that the authorities had any intention of depressing landlords or raising peasants, but that the whole established system of government was based on a certain organization of social life, and that the Government tended to maintain that organization in maintaining itself and carrying on the work of the State.[2]

This conception of degree was usually formulated in

may well be avowed by the rule of Christian sobriety: that a woman (neither exceeding the decency of fashion, nor going beyond the limits of her own estate, nor surpassing the bounds of her husband's calling) but that such a woman may wear anything' (Rich, *My Lady's Looking Glass*, 1616, p. 41).

[1] See G. M. Trevelyan, *England under the Stuarts*, p. 20. Side by side with the dislike of 'new men' who rose suddenly out of their proper station was a recognition that social advancement was possible and desirable. Both Harrison and Fuller accept the fact that yeomen often became gentlemen (*Description of England*, Book II, chap. v. *Holy State*, Book II, chap. xviii—A yeoman 'is a gentleman in ore, whom the next age may see refined; and is the wax capable of a gentle impression, when the prince shall stamp it'). And not only did merchants enter the ranks of 'the gentry', it was common for the younger sons of landed families to engage in trade; see Harrison, *loc. cit.*, and Fuller, *Holy State*, Book II, chap. xv, 'The Younger Brother'. But behind Fuller's work there is the conception of an ordered system of classes.

[2] *The Agrarian Problem in the Sixteenth Century*, p. 341.

terms of 'walking in one's vocation'—something more positive than

> God bless the squire and his relations
> And keep us in our proper stations.

'As there is no part admitted in the body that doth not work and take pain', said King Edward, 'so ought there no part of the commonwealth to be but laboursome in his vocation.'[1]

> First walk in thy vocation,
> And do not seek thy lot to change

is the burden of Crowley's *Voice of the Last Trumpet* (1550): servants, yeomen, scholars, physicians, lawyers, merchants, all are bidden 'walk in thy calling'.[2] Fifty years later Malynes' tract on usury opens by describing how the Dragon (usury)

> overthroweth the harmony of the strings of the good government of a commonwealth, by too much enriching some, and by oppressing and impoverishing some others, bringing the instrument out of tune: when as every member of the same should live contented in his vocation and execute his charge according to his profession.[3]

There are, says the same writer, two prime necessities— equality of trade between nations, and 'concord amongst the members of a commonwealth',

> when every member thereof doth live contentedly and proportionably in his vocation.   Both these are brought to con-

---

[1] Burnet, *History of the Reformation*, V, p. 98.

[2] Crowley, *Select Works*, pp. 57-104.

[3] Malynes, *Saint George for England* (1601), To the Reader.   'For albeit that equality would be the cause that every man should have enough, which made some of opinion that goods ought to be in common: yet forasmuch as the same was never used or established in any age, reason requireth that, according to the course of humane affairs, all things should be governed in the best and most assured manner that can be devised, and as it were, seeking a certainty even in uncertainties, which is called Policy' (*loc. cit.*).

fusion and utter destruction by means of this Dragon, a monster found out by covetousness, the root of all evil, whereunto ambition is annexed which moveth sedition and civil war.[1]

Brathwait's *English Gentleman* (1631), which, together with his *English Gentlewoman*, was a lengthy attempt to do for the middle classes what Peacham's *Complete Gentleman* had done for the upper, devotes a complete section to 'Vocation', which makes explicit the connexion with honourable labour.

> Now that there is a necessity of Vocation enjoined all, of what rank or degree soever, we may prove by many frequent places of Scripture, inveighing against idleness, and commending employment unto us. (Quotations from Ezekiel, Proverbs, Ecclesiasticus, the Epistles to the Thessalonians, and to Timothy, follow.) Again, that express charge given by the Apostle touching every one's distinct profession or vocation: Let every man abide in the same vocation wherein he was called. See here how much idleness is condemned, and labour commended; the former being the mother of all vices, the latter a cheerer, cherisher, and supporter of all virtues.[2]

The passage is interesting since it shows the continuity between the Puritan conception of 'the calling' and the medieval insistence on degree. 'A peculiar vocation is deputed to every one in this pilgrimage of human frailty',[3] and if each man would keep to his own the dissensions of the world would soon be cured. 'O what a golden age were this! when each performing a mutual office unto other, might so support one another, as what one wanted, might be supplied by another.'[4] Brathwait, it is true, is here pointing to the necessity of each man keeping to his own trade, rather

[1] *Loc. cit.*
[2] Richard Brathwait, *The English Gentleman* (edn. of 1633), pp. 106-107.   [3] *Ibid.*, p. 123.   [4] *Ibid.*, p. 121.

147

than to his own social rank; but the two conceptions—of a proper status, and of a particular kind of work to be done—were complementary. And rank, it is insisted, does not exempt from the obligations of a calling: 'The higher place the heavier charge', and 'None are less exempted from a calling than great men'.[1] A passage from the *Advice* which Henry Percy wrote for his son will serve as a summary:

> There are certain works fit for every vocation; some for kings; some for noblemen; some for gentlemen; some for artificers; some for clowns; and some for beggars; all are good to be known by everyone, yet not be used by everyone. If everyone play his part well, that is allotted him, the commonwealth will be happy; if not then will it be deformed; but which is fit for everyone, *quaere*? [2]

Few, however, were as sceptical as the imprisoned Earl of Northumberland.

For one brought up on nineteenth-century conceptions of 'natural equality' it is, perhaps, hard to see the virtues of a social theory which accepted as axiomatic that each man—tinker, tailor, clergyman, lawyer, nobleman—had his proper place, and that he was best employed in fulfilling the vocation to which his birth seemed to direct him. We may leave aside the question of what legal freedom and equality mean in practice to-day; what we have to remember is that in the sixteenth century the conception of degree formed part of a system of thought which stressed social responsibility as well as acquiescence in one's material fortunes.

The state was an organism (an extension of the family or

---

[1] *The English Gentleman*, p. 115.

[2] Henry Percy, *Advice to his Son* (1609, ed. G. B. Harrison), p. 119. On the kindred principle of 'One man, one trade', see Unwin, *Shakespeare's England*, I, pp. 324-325; Cheyney, *Social Changes*, p. 56; and for contemporary illustration, T. and P., I, pp. 136-140 ('A controversy between the Painters and Plasterers of London'—1601).

the gild-brotherhood), and it was the duty of each part to serve the purpose of the whole. This may seem a commonplace, but for a proper understanding of early seventeenth-century thought it is essential to realize how complete is the antithesis that it offers to the doctrine of *laissez-faire*, with its underlying principle that 'Man's self-love is God's Providence'. Those who set their own interests before the common welfare were moral offenders, and nothing is more common in the economic writings of the time than the expressed opposition between public good and private profit. To describe a class of men as 'a kind of people aiming only at their own profit' [1] was sufficient to condemn them in the eyes of the right-thinking, and the Tudor bugbears—forestallers, regrators and engrossers—were noted for their 'wicked and unsatiable greediness' in 'preferring their own private gain above the public good'.[2]

The insistence on this opposition—on the prior claim of the public good—was inherited from the Middle Ages; it survived throughout the sixteenth century, and it only decayed when the seventeenth century was well advanced. It is found—to take a few random examples—in the complaint of the London Founders in 1507 against a Warden of their Company who was said to have dealt unfairly, 'subtly intending his own singular lucre and the utter undoing' of the rest of the brotherhood;[3] in a proclamation concerning the price of sugar in 1544, when scarcity was attributed to 'the greedy appetites and affections of such as have the same sugar', and to the 'crafty conspiracies between them and other for their regular avail and lucre':[4] in a (draft) bill of 1593 which condemned 'divers evil disposed persons, com-

---

[1] A letter of the Lord Mayor and Court of Aldermen (1623) concerning cloth factors, quoted by Lipson, II, p. 27.
[2] Proclamation of 1598, quoted by Lipson, II, p. 432.
[3] T. and P., I, p. 103.   [4] *Ibid.*, p. 147.

monly called yarn choppers or jobbers of woollen yarn',
since, 'wanting the fear of God, and caring only for their
own private gain, without having any regard of the maintenance of the commonwealth', they bought up yarn and
sold it at 'unreasonable prices'; such were 'drones, idle members, and evil weeds in a commonwealth'.[1] The expressed
antithesis became almost an official formula (it occurs frequently in the drama), and the preambles of statutes made to
regulate trade and industry were as likely as not to hold up
for reprobation the 'many and sundry covetous and insatiable persons seeking their only lucres and gains . . . to
the great detriment of the commonwealth'.[2]

In the early seventeenth century it was a generally
accepted maxim that 'We all cry out on covetise and private
gain'.[3] General denunciations of evil-doers were couched
in terms of the familiar antithesis between self and state:
'We shall find how self love is settled far into every man's
heart, and that we so hotly hunt after private gain that we,
freezing coldly, seek not any public profit'.[4] On this fundamental question there was no room for doubt: 'Shall not the
rule of justice and equity be preferred, whereby the commonwealth is enriched, and the private be abolished, which

[1] T. and P., I, p. 375.
[2] *An Act to Restrain carrying of Corn Victuals and Wood over the Sea*, 1555, T. and P., I, p. 150.
Cf. T. and P., I, p. 174 ('for their private wealths, singular advan-
tages and commodities, nothing regarding the maintenance and upholding of the said City Boroughs and towns nor the common
wealth of the said handicrafts'—25 Hen. VIII, c. 18, 1534); I, p. 319
('seeking rather their own private gain than respecting any common
good'—Request of the People of Halstead, *c*. 1590); III, p. 131 ('We,
being beastly minded . . . every man seeking his own private commodity, without regard of the weal public'—William Cholmeley's Project
for Dyeing Cloth in England, 1553).
[3] Milles, *The Customer's Alphabet* (1608), Sig. F 2, v.
[4] *Grievous Groans for the Poor* (1622), p. 3.

destroyeth the kingdom? Yes, questionless.'[1] When a writer of the Protectorate period remarked, 'It is an undeniable maxim that everyone by the light of nature and reason will do that which makes for his greatest advantage. ... The advancement of private persons will be the advantage of the public,'[2] he was marking a major breach with the past.

I do not think we can doubt that this aspect of social theory in the age of Shakespeare and Jonson derived from the actual conditions of life in small communities on the one hand, and from the traditional teaching of the Church on the other. Both of these combined to foster a sense of responsibility which, in the past at all events, had been further encouraged by the organization of the gilds. When Crowley's rent-raiser replied

> That with his own he might
> Always do as he list,

he was violating an accepted code.[3] In the next epigram a usurer is reproached by a 'Prophet'.

> 'Why, sir' (quod this Usurer)
> 'It is my living'.[4]

[1] Malynes, *The Centre of the Circle of Commerce* (1623), p. 62.

[2] Joseph Lee, *A Vindication of a Regulated Enclosure* (1636), p. 9, quoted by Tawney, *Religion and Capitalism*, p. 259. The concept of 'the public good' probably influenced the development of ideas of legality in the seventeenth century. Cf.

> Never private cause
> Should take on it the part of public laws.
> (*The Revenge of Bussy D'Ambois*, III, i.)

[3] *One and Thirty Epigrams, Select Works*, p. 47.

> But immediately, I trow
> This oppressor fell sick
> Of a voice that he heard,
> 'Give account of thy bailiwick'.

[4] Compare Sir Moth Interest in *The Magnetic Lady*, II, i:

> That's my industry,
> As it might be your reading, study, and counsel.

'Yes, sir' (quod this Prophet)
But it is not your calling;
You are called to live
After twenty pound by year,
And after that rate
Ye should measure your cheer,
Till God did increase you
By his merciful ways,
By increasing your corn,
And your cattle in the leys;
Which increase with your lands
You are bound to employ,
To the profit of all them
That do dwell you by.
You are not born to yourself,
Neither may you take
That thing for your own,
Whereof God did you make
But steward and bailiff,
That shall yield a reckoning
At the Day of Judgement
For every thing.
And do ye not doubt,
But then ye shall know,
Whether ye may your goods
At your pleasure bestow.[1]

Here the conceptions of vocation, of reasonable gain, and of duty to one's neighbours are explicitly related.[2] In Greene's

[1] Crowley, *Select Works*, pp. 50-51. The usurer had sold his land in order to set up as a money-lender.
[2] Cf. 'The Gentleman's Lesson':

> Thou shalt have delight in nothing
> Saving in doing thy duty;
> Which is, under God and thy king,
> To rule them that thou dost dwell by.

The Gentleman is not allowed to do as he likes with his own, he may not raise rents at will,

> For as thou dost hold of thy king,

Quippe for an Upstart Courtier (1592) the vices of covetousness and pride are similarly opposed to the virtues of charity, hospitality and neighbourly dealing.

> Since men placed their delights in proud looks and brave attire, hospitality was left off, neighbourhood was exiled, conscience was scoffed at, and charity lay frozen in the streets: now upstart gentlemen for the maintenance of that their fathers never looked after, raised rents, racked their tenants, and imposed great fines.[1]

And the teaching of the pulpit was equally clear:

> Note here (said Latimer), that our Saviour biddeth us to say, 'us'. This 'us' lappeth in all other men with my prayer; for every one of us prayeth for another. When I say, 'Give us this day our daily bread', I pray not for myself only, if I ask as he biddeth me; but I pray for all others. Wherefore say I not, 'Our Father, give me this day my daily bread'? For because God is not my God alone, he is a common God. And here we be admonished to be friendly, loving, and charitable one to another: for what God giveth, I cannot say, 'This is my own'; but I must say, 'This is ours'. For the rich man cannot say, 'This is mine alone, God hath given it unto me for my own use'. Nor yet hath the poor man any title unto it, to take it away from him. No, the poor man may not do

> So doth thy tenant hold of thee,
> And is allowed a living
> As well as thou, in his degree.
> *(Ibid., p. 92)*

[1] Greene, *Works* (ed. Grosart), X, p. 209. The old-fashioned landlord, on the other hand, 'is mortal enemy to pride . . . he regardeth hospitality and aimeth at honour with relieving the poor. . . . He valueth fame by the report of the common sort, who praise him for his virtue, justice, liberality, housekeeping and almsdeeds. . . . His tenants and farmers would, if it might be possible, make him immortal with their prayers and praises. He raiseth no rent, racketh no lands . . . buyeth no house over his neighbour's head, but respecteth his country and the commodity thereof, as dear as his life' (*ibid.*, p. 267). Cf. *ibid.*, p. 222 ('neighbourhood and hospitality'), p. 251 ('lowliness, neighbourhood and hospitality').

so; for when he doth so, he is a thief afore God and man. But yet the poor man hath title to the rich man's goods; so that the rich man ought to let the poor man have part of his riches to help and to comfort him withal. Therefore when God sendeth unto me much, it is not mine, but ours; it is not given unto me alone, but I must help my poor neighbours withal. .... The rich man ought to distribute his riches abroad amongst the poor: for the rich man is but God's officer, God's treasurer.[1]

The Church did not confine itself to general exhortation and denunciation. Latimer's sermons against enclosers, the 'step-lords', are well known; he denounced usury as 'wicked before God, be it small or great; like as theft is wicked';[2] and he 'frankly and liberally taxed, perstringed, and openly rebuked before the King's majesty the peculiar faults of certain of his auditors'.[3] One of the Liturgies of Edward VI contained a 'Prayer for Landlords', that they might not rack rents,[4] and the tradition of public responsibility in the Church was still active in the time of Laud.[5]

Not only was there current in the sixteenth century, and

[1] Five Sermons on the Lord's Prayer, made before Lady Katherine, Duchess of Suffolk, 1552. Latimer, *Sermons* (Parker Society), I, p. 398.   [2] *Ibid.*, p. 410.

[3] Address to the Reader, before the Second Sermon preached before Edward VI, 1549, *ibid.*, p. 111.

[4] 'We heartily pray Thee that they (who possess the grounds, pastures, and dwelling-places of the earth) may not rack and stretch out the rents of their houses and lands, nor yet take unreasonable fines and incomes after the manner of covetous worldlings, but so let them out to others that the inhabitants thereof may both be able to pay the rents and also honestly to live, to nourish their families, and to relieve the poor. .... Give them grace also that they may be content with that that is sufficient and not joint house to house nor couple land to land to the impoverishment of other, but so behave themselves in letting out their tenements, lands, and pastures, that after this life they may be received into everlasting dwelling-places' (quoted by J. M. Cowper, Introduction to Crowley's *Select Works*, p. xxii).

[5] See *Religion and Capitalism*, pp. 170-175.

later, a conception of reasonable gain—'Content thyself with a living', sell your goods at a reasonable price, is Crowley's exhortation to the merchant [1]—the attitude towards wealth fostered by the Church was essentially humane. 'Humane', perhaps, is not the word to apply to some of the sermons of ecclesiastical moralists—the medieval tradition of the corruption of the flesh was incompatible with the full implications of a Greek (or modern) 'humanism'. But with regard to riches the continued insistence was that they were subordinate to the proper dignity of man. To the medieval thinker, says Dr Tawney,

> material riches are necessary; they have a secondary importance, since without them men cannot support themselves and help one another. . . . But . . . the outer is ordained for the sake of the inner; economic goods are instrumental—*sicut quaedam adminicula, quibus adjuvamur ad tendendum in beatitudinem.* 'It is lawful to desire temporal blessings, not putting them in the first place, as though setting up our rest in them, but regarding them as aids to blessedness, inasmuch as they support our corporal life and serve as instruments for acts of virtue.' Riches, as St. Antonino says, exist for man, not man for riches.[2]

This represents also the Anglican temper of the sixteenth century. In *The Sick Man's Salve* Becon makes the dying man say:

> I thank the Lord my God, I am as well contented to leave the goods of the world, as ever I was to enjoy them. And in this behalf I have to thank the Lord my God, that since I

[1] *Select Works*, pp. 86-90. Cf. The Complaint of the Lord Mayor of London against the Newcastle Coal Monopoly: 'The said inhabitants, who are not content to use the same (trade) for their moderate gain with some respect of the commonwealth, but by evil practice seek to increase and augment their gain to the hurt of other her Majesty's subjects, especially those of the poorer sort' (T. and P., I, pp. 269-270).

[2] *Religion and Capitalism*, p. 31. The quotation is from Aquinas.

came to the use of reason, and had any worldly possessions at all, I had always made them to serve me; and I never served them, but at all times could be contented to depart from them, whensoever the glory of God and the commodity of my neighbour did require.[1]

Riches, indeed, said Latimer, 'must be had, *cum tremore*, with fear; for it is a dangerous thing to have them'.[2]

Therefore, let us not set our hearts upon the riches of this world, but rather let us labour for our living; and then let us use prayer; then we may be certain of our living. Though we have no riches, yet a man may live without great riches. . . . And so you may perceive how the devil useth the good creatures of God to our own destruction: for riches are good creatures of God, but you see daily how men abuse them; how they set their hearts upon them, forgetting God and their own salvation. . . . Therefore . . . let not this affection take place in your hearts, to be rich. Labour for thy living, and pray to God, then he will send thee things necessary: though he send not great riches, yet thou must be content withal; for it is better to have a sufficient living than to have great riches.[3]

This sketch of sixteenth-century social thought—its insistence on degree and on vocation, its subordination of private profit to public good, and its suspicion of, if not hostility towards, riches—helps to explain some of the virtues of the cultural inheritance of Shakespeare's contemporaries.[4] It suggests, moreover, what was likely to be the

[1] Becon, *Works, III, Prayers, etc.* (Parker Society), pp. 116-117.
[2] *Sermons* (Parker Society), I, p. 477.
[3] *Ibid.*, p. 442. Cf. Bishop Hooper, *Later Writings* (Parker Society), p. 281.
[4] It is worth noting at this point that clerical admonitions in the sixteenth century form very much better evidence of general opinion than do the sermons of the nineteenth century. Not only were there many clerics in administrative, or semi-administrative positions, sermon-going was an important part of the education of the average Elizabethan Londoner.

common attitude towards the 'new men' whose rise to wealth and social consequence was discussed in the previous chapters. These were not content with reasonable gain, they set their own profit before the common good, and they refused to observe the limitations of degree. They were, in short (in practice, if not in theory), individualists, at a time when current opinion set the emphasis on community, order and organization.

For to the account given above must be added the contemporary insistence on an ordered trade and industry. This, as has been shown, was something that sprang from the conditions of work in the Middle Ages—conditions that were far from being entirely obsolete in the reign of James I; and the economic theory thus evolved was in harmony with the religious and political theory of the ordered state.[1] For present purposes there is no need to distinguish between the accounts given of industrial and commercial companies; nor is it necessary to summarize the early seventeenth-century debate concerning external (commercial) monopolies; the significant point is found in the terms in which such discussions were carried on.

[1] Cf. the arguments summarized by Lipson, II, p. 237, in favour of the 'stint' of trade. 'The nominal purpose of the "stint" was equality of opportunity. It was designed to ensure that "the benefit of our traffic may" be "distributed indifferently and by order among all", instead of "the overgrown and great-pursed merchant" carrying away "the living and trade of young beginners" and men of "lowly estates". The argument that it prevented the monopoly of trade falling into the hands of a few accorded with medieval ideas, and its force was not yet spent in the seventeenth century. Thus an apologist (Parker) for the (Merchant Adventurers') Company wrote in 1648: "We know well that 'tis possible for some one merchant to exceed forty others in purse or credit; yet sure it cannot be expedient for the commonwealth that one merchant should grasp too much and swell up to an excessive bulk, whilst forty other merchants being over-shadowed by him can attain to no growth at all" '. Cf. Heckscher, *Mercantilism*, I, pp. 271-276.

The traditional conception was expressed in Misselden's *Free Trade, or the Means to Make Trade Flourish* (1622). The third chapter is, 'Of governed Trade, and therein of Monopoly'. Misselden points out that order and government in trade have great advantages; and a regulated company is not a monopoly, since it is open to all, either by apprenticeship or by purchase.

> If this point were well thought upon, I presume the gracious grants and privileges of his Majesty, conferred upon Societies, would not seem so much a restraint of the common liberty, as a prudent ordering and accommodating thereof unto the public utility. For it hath ever been a policy of this state, to reduce the trades of merchants of this kingdom into Corporations and Societies, for the advancement of trade, by the benefit of order and government: well foreseeing that there cannot be any greater bane to a well-governed commonwealth, than ill-governed and disorderly trade.[1]

In Chapter IV he writes 'Of Want of Government in Trade': if trade is not ordered unskilful persons take part in it, and '*Nemo nascitur artifex*'. In the last chapter he suggests ten points for 'The Remedy for all the former Causes of decay of Trade', including the restraint of luxury and of unnecessary law-suits, the erection of *monts de piété* for the poor, and the abolition of monopolies. Finally, he writes, 'unordered' trade should be regulated and reduced to government.

> For where Trade is disordered and the Traders ungoverned, there they are like a house divided, which cannot long subsist, according to that of the Orator, *Nec domus ulla, nec Civitas, nec Societas, nec Gens, nec hominum universum genus stare, nec rerum natura omnis, nec sine imperio mundus ipse potest.*[2]

---

[1] *Free Trade*, p. 67.
[2] *Ibid.*, p. 134. The quotation is from Cicero, *De Legibus*. Elsewhere Misselden warns the reader, 'Here and there, if you meet with a little Latin or the like, which you do not like, let it alone for their sakes that understand it' (*The Circle of Commerce*, 1623, 'To the Reader').

Misselden, of course, was an official of the Merchant Adventurers' Company, but even those who disliked the privileged companies attacked what they considered their abuses rather than the conception of order which they embodied. Malynes, who answered Misselden in *The Maintenance of Free Trade*, agreed that trade should be 'ordered' and companies maintained. Those who would dissolve the companies 'have no regard, that innovations are as dangerous, as to remove the corner stones of a building'.[1] 'The providence of the state hath also a great consideration in the course of trade, under government in appointed places, especially in that of the Merchant Adventurers' Company.'[2]   In short, he agreed with the majority in the belief that 'a due order, good and ordinate rule'[3] was necessary for the proper conduct of economic affairs.

> Although the victory of the interlopers (says Lipson) registered a stage in the growth of free trade, using the term as it was then commonly employed, their own standpoint was not so different as their arguments might suggest.   They did not advocate carrying on trade 'without conduct and order'. 'We desire still a government' was the significant admission made on their behalf; and their hostility towards the Merchant Adventurers was inspired more by animus against the merchants of London, who monopolized 'the whole mass and bulk of the trade of England', than by any devotion to the abstract doctrine of economic freedom.[4]

Even Gresham remarked that, 'As the merchants be one of

[1] *The Maintenance of Free Trade*, p. 67.
[2] *Ibid.*, p. 68.   Shakespeare's lines in *Troilus and Cressida*,
> The providence that's in a watchful state
> Knows almost every grain of Plutus' gold,

had, as usual in Shakespeare, a context in contemporary thought.
[3] The phrase used here comes from the Petition of the Leather-sellers for the Amalgamation of the Glovers-Pursers into their Company (1502), T. and P., I, p. 100.
[4] Lipson, II, pp. 248-249.

the best members in our common weal, so they be the very worst if their doings be not looked unto in time; and forced to keep good order'.[1]   And this suspicion of unregulated activity directed towards one's private gain was shared by statesmen,[2] moralists and the common people.

It would, of course, be foolish to estimate the practice of the Middle Ages, of the sixteenth century, or of any other period, merely from the current social theory. But the social theory of the Elizabethan-Jacobean period has a place in this study not because of what it tells us of contemporary economic dealing but because it indicates the attitudes of 'the average man' towards his work, towards acquisition and riches, and towards his fellows. And that the traditional social morality was not a mere remote ideal is proved by the practice of the Tudor and early Stuart governments. Not that the advisers of Elizabeth and James I were philanthropists, they were practical men concerned with the practical business of government. But at least 'the system of State control had behind it the weight of a powerful tradition, which did not consider public and private interest as identical',[3] and the government of the time does seem to have been actuated not merely by a concern for public order, but by 'a genuine desire to safeguard the economic interests of the industrial population' [4] and of the lower ranges of the rural population.[5]

[1] Burgon, *Life of Gresham*, I, p. 335.   Cf. Heckscher, *Mercantilism*, II, p. 320, where the sentence is quoted.

[2] Cf. Cecil: 'Merchants have grown so cunning in the trade of corrupting, and found it so sweet, that since the 1 Henry VIII, there could never be won any good law or order which touched their liberty or state; but they stayed it, either in the Commons or higher House of Parliament or else by the Prince himself' ('An Industrial Programme', 1559, T. and P., I, p. 328).

[3] Lipson, III, pp. 4-5.   [4] *Ibid.*, p. 254.

[5] 'Yet other motives than the fear of popular outbreaks actuated

The attempts made by the Tudor governments to regulate enclosures are well known. From the time of Henry VIII statutes, commissions, and letters of the Privy Council attempted to deal with the evils of eviction and depopulation, since,

> by the same means of tillage and husbandry, the greater part of the subjects are preserved from extreme poverty in a competent estate of maintenance and means to live, and the wealth of the realm is kept dispersed and distributed in many hands.[1]

Enclosures had to be combated in order to avoid 'the great decay of people, the engrossing of wealth into few hands. . . . The balancing of the misery of the people and the decay of the realm's strength with some trifling abridgement to gentlemen hath no proportion.'[2] And state interference did not end with the accession of the Stuarts. After the riots in the Midlands in 1607 the chief offenders were summoned before the Council and bound over to rebuild houses which had fallen into decay. In 1624 all statutes

the Government. There was not wanting a genuine desire to remove hardships and alleviate suffering—it showed itself in the policy of Wolsey, who "favoured the people exceedingly and especially the poor"; in the instructions to the Council of the North to hear "the petition of the poorest man against the richest or against the greatest lord"; and in the intervention of the lords of the Privy Council on behalf of a maid-servant whose mistress was accused of "hard dealings" ' (Lipson, III, p. 448).   On 'the sincere desire' of Charles I and his ministers 'to promote the interests of the working classes', see Unwin, *Industrial Organization*, p. 143. Cf. Cunningham, II, p. 285; M. James, *Social Policy during the Puritan Revolution*, pp. 1-5; and Heckscher, *Mercantilism*, I, pp. 256-261, on 'the Stuart policy of welfare'. The Court of Requests was, of course, known as 'the Court of Poor Men's Causes'.

[1] An Act for the Maintenance of Husbandry, etc., 1597–1598, T. and P., I, p. 84. For government action, see Tawney, *Agrarian Problem*, especially Part III, chap. i; and Lipson, II, p. 398 ff.

[2] Contemporary Notes on the Act of 1597–1598 (Salisbury Collection), T. and P., I, p. 89.

against enclosures, except the two passed in 1597, were repealed, but this did not stop administrative interference, which continued fairly vigorously until the Civil War and the destruction of the central machinery of the state.[1]

But the prevention of enclosure and depopulation, as Dr Tawney remarks, 'was merely one element in a general policy, by which a benevolent government . . . was to endeavour by even-handed pressure to enforce social obligations on great and small, and to prevent the public interest being sacrificed to an unconscionable appetite for private gain'.[2] The Elizabethan government followed the medieval tradition in attempting to moderate, if it could not abolish, usury,[3] and to regulate wages and prices.[4] Its concern for the continuation of the traditional economic system is seen in the way in which it dealt with the problems of poverty and unemployment. By the Statute of Apprentices it attempted to secure long engagements of service; it exerted pressure on merchants to buy, and manufacturers to produce, even when trade was bad; it took steps to relieve the distress caused by dearth, and in the series of statutes cul-

[1] See Lipson, II, p. 403 ff.

[2] *Religion and Capitalism*, p. 173.

[3] Which it stigmatized as 'sin and detestable', 'being forbidden by the Law of God', even when allowing (with a good many precautions) a maximum rate of 10 per cent.—13 Eliz. c. 8, 1571, T. and P., II, p. 162. 'But the spirit of Tudor social policy is revealed less in statutes than in the activity, half administrative, half judicial, of the Privy Council. And the impression of conservatism is heightened if one turns from legislation to administration' (Tawney, Wilson, p. 162).

[4] Notably in the wage regulations of the Statute of Apprentices (1563) and the acts and administrative ordinances that were designed to implement it. There is some doubt as to the actual carrying out of the wage regulations—certainly wages failed to rise in proportion to prices—but 'the first century of the act was the period in which it was most commonly enforced'.—Lipson, III, p. 252 ff. For examples of price regulation see Lipson, II, p. 141 (coal), and II, pp. 424-425 (bread).

minating in the Acts of 1597 and 1601 it made provision for the relief of the destitute, the employment of the able-bodied, and the punishment of the sturdy beggar.[1] The whole policy of the governments of the period aimed at stability and a controlled order. The Statute of Apprentices embodied a conception of the proper constitution of the state that remained active for the whole of the Elizabethan and early Stuart period; it was

> an attempt on a grand scale to bring every locality (with one or two important exceptions) under the operation of a single code, to regulate the relations of all classes of the working population, whether engaged in agriculture, industry or commerce, by assigning to each class its proper place in the framework of a uniform system; and finally to provide machinery for maintaining this system in equilibrium by the periodical adjustment of the conditions of employment. The idea of a national economy finds in this great piece of Elizabethan legislation its most notable expression.[2]

In the world of practice the beginnings of modern industry can be traced to the sixteenth century; in the world of ideas the change is most clearly marked in the seventeenth century. By the reign of James I the social ideas inherited from the Middle Ages were already proving incompatible with the

[1] See Lipson, III, chap. v, section iv, and chap. vi.

[2] Unwin, *Industrial Organization*, p. 139. 'But', Unwin adds, 'from another point of view the Statute of Apprentices represented a vain endeavour to give fixity and permanence to a condition of things which already, in great part, belonged to the past.'

A contemporary Memorandum (1573?) on the Statute of Apprentices affords an interesting illustration of the prevailing concern for stability. It approves that the children of artificers 'should be applied to the trades that their parents were of before them', and upholds the ideal that 'the aged should be guides unto youth and young men should work to sustain the aged who were their bringers up', all being assured of 'a certain security'. 'Running and shifting from town to town, and from country (county) to country' is classed with 'haunting of ale-houses' and 'using of unlawful games' (T. and P., I, pp. 353-363).

demands of capitalists; and theory followed practice. 'The point in which the breach between mercantilism and the medieval outlook was widest and most decisive', says Dr Heckscher, 'was certainly in the domain of the ethical.'[1] Or, as Dr Tawney more forcibly puts it, 'The creed of the commercial classes was a doctrineless individualism. By the reign of James I they had almost come to their own.'[2] But for the bulk of the population in the age of Jonson the traditional ideas were far from being meaningless, as the following chapters will help to show.

A Note on Usury

A few illustrations of the contemporary attitude towards usury, 'that controversial sin',[3] will help to show both the prevailing conservatism and the general sense of corporate responsibility discussed above.

Leaving aside certain medieval distinctions with regard to

[1] *Mercantilism*, II, p. 285. 'We may say that the mercantilists were amoral in a two-fold sense, both in their aims as also in the means for the attainment of their ends. This two-fold amorality arose from their widespread indifference towards mankind, both in its capacity as a reasoning animal, as also in its attitude towards the eternal. Hobbes' Leviathan or "Mortal God", the state, dominated the arguments of the mercantilists to such a degree that in the place of an interest in human beings came the interest in the state' (*loc. cit.*). The pre-mercantilist theories of Tudor statesmen combined a modern insistence on the strong state with an inherited concern for the individual. 'The whole tendency of mercantilism made economic policy antagonistic to the church and priesthood, and on the other hand brought these into harness against mercantilism. Petty could seldom speak of priests without adding some malicious remark. Colbert from the start was in opposition to the interests of the church' (*ibid.*, II, p. 302). This forms another obvious contrast with Tudor times.

[2] Tawney, Wilson, p. 170.

[3] The phrase is from D'Ewes' *Autobiography* (ed. Halliwell), I, p. 46. D'Ewes believed that when his father's house was burned down it was a divine punishment for having accepted interest for a loan.

rent charges, cases of *lucrum cessans, damnum emergens*, and the like, the medieval argument can be summarized:

> To take usury is contrary to Scripture; it is contrary to Aristotle; it is contrary to nature, for it is to live without labour; it is to sell time, which belongs to God, for the advantage of wicked men; it is to rob those who use the money lent, and to whom, since they make it profitable, the profits should belong; it is unjust in itself, for the benefit of the loan to the borrower cannot exceed the value of the principal sum lent him; it is in defiance of sound juristic principles, for when a loan of money is made, the property in the thing lent passes to the borrower, and why should the creditor demand payment from a man who is merely using what is now his own? [1]

During the Elizabethan and early Stuart period the old arguments were repeated almost verbatim, and the same sentiments were appealed to. The usurer was still accused of selling time, which is God's.[2] Money by itself is barren, whereas 'he puts his money to the unnatural act of generation'.[3] 'The usurer lives by the lechery of money, and is bawd to his own bags, taking a fee, that they may engender.' [4] The usurer, said another character-writer,

> must be drawn like to those pictures that have a double aspect, which if you behold one way seems to be a man, but the other way a devil. . . . To conclude, he's one that makes

---

[1] *Religion and Capitalism*, p. 43.   Cf. Ashley, I, chap. iii, section 17; II, chap. vi, sections 65-70.

[2] See, for example, John Davies of Hereford, *The Scourge of Folly* (1611), Epig. 147.

[3] Overbury, *Characters* (1614), 'A Devilish Usurer'.   'Friendship he accounts but a word without any signification; nay, he loves all the world so little, that, if it were possible, he would make himself his own executor; for certainly he is made administrator to his own good name, while he is in perfect memory, for that dies long afore him; but he is so far from being at the charge of a funeral for it, that he lets it stink above ground' (*ibid.*).

[4] Dekker, *The Seven Deadly Sins of London* (1606), *Non-Dramatic Works* (ed. Grosart), II, p. 28.

haste to be rich, and therefore cannot be innocent. Like thieves he undoes men by binding them. And lastly his estate is raised out of the ruin of whole families, which first sends him in ill getting it, and afterward his son in ill spending it, both to the devil; and there I leave them.[1]

Usury was 'the city's scourge', whose prevalence rightly called down the wrath of heaven.[2]

Malynes' *St. George for England* (1601) is completely medieval in outlook. Malynes will allow no compromise with usury; one might as well tolerate thieves and murderers as the money-lender.[3] The medieval doctrine of absolute values inspires his argument

> that money was ordained as a pledge or right betwixt man and man, and in contracts and bargaining a just measure and proportion, which measure is by them falsified: and this monster causeth them to incorporate the same, so that no man can come by it without their consent and paying for it, falsifying and altering the same.[4]

He, too, quotes Scripture, and puts forward the old argument that the usurer

> demandeth consideration for that which is none of his own,

---

[1] Wye Saltonstall, *Picturae Loquentes* (1631), the thirteenth Character. Cf. the rhyme, which survived the Restoration,

> Here lies ten i' th' hundred fast ramm'd
> 'Tis a hundred to ten but his soul is damn'd.

Quoted by William London, *A Catalogue of the most Vendible Books in England* (1657), Sig. E 3, v.

[2]   O usury,
> Thou art the city's scourge. How much have we
> Occasion to proscribe thee from our land,
> Since by thy means have we felt heaven's hand
> More heavy and revenging than before;
> Whose wrath has vials ever laid in store
> To punish impious men; it's thou (foul sin)
> Which hast hal'd down the infection we have seen
> Rage in this famous isle.

(Richard Brathwait, *A Strappado for the Devil*, 1615, p. 20.)

[3] *St. George for England*, p. 59.   [4] *Ibid.*, p. 60.

and moreover two recompenses for one entire thing: by reason whereof he bringeth forth inequality for his advantage, making men to forget that ever they lived without him, by that which they were born and bred unto.[1]

All the evils of the time are attributed to usury. 'But let this monster be destroyed, and every man will return unto his quietness, and live within his bounds and calling, using such trade as he ought to do.'[2]

Commercial opinion insisted that 'the mischief is of the excess, not otherwise. . . . It is the biting and over-sharp dealing which is disliked and nothing else',[3] and no doubt 'the practice of claiming as a right the power to receive profit from one's property, whatever form it took' was 'inevitable'.[4] But during the first part of the seventeenth century the bulk of public opinion continued to regard the taking of interest with unqualified hostility. The most numerous classes of borrowers, we have seen, were peasants, small tradesmen and needy gentlemen, who borrowed out of necessity and with no expectations of speedy or large returns.[5] Money-lending, moreover, was often only a subsidiary business, and the usurer contravened the principle of 'one man, one trade'. 'What was characteristic of Wilson's day', says Tawney, 'was less the development of banking than its informal, almost furtive character.'[6] Shopkeepers, scriveners, and goldsmiths made loans in the towns; in the woollen industry many of the small weavers were in almost perpetual debt to the more wealthy woollen factors; the peasant had frequently to borrow money from his more successful neighbour. In the circumstances that have

[1] *Ibid.*, p. 64.   [2] *Ibid.*, p. 64.
[3] Debate on the Usury Bill in the House of Commons, 1571, T. and P., II, p. 155.
[4] Robertson, *Economic Individualism*, p. 199.
[5] Tawney, Wilson, II, i, 'The Peasant and Small Master'; ii, 'The Needy Gentleman'.   [6] *Ibid.*, p. 102.

been described [1] there was plenty of opportunity for extortion, and the old moral arguments lost none of their force. It was a public duty to deliver the poor from the 'daily devouring jaws of that Monster of Crete and Bawd of Bankers',[2] since it was a principle of statecraft that 'ever a state flourisheth where wealth is more evenly spread',[3] just as it was a principle of religion that a man should not grow rich at the expense of his neighbours. The usurer offended in both these respects.

> The chief cause of poverty is usury, which doth too much enrich some few, and doth impoverish too much a great many. So that men cannot live contentedly and proportionably in their vocation, according to their profession, taking away the chiefest comfort of the poor, which is the quietness of their minds, and giving ability to the rich to do all the mischief that can be devised.[4]

This, like many of the pronouncements on the subject, was an over-simplification, but it illustrates fairly enough the principles involved in the long-continued debate on usury.

[1] See above, pp. 128-130.
[2] Milles, *The Customer's Alphabet* (1608), Sig. F 2.
[3] Bacon, *Essays*, 'Of Usury'.
[4] Malynes, *St. George for England* (1601), p. 80.

THE DRAMATISTS

CHAPTER FIVE

DRAMA AND SOCIETY

In some respects many of the plays that will be considered here form part of 'the last great literary expression of the appeal to the average conscience which had been made by an older social order'.[1] We have to see them, that is, in a context of sermons, pamphlets and satires, which, in the face of the newer economic developments, formulate and clarify those 'dimly conceived presuppositions as to social expediency'[2] inherited from the Middle Ages.

But why is it, we ask, that themes of this kind only enter into the drama in the last years of the sixteenth century, and then provide subjects of such intense interest for a period of twenty-five or thirty years? The answer has to be sought partly in the history of the drama itself, partly in the economic development of the times.

In the first place, neither drama nor poetry was made the vehicle for the keenest human interests until the last decade of the sixteenth century. The bulk of Elizabethan non-dramatic poetry has to be regarded not as the intense expression of important thoughts and feelings, but as an accomplishment. With a few exceptions Elizabethan lyric poetry, closely associated with music, was a superior pastime. As such it has its own value; but it is only with Donne—whose start is from the satire of the 'nineties—that lyric poetry becomes something which engages our more important interests. (Spenser has his own place, but *The Faerie Queene*

[1] *Religion and Capitalism*, p. 66.
[2] Tawney, *Agrarian Problem*, p. vii.

171

—despite the political allusions behind the allegory—is only remotely connected with the actual world.) So also with the drama. There had been plays whose function corresponded roughly to that of *Euphues*, some that corresponded roughly to the news ballads, others that provided the easiest forms of popular entertainment; but of the twenty or thirty 'Elizabethan' plays that we read and reread only a few fall much before the end of the century. Shakespeare's progress from *Romeo and Juliet* to *King Lear* was not *merely* a personal development.

Amongst the earlier Elizabethan dramatists the exceptional intelligence of Marlowe makes him stand out far above Lyly, Greene, Peele and the rest; but in spite of *Faustus* and *The Jew of Malta* his genius counts mainly as an influence on others. What Marlowe serves to remind us is that (to use a previous formulation [1]) the achievement of the great period of English drama was due to the bringing together and the lively interplay of many important contemporary interests. If Marlowe 'gets into blank verse the melody of Spenser',[2] the satirists and epigrammatists—Hall, Marston, Donne, Rowlands, Bastard, Guilpin—focus attention on the familiar world. The long-continued war with Spain fosters an alert political interest, whilst the growth of religious controversy reinforces the already popular demand for moral instruction. These of course are vague pointers. A full account of the strength of the late Elizabethan and Jacobean drama would embrace a study of Shakespeare's language (an examination of the way in which it draws its strength from the life of the community) on the one hand, and of the constitution and tastes of the theatre audiences and the general reading public on the other. It would, I

[1] See pp. 10-11 above.
[2] T. S. Eliot, *Elizabethan Essays*, p. 27.

think, lead us directly to the nerve centres of the social life of the time.[1]

From the first there had been patriotic plays and plays reinforcing particular social attitudes (some of them are discussed later), but—to make the point heavily—social criticism cannot be effective in a tenth-rate play like *The Troublesome Reign of King John*. It is possible to discuss the social themes of the Jacobean drama because then there were half a dozen dramatists capable of dealing in an interesting way (though not with equal success) with major issues.

There were, besides, especial reasons why the economic and social changes should be sharply focused in the public attention about the year 1600. Partly, of course, the general processes of the sixteenth century were by then sufficiently developed to be obvious to all; and they were processes, as I have tried to show, that were vastly accelerated in the last thirty or forty years of the century. More particularly, the depression which culminated in the last five years of Elizabeth's reign made economic problems unavoidably obtrusive, 'placing in relief the individual struggle to retain some control over one's worldly condition'.[2] From the petition against monopolies in 1597 until the Statute of Monopolies in 1624 Parliament was preoccupied with specific economic issues to an extent which—perhaps excepting the period of the enclosure controversy under Henry VIII—it had never been before. The interests represented by most of the dramatists were not the same as those represented by most members of the House of Commons: the latter tended more and more to express the new commercial opinion, whilst the enlightened conservatism of the better

---

[1] See Appendix A, 'Elizabethan Prose'. I may refer, too, to my 'Education and the Drama in the Age of Shakespeare', *The Criterion*, July 1932.

[2] Robertson, *Aspects of the Rise of Economic Individualism*, p. 184.

playwrights drew upon traditional opinions and attitudes that were more potent in the Privy Council than in Parliament. But the point is that the depression created, or brought to a head, economic grievances, and the financial necessities of the Crown made those grievances vocal. Nor did the ending of the depression solve the deeper problems of general welfare. The reign of James I included the Midland riots of 1607 and the disorganization of the staple woollen industry in 1616, and ended in another major depression; whilst the continued abuses of the patent system were of a kind that touched the interests of every level of the population. The history of the time contains sufficient reasons for the part played by social themes in a drama that was alive to contemporary issues.

And economic problems were accentuated by the glaring contrast between the fortunes that were amassed in, say, the East India trade (in the middle years of the reign the minimum return on a single voyage, we remember, was 121 per cent.) or that could be snapped up by a fortunate projector, on the one hand, and the destitution and economic uncertainty of many thousands, on the other.[1] The gulf between wealth and poverty had been clearly enough marked in all previous periods, but the Middle Ages had known

---

[1] 'Side by side with the industrial distress and decay of trade and monetary scarcity . . . it must be admitted that considerable prosperity existed also. Large fortunes were amassed by many of the London merchants, especially by those engaged in the East India trade. Such undertakings, by private enterprise, as the construction of the New River by Hugh Myddleton, to supply London with water; the foundation of the Charter House School by Sutton, etc., give evidence of wealth and prosperity. Moreover the same is witnessed in the rapid growth of London, which took place at this time . . .' (Durham, *The Relations of the Crown to Trade under James I, Transactions of the Royal Historical Society*, N.S. XIII, p. 246). It is the 'side by side' that is important. In Jacobean London the East End and the West End were not so far apart as they are to-day.

nothing comparable to the opportunities for luxurious display provided by the opening up of a world trade. And the men who secured the lion's share of commercial and industrial profits (profits resulting from the same general process that created the rootless poverty of the lowest classes of Jacobean London) were men who stood outside the current traditions. Hence, in part, the attacks on the new men and the questioning of the whole order which they represented.

Gifford claimed that the Jacobean dramatic poets were 'the most clear-sighted politicians of those troublous times',[1] and if this book establishes anything it should be that the reactions of a genuine poet to his environment form a criticism of society at least as important as the keenest analysis in purely economic terms; that the intelligence and perception that help to make great poetry do not function in a special 'poetic' sphere, but are immediately relevant to all questions of 'the good life'. Which is not to say that Gifford's phrase can be accepted uncritically.

I shall try to explain the nature of that 'criticism of society'. Obviously it does not consist in analysis at the level of economics. From the fifteenth century onwards, says Lipson, 'the conflict of capital and labour was fought out over three main grievances—low wages, payment in kind, and unemployment'.[2] None of these three main grievances has any prominence in the drama of Jonson and his contemporaries. All of them attack usurers, but they show no interest in the place of credit transactions in a capitalist economy; they attack monopolists and patentees, but, as one would expect, they show no signs of recognizing the element of monopoly in the older organizations, or of appreciating the attempts to regulate trade and industry by means of patents.

[1] Ben Jonson, *Works* (ed. Gifford and Cunningham), V, p. 11.
[2] Lipson, III, p. 249.

There were of course good reasons why the only economic 'diagnosis' that we find on the Jacobean stage should take the form of satire on particular individuals or classes of individuals; it was not merely that the outwitting of the usurer on the stage had a sure popular appeal. A character in one of Dos Passos's novels remarks: 'Don't blame people for things; it's the system'. This could not have been said in the reign of James I. The capitalist 'system' was taking shape, and 'impersonal' causes were already responsible for a good deal; but the individuals who were helping to form that system were, I think, more prominent, more obviously capable of exerting economic pressure, than their successors in the nineteenth century, who could claim, with at least a show of reason, that they were obeying the 'laws' of supply and demand and so on. Therefore attacks on the new order took the form of attacks on individuals (I am not referring merely to recognizable caricature); the diagnosis was moral rather than economic. Or, to put it another way, the dramatic treatment of economic problems showed them as moral and individual problems—which in the last analysis they are.

So far I have spoken of the dramatists' 'concern with social and economic themes', of 'social criticism', and of 'attacks on individuals or classes of individuals'. All of these phrases could be illustrated, but none of them explains the fundamental importance of, say, *Volpone*, or *The City Madam*, for an understanding of the possibilities of living, then and at all times. What it comes to is this. 'Facts about' a period give us only a vague general impression of its life. The ideas current in that period *point to* the qualities that were considered valuable, but they do no more than that. But each of the greater plays of this period exhibits certain valuable qualities of human experience *in the con-*

crete; and the finer the play *as poetry*, as literature, the more completely, the more precisely, is the stuff and substance of a particular experience evoked.

Now the possibilities of living at any moment are not merely an individual matter; they depend on physical circumstances and (what is less of a commonplace) on current habits of thought and feeling, on all that is implied by 'tradition'—or the lack of it. The poet who is able to draw on a living tradition embodies it in a particular, comprehensible form; and for us to grasp that form is to work our way into those extra-personal conditions which combined with the writer's genius to make his work.

The claim that I am making is that the essential life of a period is best understood through its literature; not because of what that literature describes, but because of what it embodies. If this is so the whole of Elizabethan and Jacobean literature should be considered in a study of this kind. Actually plays with a more or less overt social reference have been selected in order to make the investigation manageable. I have tried to present a certain class of facts about the Jacobean environment, and to sketch the main ideas that were current in the social tradition. Now I wish to examine a selection of plays that embody an attitude towards those facts and to the human qualities that produced them, and to show how, in a few great plays, 'that living body of assumptions as to the right conduct of human affairs' [1] helped to nourish qualities that we can admire.

In spite of the imposed limitations the approach is mainly the literary-critical one, for the reasons that I have given. It is easy to collect and classify references to usurers, patentees, the newly rich, and so on. But for an investigation of this kind we need more delicate tools, and a method of approach that keeps constantly before us the question of relevance.

[1] Tawney, *Agrarian Problem*, p. 347.

177

If Ben Jonson appears to have a disproportionate amount of space, it is because he seems to me so immeasurably superior to all his contemporaries—with the one obvious exception—and because his greatness as a poet makes clear the value of the popular tradition which is only dimly apprehended in the work of the lesser men such as Dekker and Heywood.

CHAPTER SIX

TRADITION AND BEN JONSON

I hate traditions;
I do not trust them. (*Ananias*)

RECENT revivals of *Volpone* and *The Alchemist* occasioned
some surprise—surprise that they were such good 'theatre'.
The general impression seems to have been that in these
plays Jonson had, somehow, triumphed over his 'weight of
classical learning', had in fact forgotten it, and had provided
some very good fun instead of his usual pedantries. It may
not be quite fair to the dramatic critics to suggest that their
delight at being entertained instead of bored showed how
little Jonson is read, but certainly the reception given to
those plays implied a still widespread misconception both of
Jonson's intrinsic merits and of the extent and kind of his
indebtedness to the Classics.

Ben Jonson is a very great poet—more finely endowed, I
think, than any who succeeded him in the seventeenth century—and he read deliberately and widely. It was to be
expected, therefore, that the effects of his reading would be in
some manner present in his verse. Dryden said of him that
he was a learned plagiary of all the ancients: 'you track him
everywhere in their snow'. But this, the common view,
violently distorts the sense in which Jonson is 'traditional';
it not only makes him appear to owe to the Greek and Latin
writers a mere accumulation of thoughts and phrases, it
completely hides the native springs of his vitality. The aim
of this chapter is to correct the perspective, to show that

179

Jonson's art is intimately related to the popular tradition of individual and social morality.

A study such as this lies largely outside the field of strict literary criticism; but without a background of criticism to refer to it is impossible to say anything at all, and I propose to begin (without more apology for the indirect approach) by selecting one play and merely trying to explain why I find it admirable.

Sejanus is chosen not only because it is commonly under-rated, but because it is the first play in which Jonson finds his proper scope: the early 'Humour 'plays were mere experiments. Although here the typically Jonsonian method is deployed with less subtlety and richness than in, say, *Volpone*, the parallels between this 'tragedy' and the later 'comedies' are obvious and important.

The stuff of the play is the lust of political power and the pettiness that so often accompanies political greatness. The world with which we are presented is completely evil. Tiberius and Sejanus are equal in cruelty and cunning; Macro, the agent of Sejanus' overthrow, is, like others besides the principals, explicitly 'Machiavellian'; the satellites and senators are servile and inconstant; the mob tears the body of the fallen favourite,

> And not a beast of all the herd demands
> What was his crime, or who were his accusers.[1]

The 'good' characters are choric and denunciatory merely, representing no positive values. How carefully anything that might bring into play sympathetic feelings is excluded is seen in the treatment of Agrippina; the meeting of her adherents, for example, is described (II, ii) in terms that reduce it to a gathering of fractious gossips. And this exclusion

[1] V, x (III, 147) (the references in brackets are to the volume and page of the Gifford-Cunningham edition of Jonson's *Works*, 1875).

operates in the smallest details—in Tiberius' remark about
dedicating

> A pair of temples, one to Jupiter
> At Capua; th'other at Nola to Augustus,[1]

or in Sejanus' contempt for 'all the throng that fill th'
Olympian hall'.[2]

But in drama substance and criticism of that substance
are inseparable, and the world of *Sejanus* exists only in the
light of a particular vision. The most obvious device for
determining the angle of presentation is found in the vein of
farce that runs throughout: there is a violent juxtaposition
of contrasts. After the heroics of Sejanus' 'love-making'
Livia turns to her physician:

> How do I look to-day?
> *Eudemus.* Excellent clear, believe it. This same fucus
> Was well laid on.
> *Livia.* Methinks 'tis here not white.
> *Eudemus.* Lend me your scarlet lady. 'Tis the sun
> Hath giv'n some little taint unto the ceruse. . . .
> *(Paints her cheek.)*[3]

Here, and in the other scenes of stylized farce (for instance,
V, iii, or V, vii, where the secret is passed round) there are
obvious theatrical possibilities. Perhaps the most effective
scene would be the last, where the senators first cluster
round Sejanus—indicating by their verbal *feu de joie* the
kind of stylization demanded—then edge away as the drift of
Tiberius' riddling letter becomes clear, leaving only Haterius,
kept 'most miserably constant' by his gout. But the whole
of the last act, with its controlled confusion leading swiftly
to an exciting climax, would act well; and for more subtle
dramatic play we can turn to the scene (III, ii) where Tiberius
and Sejanus manœuvre against each other under cover of

---

[1] III, iii (III, 86).   [2] V, i (III, 113).   [3] II, i (III, 41).

friendship; the variations gain from the surface rigidity of the characters.

The essential Jonsonian mode, however, is determined by something more fundamental than the separable elements of farce: it is determined by the verse—a dramatic medium in which exaggeration is controlled by a pervasively implicit sardonic mood. The exuberance of 'Swell, swell, my joys . . .' (V, i) is followed by

> . . . 'Tis air I tread;
> And at each step I feel my advanced head
> Knock out a star in heaven.

It is 'knock out'—the slight twist given to 'sublimi feriam sidera vertice'—that finally determines our attitude. But a longer quotation is in place here. In Act II, scene ii, Sejanus addresses Drusus in soliloquy:

> Thy follies now shall taste what kind of man
> They have provoked, and this thy father's house
> Crack in the flame of my incensed rage,
> Whose fury shall admit no shame or mean.—
> Adultery! it is the lightest ill
> I will commit. A race of wicked acts
> Shall flow out of my anger, and o'erspread
> The world's wide face, which no posterity
> Shall e'er approve, nor yet keep silent: things
> That for their cunning, close, and cruel mark,
> Thy father would wish his: and shall, perhaps,
> Carry the empty name, but we the prize.
> On then, my soul, and start not in thy course;
> Though heaven drop sulphur, and hell belch out fire,
> Laugh at the idle terrors: tell proud Jove,
> Between his power and thine there is no odds:
> 'Twas only fear first in the world made gods.

In the sentiments, and in the vigorous development of a single dominant impulse, there is an obvious resemblance to *Tamburlaine*. But the attitude of sophisticated detachment

182

towards the words, present in those words, suggests what Jonson had learnt from *The Jew of Malta* (a relationship first stated in *The Sacred Wood*): with that play in mind we are not likely to accept Coleridge's verdict of 'absurd rant and ventriloquism'—or not as he intended it.   It is equally obvious that the speech is not by Marlowe, that in its combination of weight and vigour it looks forward to the finer poetry of *Volpone* and *The Alchemist*.

The means by which Jonson achieves that combination are here immediately apparent.   The alliteration not only adds to the general critical-exaggerative effect, it secures the maximum of direct attention for each word:

> Sleep,
> Voluptuous Caesar, and security
> Seize on thy stupid powers.

More generally, we may say that whereas the auditory qualities of Shakespeare's verse arouse a vibrating responsiveness, help to create a fluid medium in which there is the subtlest interplay, the corresponding qualities in Jonson cause the words to separate rather than to coalesce. ('Separate', of course, is only a way of laying the stress.)   Everything is said deliberately—though there is no monotony in the varying rhythm—and, following Jonson's own precepts for 'a strict and succinct style',[1] with the greatest economy. The economy of course is not Shakespeare's.   There are no overlaying meanings or shifts of construction; the words gain their effect by their solidity, weight and unambiguous directness of expression.   How poetically effective that weighted style can be is demonstrated again and again in the present play.

> There be two,
> Know more than honest counsels; whose close breasts,

[1] *Discoveries*, cxxix.

Were they ripp'd up to light, it would be found
A poor and idle sin, to which their trunks
Had not been made fit organs.   These can lie,
Flatter, and swear, forswear, deprave, inform,
Smile, and betray; make guilty men; then beg
The forfeit lives, to get their livings; cut
Men's throats with whisperings. . . .[1]

Jonson's metaphors and similes tend to fall into one of three classes.   Many, perhaps the majority, are straight-forwardly descriptive.   ('Metaphors far-fet,' he said, 'hinder to be understood.')

The way to put
A prince in blood, is to present the shapes
Of dangers greater than they are, like late
Or early shadows.

Did those fond words
Fly swifter from thy lips, than this my brain,
This sparkling forge, created me an armour
T'encounter chance and thee?[2]

A second class is formed by those metaphors that, like the 'race of wicked acts . . .' in Sejanus' soliloquy, heighten the effect of caricature.   But Jonson's most striking figures are magnificently derogatory.

Gods! how the sponges open and take in,
And shut again! look, look! is not he blest
That gets a seat in eye-reach of him? more
That comes in ear, or tongue-reach?   O but most
Can claw his subtile elbow, or with a buz
Fly-blow his ears?

[1] I, i (III, 14).
[2] This second image is bright and clear, but its surface quality is emphasized if we put beside it the line from *Henry V*,
    In the quick forge and working-house of thought,
where the rhythm, the double meaning of 'quick' and the fused impression of swift movement and ordered labour evoke a far more complex activity of the mind.

184

Jonson's triumph, we have been told, is a triumph of consistency, and the habit of mind behind this last quotation provides the dominant tone of the play. I have already commented on the exclusion of irrelevant moods and associations, and there only remains to notice the characteristic linking together of words that usually invite sympathy or admiration with those demanding an exactly contrary response.

> Like, as both
> *Their bulks and souls* were bound on Fortune's wheel. . . .

> He . . . gives Caesar leave
> To hide his *ulcerous and anointed* face. . . .[1]

One does not need to look up the various suggestions of weight and clumsiness under 'cob' in the Oxford Dictionary to feel the effect of 'a cob-swan, or a high mounting bull' in the most famous speech from *Catiline*.

It should be plain by now that the appreciation of Jonson starts from the appreciation of his verse: it could start from nothing else; but it does not seem to be realized how clogging are the discussions of 'humours' which, in histories of English literature, fill up the pages on Jonson. His plays have the tightness and coherence of a firmly realized purpose, active in every detail, and a commentary on Jonson's technical achievements—the weight and vigour of his verse, the intensive scrutiny that it invites—is only one way of indicating his essential qualities.

Sejanus, like the other greater plays, is the product of a unique vision; but in stressing the uniqueness one has to avoid any suggestion of the idiosyncratic. It is not merely

---

[1] That the corresponding phrase in Tacitus is 'Facies ulcerosa ac plerumque medicaminibus interstincta', is, I think, irrelevant.

that the matter on which the poet works is provided by the
passions, lusts and impulses of the actual world, the firmly
defined individual spirit which moulds that matter springs
from a rich traditional wisdom; it relies, that is to say, on
something outside itself, and presupposes an active relationship with a particular audience.

The point can be made by examining a passage that is
commonly recognized as 'great poetry'.

> See, behold,
> What thou art queen of; not in expectation,
> As I feed others: but possess'd and crown'd.
> See, here, a rope of pearl: and each more orient
> Than that the brave Ægyptian queen caroused:
> Dissolve and drink them. See, a carbuncle,
> May put out both the eyes of our St. Mark;
> A diamond, would have bought Lollia Paulina,
> When she came in like star-light, hid with jewels,
> That were the spoils of provinces; take these,
> And wear, and lose them: yet remains an ear-ring
> To purchase them again, and this whole state.
> A gem but worth a private patrimony,
> Is nothing: we will each such at a meal.
> The heads of parrots, tongues of nightingales,
> The brains of peacocks, and of estriches,
> Shall be our food: and, could we get the phœnix,
> Though nature lost her kind, she were our dish.[1]

Mr Palmer, supporting a general thesis that Jonson 'wrote
for a generation which had still an unbounded confidence in
the senses and faculties of man. England had not yet
accepted the great negation . . .', remarks: 'In the figure
of Volpone Jonson presents the splendours of his theme.
Was ever woman so magnificently wooed as the wife of
Corvino?'[2] This is to miss the point completely. The
poetic force of Volpone's wooing has two sources. There

[1] *Volpone*, III, vi (III, 249).   [2] *Ben Jonson*, pp. x and 175.

is indeed an exuberant description of luxury—'Temptations are heaped upon temptations with a rapidity which almost outstrips the imagination'—and the excited movement seems to invite acceptance. But at the same time, without cancelling out the exuberance, the luxury is 'placed'. We have only to compare passages (from the early Keats, for example) in which the imagined gratification of sight, taste and touch is intended as an indulgence merely, to see how this placing is achieved. It is not merely that the lines quoted have a context of other swelling speeches (compare *Sejanus*), so that by the time we reach them the mode is established, the exaggeration, which reaches a climax at 'phœnix', is itself sufficient to suggest some qualification of Mr Palmer's 'splendours'. The verse demands the usual scrupulous inspection of each word—we are not allowed to lapse into an impression of generalized magnificence—and the splendours, in 'caroused', 'spoils of provinces', 'private patrimony', are presented clearly enough as waste. 'Though nature lost her kind', at least, implies a moral judgement; and the references to Lollia Paulina and Heliogabalus (Gifford quotes 'Comedit linguas pavonum et lusciniarum'), which would not be unfamiliar to an Elizabethan audience, are significant.

The manner of presentation (relying on a response which later criticism shows is neither obvious nor easy) suggests that the double aspect of the thing presented corresponds to a double attitude in the audience: a naïve delight in splendour is present *at the same time as* a clear-sighted recognition of its insignificance judged by fundamental human, or divine, standards. The strength of this attitude is realized if we compare it with a puritanic disapproval of 'the world' on the one hand, or a sensuous abandonment on the other. It is the possession of this attitude that makes Jonson 'classical', not his Greek and Latin erudition. His classicism is an equanimity and assurance that springs — 'here at home'[1] — from the strength of a native tradition.

For Jonson's knowledge, and use, of the native literary tradition there is, I believe, evidence of the usually accepted kind. One could consider his references (explicit and otherwise) to earlier poets and prose-writers from Chaucer onwards; his avowed interest in the *Vetus Comoedia*;[2] the obvious 'morality' influence in such plays as *The Devil is an Ass* and *The Magnetic Lady*;[3] the popular source of the jog-trot rhythms used for Nano, Androgyno and the Vice, Iniquity. But when we are dealing with a living tradition such terms are hopelessly inadequate, and exploration can be more profitably directed, in the manner suggested by the analysis above, towards Jonson's handling of his main themes, lust and the desire for wealth and their accompanying vanities.

In *The Devil is an Ass* the satire is more than usually direct. But the play provides more than a succession of satiric comments on the first period of intensive capitalistic activity in England; it formulates an attitude towards acquisition. The word 'formulates' is used advisedly. The outlook is a particular one, is Jonson's own; but it is clear that the satire presupposes certain general attitudes in the audience, and that it builds on something that was already

[1]   And make my strengths, such as they are,
         Here in my bosom, and at home.
                            (*A Farewell to the World*)
[2] English, not Roman. See *Conversations*, 16.
[3] An influence that was active in other playwrights. It is some time since Sir Arthur Quiller-Couch suggested that Henry IV was Shakespeare's rehandling of a morality play ('Contentio inter Virtutem et Vitium de Anima Principis'). The subject generally is of more than academic interest; those who are interested can consider such different plays as *Troilus and Cressida* (Pandarus is demonstrably 'the Pander'), *Old Fortunatus*, *Michaelmas Term* or any of Middleton's comedies.

there. Fitzdottrel, immersed in his schemes for making money, believes that he has surprised his wife making love with Wittipol, and (II, iii) reproaches her:

> O bird,
> Could you do this? 'gainst me! and at this time now!
> When I was so employ'd, wholly for you,
> Drown'd in my care (more than the land, I swear,
> I have hope to win) to make you peerless, studying
> For footmen for you, fine-pace huishers, pages,
> To serve you on the knee. . . .
> You've almost turn'd my good affection to you;
> Sour'd my sweet thoughts, all my pure purposes. . . .

Fitzdottrel is an ass and it is quite unnecessary to say that there is not a hint of pathos, though it is easy to imagine the temptations of a nineteenth-century novelist in such a scene. (Compare the exaggerated significance that is given to Mrs Dombey's jewels—'She flung it down and trod upon the glittering heap', etc.) The point is that Jonson evidently relies upon his audience immediately despising those 'pure purposes'; what these are—the way in which the money acquired would be employed—is magnificently brought out in the Tailbush-Eitherside scene (IV, i: 'See how the world its veterans rewards . . .'). It is, of course, the tone and manner of presentation that is commented on here.   As one learns to expect, that tone is consistent throughout and one has to be alive to its implications even in the smallest particulars. The 'Spanish lady' is

> such a mistress of behaviour,
> She knows from the duke's daughter to the doxy,
> What is their due just, and no more.

Here the scornful alliteration acts as a leveller (we have seen something similar in *Sejanus*): Jonson, that is, takes his stand on a scheme that shows duke's daughter and doxy in proper perspective.   It was not merely that Jonson as an

189

individual 'never esteemed of a man for the name of a Lord'; [1] his values were a part of the national life. We have only to turn up Bunyan's account of By-End's ancestry and connexions: 'My wife . . . came of a very honourable family, and is arrived to such a pitch of breeding, that she knows how to carry it to all, even to prince and peasant'. The tone and method are identical. [2]

In *The Devil is an Ass*, in *Volpone* and *The Alchemist* Jonson is drawing on the anti-acquisitive tradition inherited from the Middle Ages. But this account is too narrow; the tradition included more than a mere distrust of, or hostility towards, riches. Understanding is, perhaps, best reached by studying (with Volpone in mind) the speeches of Sir Epicure Mammon. Each of them, it seems to me, implicitly refers to a traditional conception of 'the Mean'. Mammon, wooing Doll, describes their teeming pleasures:

> and with these
> Delicate meats set our selves high for pleasure,
> And take us down again, and then renew
> Our youth and strength with drinking the elixir,
> And so enjoy a perpetuity
> Of life and lust! And thou shalt have thy wardrobe
> Richer than nature's, still to change thy self,
> And vary oftener, for thy pride, than she. [3]

The reference to 'nature', which give the proper angle on 'a perpetuity of life and lust', is important. The accepted

---

[1] *Conversations*, 14. I know that Jonson was capable of writing fulsome dedications: but before we make much of that charge we need to enquire, in each instance, the grounds of his praises. Many of the Elizabethan aristocracy had a decent sense of responsibility, literary and other.

[2] Dr G. R. Owst's *Literature and Pulpit in Medieval England* (pp. 97-109) gives an admirable account of the long popular and religious tradition behind Bunyan, reinforcing the conclusions that one would draw from reading *The Pilgrim's Progress* itself.

[3] *The Alchemist*, IV, i (IV, 120).

standard is 'natural', and although exact definition would
not be easy we may notice the part played by that standard
throughout Jonson's work. An instance from *Volpone*
has been quoted. Mammon's folly is that he expects
Subtle to

> teach dull nature
> What her own forces are.[1]

Similarly in the masque, *Mercury Vindicated*, the alchemists
'pretend . . . to commit miracles in art and treason against
nature . . . a matter of immortality is nothing'; they 'profess
to outwork the sun in virtue, and contend to the great act of
generation, nay almost creation'.[2]   The obviously expected
response is similar to that given to the description of Mammon's jewels whose light shall 'strike out the stars'.   Who
wants to strike out the stars, anyway?

The Staple of News, that odd combination of morality
play and topical revue, is generally spoken of as a 'dotage';
but, apart from the admirably comic Staple scenes, it contains passages of unusual power, and all of these, we notice,
are informed by the same attitude.   In a speech of Pennyboy Senior's the anti-acquisitive theme (the play is mainly
directed against the abuse of 'the Venus of our time and
state, Pecunia') is explicitly related to the conception of a
natural mean:

> Who can endure to see
> The fury of men's gullets, and their groins?
> . . . What need hath nature
> Of silver dishes, or gold chamber-pots?
> Of perfumed napkins, or a numerous family
> To see her eat? poor, and wise, she requires
> Meat only; hunger is not ambitious:
> Say, that you were the emperor of pleasures,
> The great dictator of fashions, for all Europe,
> And had the pomp of all the courts, and kingdoms,

[1] *Ibid.* (IV, 116).   [2] (VII, 236-238).

191

Laid forth unto the shew, to make yourself
Gazed and admired at; you must go to bed,
And take your natural rest: then all this vanisheth.
Your bravery was but shown; 'twas not possest:
While it did boast itself, it was then perishing.[1]

We have seen something of the background that all these passages imply. That a sense of the mean, an acceptance of natural limitations, was a part of the inheritance of Jonson and his contemporaries, can be demonstrated from medieval and sixteenth-century sermons and the writings of moralists. But it was not something imposed from above; it sprang from the wisdom of the common people, and it was only indirectly that it found its way into writing.[2] The anti-acquisitive attitude had been more explicitly formulated. It was not only a part of the life of the small local communities of the Middle Ages, it was the basis of the Canon Law on such subjects as usury. And although the age of Jonson was also the age of Sir Giles Mompesson and Sir Arthur Ingram it was still, we remember, a commonplace, accepted by the worldly Bacon, that 'The ways to enrich are many, and most of them foul'.[3]

In a well-known passage in *Discoveries* Jonson speaks of following the ancients 'as guides, not commanders': 'For to all the observations of the ancients, we have our own

---

[1] *The Staple of News*, III, ii (V, 244).

[2] An essay by John Speirs on 'The Scottish Ballads' (*Scrutiny*, June 1935) is relevant here. There it is remarked, for example, that in the Ballads, 'The images of finery . . . possess a symbolical value as profound as in Bunyan (". . . he that is clad in Silk and Velvet"). That finery is associated with folly, pride and death. It is Vanity.'— The relation between popular thought and medieval sermon literature is brought out by Dr Owst.

[3] *Essays*, 'Of Riches'. See Chapter IV, above.

experience; which, if we will use, and apply, we have better means to pronounce'.[1] That this was not a mere assertion of independence (or a mere translation—see M. Castelain's learned edition) is shown by every page on which he seems to draw most directly on the classics. Wherever the editors suggest parallels with Horace or Catullus, Tacitus or Suetonius, the re-creation is as complete as in—to take a modern instance —Mr Pound's *Propertius*, so complete as to make the hunt for 'sources' irrelevant. When Fitzdottrel is gloating over the prospect of obtaining an estate on which his descendants shall keep his name alive, Meercraft, characteristically speaking 'out of character', reminds him of the revolution of the times:

Fitzdottrel.　　　　　　'Tis true.
　　DROWN'D LANDS will live in drown'd land.
Meercraft.　　　　　　Yes, when you
Have no foot left; as that must be, sir, one day.
And though it tarry in your heirs some forty,
Fifty descents, the longer liver at last, yet,
Must thrust them out on't, if no quirk in law
Or odd vice of their own not do it first.
We see those changes daily: the fair lands
That were the client's, are the lawyer's now;
And those rich manors there of goodman Taylor's,
Had once more wood upon them, than the yard
By which they were measured out for the last purchase.
Nature hath these vicissitudes. She makes
No man a state of perpetuity, sir.[2]

Here is the passage in Horace (*Satires*, II, 2) that the speech 'derives' from:

nam propriae telluris erum natura neque illum
nec me nec quemquam statuit: nos expulit ille,

---

[1] *Discoveries*, xxi, *Non nimium credendum antiquitati.*
[2] *The Devil is an Ass*, II, i (V, 58).

illum aut nequities aut vafri inscitia iuris,
postremo expellet certe vivacior heres.

Even in the lines that come nearest to translation there is a
complete transmutation of idiom: 'nequities' has become
'some odd vice', and 'ignorance of the subtle law', the sardonically familiar 'quirk in law'. But as Horace is left
behind the presence of everyday life is felt even more immediately, in 'daily', 'those rich manors there' and 'goodman Taylor's', followed as these are by a kind of country wit
about the yardstick. The strength of the passage—it is
representative—lies in the interested but critical inspection
of a familiar world.

In pointing to the idiom we are of course noticing very
much more than 'local colour'; we are noticing ways of
thought and perception. Jonson's idiom—his vocabulary,
turns of phrase and general linguistic habits—might form a
study in itself. It was Coleridge who spoke of 'his sterling
English diction' [1]—which seems a sufficient rejoinder to the
description, 'ponderous Latinism', applied by a recent
anthologist of the seventeenth century. It is easy, as Gifford
pointed out, to exaggerate the extent of Jonson's latinized
formations when we forget the similar experimenting of his
contemporaries. (And it was not Jonson who tried to in-
troduce 'lubrical', 'magnificate', 'ventosity' and the rest.)
But whereas these have had too much attention, a more
striking characteristic had had none. Important as Jonson
was as a formative influence on the Augustan age, his
English is not 'polite'; it is, very largely, the popular English
of an agricultural country. It is not merely a matter of
vocabulary—'ging' (gang), 'threaves', 'ding it open': one
could go on collecting—his inventive habits are of a kind
that can still be paralleled in country life. There is the

[1] *Lectures on Shakespeare* (Bohn edition), p. 397.

delighted recognition of those elements of caricature that man or nature supplies ready made: 'It is now such a time . . . that every man stands under the eaves of his own hat, and sings what pleases him'.[1] There are those derisive compounds: 'Honest, plain, livery-three-pound-thrum'. There is a predilection for alliterative jingles:

> You shall be soaked, and stroked, and tubb'd and rubb'd,
> And scrubb'd, and fubb'd, dear don.

And if this kind of clowning is thought unworthy of serious criticism we can point to the easy alliterative run of 'the tip, top, and tuft of all our family', or half the speeches quoted from *Sejanus*. But even the pleasantries reveal a natural bent, and the boisterous coining of nicknames—'His great Verdugoship'—was more than a rustic habit; 'old Smug of Lemnos', 'Bombast of Hohenhein' (Vulcan and Paracelsus) indicate an attitude, similar to Nashe's,[2] of familiar disrespect towards text-book worthies. And the amazing fertility that reveals itself now in a popular fluency

> —our Doll, our castle, our cinque port,
> Our Dover pier—

now in Volpone's mountebank oration, now in Mammon's description of luxury, is an index of a native vigour that we recognize as 'typically Elizabethan'. The more we study Jonson in minute detail the more clearly he appears both intensely individual and—the paradox is justifiable—at one with his contemporaries.

The speech last quoted from *The Devil is an Ass* has a further significance; it represents an outlook that is present

[1] *Pleasure Reconciled to Virtue* (VII, 300).

[2] 'The gods and goddesses all on a row, bread and crow, from Ops to Pomona, the first applewife, were so dumpt with this miserable wrack . . .' (*Nashe's Lenten Stuff*).

even in such pure entertainment as *The Silent Woman* (See
Truewit on Time in I, i), and that combines easily with
hilarious comedy, as in Volpone's ludicrously inadequate
modesty:

> *Mosca.* That, and thousands more,
> I hope to see you lord of.
> *Volpone.* Thanks, kind Mosca.
> *Mosca.* And that, when I am lost in blended dust,
> And hundred such as I am in succession—
> *Volpone.* Nay, that were too much, Mosca.[1]

Meercraft's speech, that is, forms part of the permanent
sombre background of which we are made aware in all of
Jonson's comedies.   But the insistence on mortality has the
very opposite effect of the introduction of a death's head at a
feast; it is not for the sake of a gratuitous thrill.

> Nature hath these vicissitudes.   She makes
> No man a state of perpetuity, sir.

It is the tone—the quiet recognition of the inevitable—that
is important; and the clearly apprehended sense of muta-
bility heightens, rather than detracts from, the prevailing
zest.

It is here, I think, that a genuine 'classical influence', or at
least the influence of Horace, can be traced.

> iam Cytherea choros ducit Venus imminente luna,
>   iunctaeque Nymphis Gratiae decentes
> alterno terram quatiunt pede . . .

> pallida Mors aequo pulsat pede pauperum tabernas
>   regumque turris.[2]

The potency of the evocation of the nymphs' flying feet is
not lessened because they are also the feet of Time.   But
even here it is plain that the Jonsonian attitude is not
acquired but inherited.   There is no need to stress the

---

[1] *Volpone*, I, i (III, 178).   [2] *Odes*, I, iv.

medieval and sixteenth-century insistence on wormy circumstance [1] (a good deal of it was pathological), but we need
to keep in mind the way in which, in the popular literature of
those periods, death and life are vividly juxtaposed.

And the ability to see life under two opposed aspects
simultaneously was part of the natural equipment of the
poets of the seventeenth century before the Restoration. It
is expressed in Marvell, in the recognition of conflicting
claims in the *Horatian Ode*, in the concluding lines of the
Coy Mistress:

> And tear our pleasures with rough strife
> Through the Iron gates of Life.

The aspects of experience represented by 'the Iron gates'
would hardly be present in a nineteenth-century 'love poem',
or, if present, would have a totally different intention and
effect. It was in connexion with Marvell, we remember,
that Mr Eliot defined Wit: 'It involves a recognition, implicit in the expression of every experience, of other kinds of
experience which are possible'.[2] Jonson had not a meta-
physic wit and he was not Donne, but it is a similar recognition, implicit or explicit, of the whole range of human life,
that explains his tough equilibrium.

How little a mere classicizing can produce that equilibrium
a final comparison may show. When Jonson's verse seems
to catch an Horatian inflexion it is not because he has
assumed it:

> dum loquimur, fugerit invida
> aetas[3]

becomes, quite naturally,

> think,
> All beauty doth not last until the autumn:
> You grow old while I tell you this.[4]

---

[1] See Appendix B, pp. 319 ff., below.   [2] *Selected Essays*, p. 289.
[3] *Odes*, I, xi.   [4] *The Devil is an Ass*, I, iii (V, 31).

On the other hand there is Landor:

> occidit et Pelopis genitor, conviva deorum,
> Tithonusque remotus in auras. . . .
>
> . . . sed omnis una manet nox
> et calcanda semel via leti.[1]

Laodameia died; Helen died; Leda, the beloved of Jupiter went before. . . . There is no name, with whatever emphasis of passionate love repeated, of which the echo is not faint at last.[2]

In this affected mimicry the Horatian tone ('durum: sed levius fit patientia'), all, in fact, that gives value to the recognition of a common night, has completely evaporated, and we are left with as orotund a piece of self-indulgence as ever found its way into anthologies. Jonson's tone is that of a man who has seen many civilizations, and is at home in one.

I have tried to show that, in Jonson's audience, we may postulate a lively sense of human limitations. When Mammon declared of the elixir that, taken by an old man, it will

> Restore his years, renew him, like an eagle,
> To the fifth age; make him get sons and daughters,
> Young giants; as our philosophers have done,
> The ancient patriarchs, afore the flood,
> But taking, once a week, on a knife's point,
> The quantity of a grain of mustard of it,

they had a right to laugh as our modern seekers after youth have not.[3] But it was not a sense that incapacitated from

[1] Horace, *Odes*, I, xxviii.
[2] *Imaginary Conversations*, 'Aesop and Rhodope'.
[3] *The Alchemist*, II, i (IV, 46). Gifford quotes Hurd (IV, 180): 'The pursuit so strongly exposed in this play is forgotten, and therefore its humour must appear exaggerated'. It would have pleased Gifford to refute Hurd by quoting from our newspapers and upper-class periodicals, with their appeals to 'Banish middle age', etc.

living in the present. One does not need to search for illustration of Jonson's lively interest in every aspect of his environment. Meercraft's speech comes from a play which, as we shall see, forms the most striking indictment of the newer forms of economic parasitism. It would be good to see *The Devil is an Ass* acted; it would be good to see *Sejanus*—which has a contemporary relevance not merely because it is a study of tyranny ('We shall be marked anon, for our not Hail' [1]), but it would be better if one could feel assured that they were widely read. Jonson's permanent importance is beyond question, but the discipline that a thorough assimilation of his work imposes is an especial need of the present day. It is not merely that poets might profitably study his verse as well as Donne's and Hopkins', Skelton's and *The Seafarer* (I am not suggesting anything so foolish as direct imitation); not merely that practitioners of 'the poetic drama' might learn something of effective stylization (the result of an emotional discipline) from his plays: these matters, in any case, are best left to poets. But for all of us he is one of the main channels of communication with an almost vanished tradition. That tradition cannot be apprehended in purely literary terms, but we can learn something of it through literature, just as to feel our way into the technique of Jonson's verse is to share, in some measure, that steady, penetrating scrutiny of men and affairs.

[1] *Sejanus*, V, viii (III, 132).

CHAPTER SEVEN

JONSON AND THE
ANTI-ACQUISITIVE ATTITUDE

I HAVE tried to show that the vitality of Jonson's plays draws on a popular source. However much he might flaunt 'the vulgar' in his prologues and inter-means, his code formed part of a healthy tradition which his audience helped to keep alive. The most effective way of demonstrating the value of the inherited standards of the period is to examine those masterpieces of Jonson's in which they are present as a living force. More, of course, goes to the making of a great comedy than an acceptable moral code. In *Volpone* and *The Alchemist* Jonson's general anti-acquisitive attitude combines with powerful emotions, with subtle observation, with all those constituents of value that are only susceptible to literary analysis. But here I shall single out only a few strands of that rich combination. Since they represent aspects of Jonson's art which have been largely neglected, the emphasis may help to make possible a more complete assimilation of his work.

In *Volpone*, Jonson's greatest comedy, played at the Globe in 1606, the sardonically alert criticism of accumulation is so obvious as to need merely a brief illustration. Herford and Simpson show that Jonson found the theme of legacy-hunting in Lucian and Petronius, and proceed:

> In choosing such a subject as this Jonson, then, necessarily abandoned one of his surest holds upon the play-going public, his powerful presentment of the London life at their doors.

200

In Jacobean London similar concoctions of greed, cunning, and credulity, were not perhaps much less rife than in imperial Rome; but this particular variety of them was not yet at home there. Yet the very unfamiliarity of this 'folly' touched the vein of a Jacobean audience at another point. If they enjoyed seeing London gallants and prentices, country simpletons and City wives, made sport of, they were at least as accessible to the romantic fascination of strange or exotic crime.[1]

'The romantic fascination of strange or exotic crime' is utterly beside the point. Whether 'fishing for testaments' was actually one of the contemporary forms of fortune-hunting or not, its significance here is solely as a manifestation of human greed, peculiarly appropriate in the era that was then beginning.[2]

The general construction can be paralleled in most of Jonson's plays. The main theme is focused in a sharp, strong light. Behind it, as it were, there is, first, a representation of minor follies (the songs of Nano, etc., on the one hand, and Sir Politick and Lady Would-be on the other)—variations which help to shape our attitude towards the main theme; then the final sombre setting—'When I am lost in blended dust',[3]

> So many cares, so many maladies,
> So many fears attending on old age.[4]

With *Sejanus* in mind we can understand the sense in which *Volpone* represents 'the creation of a world'.[5] It draws potently enough upon the actual, but there is a similar exclusion, a similar concentration upon one dominant group of impulses, 'a unity of inspiration that radiates into plot and personages alike'.[6]

---

[1] Ben Jonson (ed. C. H. Herford and Percy Simpson), *The Man and his Work*, II, p. 53. [2] See above, pp. 121 ff.
[3] I, i (III, 178). [4] *Ibid.* (III, 189).
[5] T. S. Eliot, *Elizabethan Essays*, p. 79. [6] *Ibid.*, p. 77.

The nature of that inspiration I tried to make clear in my analysis of 'See, behold, what thou art queen of . . .'. The greed that forms the subject of *Volpone* includes both the desire of sensuous pleasure as an end in itself, and the desire for riches; and the expression of each makes similar demands upon the reader.

> Good morning to the day; and next, my gold!
> Open the shrine, that I may see my saint.
> (*Mosca withdraws the curtain, and discovers piles of gold,*
>   *plate, jewels, etc.*)
> Hail the world's soul, and mine! more glad than is
> The teeming earth to see the long'd for sun
> Peep through the horns of the celestial Ram,
> Am I, to view thy splendour darkening his;
> That lying here, amongst my other hoards,
> Shew'st like a flame by night, or like the day
> Struck out of chaos, when all darkness fled
> Unto the centre.   O thou son of Sol,
> But brighter than thy father, let me kiss,
> With adoration, thee, and every relick
> Of sacred treasure in this blessed room. . . .[1]

There is no need to repeat the criticism of the previous chapter, but we may remark that this 'morning hymn to gold' does *not* 'transfigure avarice with the glamour of religion and idealism'.[2]   It brings the popular and religious tradition into play, but that is a different matter; religion and the riches of the teeming earth are there for the purpose of ironic contrast.

Volpone himself may
>   glory
> More in the cunning purchase of my wealth,
> Than in the glad possession,[3]

but the suitors are solely personifications of greed. 'Raven,

---

[1] I, i (III, 166).   [2] Herford and Simpson, II, p. 58.
          [3] I, i (III, 167-168).

crow, vulture, they represent but a narrow class even among birds of prey. They differ in their circumstances, not in their bent.'[1]   And in order that the theme may be complete and whole the four judges, the Avocatori, are made to represent anything but justice. Their complacent fatuity is apparent in their stilted and tautological comments. (The court scene, like the meeting of the Senate in *Sejanus*, is highly stylized.)

   1. *Avoc.* The like of this the senate never heard of.
   2. *Avoc.* 'Twill come most strange to them when we
      report it.[2]

They display a new-found politeness to Mosca when it seems that he is the heir,[3] and the Fourth Judge considers this 'proper man . . . a fit match for my daughter'.[4]   As for Celia and Bonario, they are completely, and intentionally, null, and there is no point in talking about their 'white innocence'.[5]   The one mode is maintained consistently to the end.

>   Why, your gold
> Is such another med'cine, it dries up
> All those offensive savours: it transforms
> The most deformed, and restores them lovely,
> As 'twere the strange poetical girdle. Jove
> Could not invent t'himself a shroud more subtle
> To pass Acrisius' guards. It is the thing
> Makes all the world her grace, her youth, her beauty.[6]

Volpone is a work of art, a particular experience, and in reading it we are concerned solely with those passions that Jonson chooses to exhibit, and the particular way in which

---

[1] Herford and Simpson, II, p. 63.   [2] IV, ii (III, 273).
[3] V, vi (III, 309).   [4] V, viii (III, 314).
[5] 'The rank and uniform depravity of the rogues and dupes is set off by the white innocence of Celia and Bonario, who to tell the truth are, as characters, almost as insipid as they are innocent' (Herford and Simpson, II, pp. 63-64).   [6] V, i (III, 289).

he exhibits them. But it is worth noticing how many variations are, at different points, explicitly related to the main
themes. The Third Act opens with Mosca's praise of his
profession in typical hyperbole:

> O! your parasite
> Is a most precious thing, dropt from above,
> Nor bred 'mongst clods and clodpoles, here on earth. . . .
>   . . . And, yet,
> I mean not those that have your bare town-art,
> To know who's fit to feed them; have no house,
> No family, no care, and therefore mould
> Tales for men's ears, to bait that sense; or get
> Kitchen invention, and some stale receipts
> To please the belly and the groin; nor those,
> With their court-dog-tricks, than can fawn and fleer,
> Make their revenue out of legs and faces,
> Echo my lord, and lick away a moth:
> But your fine elegant rascal. . . .[1]

All the forms of parasitism that Mosca does *not* mean are
here brought within the scope of the same trend of feeling as
that which is aroused towards Mosca himself.[2] There is
a similar effect in the praise of Volpone's craft:

> *Volpone.*   I gain
> No common way; I use no trade, no venture;
> I wound no earth with plough-shares, fat no beasts,
> To feed the shambles; have no mills for iron,
> Oil, corn, or men, to grind them into powder:
> I blow no subtle glass, expose no ships
> To threat'nings of the furrow-faced sea;
> I turn no monies in the public bank,
> No usure private.
> *Mosca.*   No, sir, nor devour
> Soft prodigals. You shall have some will swallow

[1] III, i (III, 225).
[2] Compare W. Empson, *Seven Types of Ambiguity*, pp. 261-262,
where the examples, although very different from this, illustrate the
affirmative possibilities of 'not'.

A melting heir as glibly as your Dutch
Will pills of butter, and ne'er purge for it;
Tear forth the fathers of poor families
Out of their beds, and coffin them alive
In some kind clasping prison, where their bones
May be forthcoming, when the flesh is rotten:
But your sweet nature doth abhor these courses;
You loathe the widow's or the orphan's tears
Should wash your pavements, or their piteous cries
Ring in your roofs, and beat the air for vengeance.[1]

What we are forced to notice here is the magnificently adroit transition from the legitimate forms of gain (that Volpone neglects these reflects only on himself) to those which stand there for bitterly derisive contemplation. The change is marked in the fifth line

> . . . have no mills for iron,
> Oil, corn, *or men*, to grind them into powder,

and in Mosca's rejoinder grim caricature is followed by the emphatic moral indignation of,

> Tear forth the fathers of poor families
> Out of their beds, and coffin them alive
> In some kind clasping prison.[2]

Mr Eliot says that 'the worlds created by artists like Jonson . . . are not fancy, because they have a logic of their own; and this logic illuminates the actual world, because it gives us a new point of view from which to inspect it'.[3] Mr Eliot's essay is the finest criticism of Jonson that we have,

---

[1] I, i (III, 168).

[2] Compare Jonson's attitude towards enclosures as expressed in *King James's Entertainment in Passing to his Coronation*, 1603 (VI, 425):

> Now innocence shall cease to be the spoil
> Of ravenous greatness, or to steep the soil
> Of rased peasantry with tears and blood.

[3] *Elizabethan Essays*, p. 79.

205

but the connexion between Jonson's plays and 'the actual world' is very much closer than that sentence allows. The attitude expressed in the passage last quoted informs the whole of *Volpone*, and it is, strictly, a moral attitude. Great literature cannot be discussed in purely moral terms, for the reason that these, at best, are too broad and general. But literary analysis is the keenest instrument we possess for the exploration of human values, and *Volpone*—a masterpiece of literary art—serves to make the point on which other great artists, besides Jonson, have been emphatic: 'The essential function of art is moral. Not aesthetic, not decorative, not pastime and recreation, but moral.'[1] The comedy of *Volpone* is universal, but it would be perverse not to relate it to the acquisitiveness of a particular time and place.

In order to understand the contemporary background of *The Alchemist* (1610) we need to know more about the various forms of fortune-hunting of the period than about the history of alchemy. We have to realize, of course, that alchemy was not a back-street fraud. Not long before Jonson wrote Dr Dee had been consulted by half the fashionable society in London, and Edward Kelly had been, for a time, the favourite of the Imperial Court. Elizabeth allowed an alchemist to experiment in Somerset House, and Burghley hoped that Kelly might 'send her majesty for a token some such portion (of gold), as might be to her a sum reasonable to defer her charges for this summer for her navy'. In 1610 Dr Simon Forman, 'who combined alchemy with astrology, medicine, necromancy, and other crafts . . .

[1] D. H. Lawrence, *Studies in Classic American Literature*, p. 117. Compare Jonson on 'the impossibility of any man's being the good poet, without first being a good man'.—Dedication of *Volpone* (III, 156), and the Prologues and Inductions generally.

was at the height of his reputation'.[1]   But for Jonson alchemy not only provided examples of quackery and credulity; it symbolized the desire for infinite riches.

   The Alchemist, like *Volpone*, is built on the double theme of lust and greed, and the whole play is constructed so as to isolate and magnify the central theme.   The extraordinary complications of the plot all centre on Subtle and Face, and all work to one end.   The play is completely self-consistent; all of the simplified characters are actuated by variations of the one motive, and no extraneous passions are allowed to enter.   To put it another way, all the interests aroused in the reader point in one direction, so that effects of exaggeration are possible here as they would not be in a 'realistic' play or in a play involving more complicated emotions.   In a world of caricature the speeches of Sir Epicure Mammon do not appear 'unnatural'; they are merely a characteristic heightening of the effect.

> Come on, sir.   Now, you set your foot on shore
> In *Novo Orbe*; here's the rich Peru:
> And there within, sir, are the golden mines,
> Great Solomon's Ophir! he was sailing to't,
> Three years, but we have reach'd it in ten months.
> This is the day, wherein, to all my friends,
> I shall pronounce the happy word, BE RICH;
> THIS DAY YOU SHALL BE SPECTATISSIMI.
> You shall no more deal with the hollow dye,
> Or the frail card.   No more be at charge of keeping
> The livery-punk for the young heir. . . .
> No more of this.   You shall start up young viceroys,
> And have your punks, and punketees, my Surly.[2]

Mammon's first speech is representative.   There is the typical inflation, containing within itself the destructive

   [1] Herford and Simpson, II, pp. 88-93; Ralph Sargent, *At the Court of Queen Elizabeth*, chap. vii, where Burghley's letter is quoted, p. 115.   [2] II, i (IV, 43).

irony, and exploding when the height of ambition and the
commonest sin are linked together in the concluding lines.
Our response is the sardonic contemplation that we give to
the 'cob-swan', 'the holy purse', or Caesar's 'ulcerous and
anointed face'. The effect is pervasive:

> I will have all my beds blown up, not stuft;
> Down is too hard: and then, mine oval room
> Fill'd with such pictures as Tiberius took
> From Elephantis, and dull Aretine
> But coldly imitated. Then, my glasses
> Cut in more subtle angles, to disperse
> And multiply the figures, as I walk
> Naked between my succubæ . . .
>   . . . Where I spy
> A wealthy citizen, or a rich lawyer,
> Have a sublimed pure wife, unto that fellow
> I'll send a thousand pound to be my cuckold.
> . . . I'll have no bawds,
> But fathers and mothers: they will do it best,
> Best of all others. And my flatterers
> Shall be the pure and gravest of divines,
> That I can get for money. My mere fools,
> Eloquent burgesses.[1]

The exaggeration is of course the very opposite of simple
hyperbole. The astonishing comparisons ('dull Aretine'),
the violent alignment of characters which convention
assumes are natural opposites (flatterers: divines; fools:
eloquent burgesses), generate an intensely critical activity in
the reader, make him aware that he is called on to judge a
mode of experience as well as to enjoy the representation.

Mammon's speeches are central; every other scene, although an end in itself, leads up to them, and they in turn
reflect on the whole course of the action. There is no need
to comment on Drugger, Dapper and Kastrill—

[1] II, i (IV, 52).

> A gentleman newly warm in his land,
> Scarce cold in his one and twenty, that does govern
> His sister here; and is a man himself
> Of some three thousand a year, and is come up
> To learn to quarrel and to live by his wits,
> And will go down again, and die in the country[1]

—but the Puritans, Ananias and Tribulation Wholesome, have a special significance. They stand not merely for hypocrisy, but for acquisition with a good conscience. Subtle explains that

> Such as are not graced in a state,
> May, for their ends, be adverse in religion,
> And get a tune to call the flock together,[2]

[1] *Ibid.* (IV, 85). This is not the only place where Jonson expresses scorn (admirably effective in the flat movement of the last line) for the parasite-landlord. Compare La-Foole in *Epicœne* I, i (III, 351): 'I . . . shew'd myself to my friends in court, and after went down to my tenants in the country, and surveyed my lands, let new leases, took their money, spent it in the eye o' the land here, upon ladies:— and now I can take up at my pleasure'. The standard by which such creatures are judged is the old one which associated landed wealth with obligations:

> Ay, that was when the nursery's self [the nursery of nobility]
>   was noble,
> And only virtue made it, not the market,
> That titles were not vented at the drum,
> Or common out-cry; goodness gave the greatness,
> And greatness worship: every house became
> An academy of honour, and those parts
> We see departed in the practice now
> Quite from the institution.
>
>   (*The New Inn* (1629), I, i (V, 313).)

All these passages are relevant to the question of 'housekeeping' and aristocratic responsibility discussed in Chapter III, above. It is Carlo Buffone who remarks: 'To be an accomplished gentleman, that is, a gentleman of the time, you must give over housekeeping in the country, and live altogether in the city amongst gallants' (*Every Man out of his Humour*, I, i (II, 30)).

[2] *The Alchemist*, III, ii (IV, 91).

and certainly the hypocrisy is there ('casting of dollars is concluded lawful'[1]). But there is also a complacence in Tribulation's willingness to ally himself and 'the holy brethren of Amsterdam' with riches,

> weighing
> What need we have to hasten on the work
> For the restoring of the silenced saints,
> Which ne'er will be, but by the philosopher's stone.
> And so a learned elder, one of Scotland,
> Assured me; *aurum potabile* being
> The only med'cine for the civil magistrate,
> T'incline him to a feeling for the cause;
> And must be daily used in the disease.[2]

Indeed,

> We may be temporal lords ourselves, I take it.[3]

Neither Ananias nor Tribulation 'represents' Puritanism, but their concern with the stone, their shrewd dealing, and Subtle's ironic catalogue of their offences—

> (You) take the start of bonds broke but one day,
> And say, they were forfeited by providence[4]—

caricature an absorption in worldly business against which the Protestantism of the new business classes was insufficiently armed.

In *The Devil is an Ass* (1616) Jonson handles, with a difference, the devil theme that had proved so popular in such plays as *Grim the Collier of Croydon* and the 'dear

---

[1] IV, iv (IV, 146). Herford and Simpson point out (II, 104) that 'when Ananias introduces himself as "a faithful Brother" and Subtle affects to understand by this a devotee of alchemy, the two professions at once assume an air of parallel fraternities'.

[2] III, i (IV, 88).   [3] III, ii (IV, 91).   [4] *Ibid.* (IV, 92).

delight' of theatre audiences, *The Merry Devil of Edmonton*. Pug, the devil, who obtains leave of absence from Hell to try his tricks on earth, is an ass because he is so ineffectual. Satan has warned him that their 'breed and trade' is likely to decay, since vices are bred more quickly in the upper world than in the lower, and Pug, after a bad time among the gallants and ladies of fashion, is glad to return to comparative peace below.

> You talk of a university! Why, hell is
> A grammar school to this![1]

The satire is lively, varied and direct; it includes the jealous husband, the greedy and ambitious citizen, the foolish justice, idle ladies aping court manners, believers in witchcraft, and London vice in general. But the main theme is provided by the projectors, monopolists and patentees whose activities had increased so alarmingly by the middle of the reign of James I. The play was produced in 1616, and it is worth recalling that this was the boom period for projectors and monopolists, culminating in parliamentary action in 1621 and 1624. In 1614 'it was reported that, "as a garden, clean weeded, weeds again next year", so since 1611 a fresh crop of objectionable grants had sprung up';[2] the reluctance of Parliament to vote supplies had forced James to take further advantage of the opportunities that monopolies seemed to offer for filling the royal purse, and in this he was aided by Bacon, who became Chancellor in 1616, the year in which Cockayne's experiment collapsed. There is no doubt that *The Devil is an Ass*

---

[1] *The Devil is an Ass*, IV, i (V, 109). Cf. Lucifer's comment in Middleton's *The Black Book* (1604):
> And were it numbered well
> There are more devils on earth than are in hell.
> (*Works*, ed. Bullen, VIII, p. 7)

[2] Scott, I, p. 141. And see above, pp. 71 ff. and p. 87.

reflects popular opinion, just as it anticipated the parliamentary action of 1621 which exposed some of the worst of the projectors.

In all of Jonson's plays we are conscious that he is observing a contemporary world, but never before had he handled a major political issue so effectively.[1] Its effectiveness is due to the fact that it is so much more than a political pamphlet. The method is similar to that of the greater plays; like them it draws upon and refines the healthy instincts of its audience, and gives point and coherence to a vague popular sentiment. But whereas *Volpone* had been concerned with attitudes and impulses permanent in human nature, though liberated and enforced by contemporary events, *The Devil is an Ass* brings the events themselves upon the stage. Unwin, who was better qualified to speak than most, remarked that, 'A study of the leading characters in *The Devil is an Ass* . . . would be by far the best introduction to the economic history of the period',[2] and one of the best ways of appreciating its qualities is to examine the satire on projectors, its scope and method.

Fitzdottrel is the born dupe, the greedy prey.[3] Wittipol's account of him is that he loves the devil (Pug has taken service with him),

> for hidden treasure
> He hopes to find; and has proposed himself
> So infinite a mass, as to recover,
> He cares not what he parts with, of the present,
> To his men of art, who are the race may coin him.[4]

Temporarily deserting the alchemists he lends a ready ear to

---

[1] The play's immediate implications were noted, and Jonson was 'accused' on account of it. '*Parergos* is discoursed of the Duke of Drownland: the King desired him to conceal it' (*Conversations*, 16 (IX, 400)).   [2] *Shakespeare's England*, I, p. 339.

[3] 'The Dottrel (Fuller tells us) is . . . a mirth-making bird . . . that is easily caught, or rather catcheth himself by his own over-active imitation'—Gifford's note. (V, 50.)   [4] I, iii (V, 26).

Meercraft, 'the wit, the brain, the great projector', who 'is newly come to town',[1]

> one that projects
> Ways to enrich men, or to make them great,
> By suits, by marriages, by undertakings:
> According as he sees they humour it.[2]

The scheme that Meercraft proposes—the recovery of drowned lands, or fen drainage—happens to be completely bogus, and Fitzdottrel does his best to ruin himself, but the bogusness does not matter. What is remarkable is the extent of Jonson's knowledge of the intricate machinery that is set at work by the patent seekers. Money has to be raised—

> We'll take in citizens, commoners and aldermen,
> To bear the charge, and blow them off again,
> Like so many dead flies, when it is carried,[3]

—and the Crown has to be promised

> a moiety,
> If it be owner; else the crown and owners
> To share that moiety, and the recoverers
> To enjoy the other moiety for their charge.[4]

Jonson is aware of the whitewash of 'reward for invention'; Meercraft says of Lady Tailbush:

> She and I now
> Are on a project for the fact, and venting
> Of a new kind of fucus, paint for ladies,
> To serve the kingdom: wherein she herself
> Hath travailed, specially, by way of service
> Unto her sex, and hopes to get the monopoly
> As the reward for her invention.[5]

---

[1] *Ibid.* (V, 36).   [2] *Ibid.*   [3] II, i (V, 39).   [4] *Ibid.* (V, 40).
[5] III, i (V, 87). Wittipol asks, 'What is her end in this?' and Jonson answers through Meercraft,

> Merely ambition,
> Sir, to grow great, and court it with the secret,
> Though she pretend some other.

There is share-dealing, with pickings for the favoured, and corruption of officials:

> She's dealing
> Already upon caution for the shares;
> And master Ambler he is named examiner
> For the ingredients, and the register
> Of what is vented, and shall keep the office.
> Now if she break with you of this, (as I
> Must make the leading thread to your acquaintance,
> That, how experience gotten in your being
> Abroad, will help our business,) think of some
> Pretty additions, but to keep her floating.[1]

And then there is the unofficial side of the business. For a patent to be successful it needs the 'countenance' of great men;[2] Meercraft tells two other of his dupes of his 'pains at court, to get you each a patent',[3] and Lady Tailbush's time is taken up with visits at court to oil the wheels:

> *Lady Tailbush.*　　　　I swear I must to-morrow
> Begin my visits, would they were over, at court:
> It tortures me to think on them.
> *Lady Eitherside.*　　　I do hear
> You have cause, madam, your suit goes on.[4]

Society advertising plays its part. Tailbush is

> 　　　　　　　　infinitely bound
> Unto the ladies, they have so cried it up,[5]

and Eitherside, who helps to set the fashion for the new fucus, is to get 'every month a new gown out of it'.[6] The flashy Everill is kept in 'Scarlet, gold-lace, and cut-works' by Meercraft, and haunts fashionable eating-houses[7] so that he may

> 　　　　　　　　　　　Stand
> Your name of credit, and compound your business,

---

[1] III, i (V, 87).　　[2] II, i (V, 39).　　[3] V, iii (V, 129).
[4] IV, i (V, 98).　[5] IV, i (V, 95).　[6] IV, i (V, 98).　[7] III, i (V, 76).

> Adjourn your beatings every term, and make
> New parties for your projects.[1]

Meercraft has little to learn from modern copy-writers. Another of his projects is,

> For serving the whole state with tooth-picks;
> Somewhat an intricate business to discourse: but
> I show how much the subject is abused,
> First, in that one commodity; then what diseases
> And putrefactions in the gums are bred,
> By those are made of adulterate and false wood;
> My plot for reformation of these, follows:
> To have all tooth-picks brought unto an office,
> There seal'd; and such as counterfeit them, mulcted.[2]
> And last, for venting them, to have a book
> Printed, to teach their use, which every child
> Shall have throughout the kingdom, that can read,
> And learn to pick his teeth by: which beginning
> Early to practise, with some other rules,
> Of never sleeping with the mouth open, chewing
> Some grains of mastick, will preserve the breath
> Pure and so free from taint.[3]

Everything, in short, is there, and Unwin's statement is no exaggeration.

But if the play were merely a satiric catalogue of economic abuses there would be less reason to read it to-day. It is the method, the angle at which the abuses are presented, that is important. The method is indicated in the quotations that have been given; the list of projects makes it clear. Off-hand, after a first reading, one would probably say that all of Meercraft's schemes were fanciful caricatures of reality. But they include not only projects for making gloves of dogskins and wine of blackberries,[4] but also sensible-sounding schemes ('a patent . . . for the laudable use of forks'[5]), and plans for a rationalized industry:

[1] III, i (V, 84). [2] Compare the New Draperies, etc.
[3] IV, i (V, 99). [4] II, i (V, 42-44). [5] V, iii (V, 129).

215

I will save in cork,
In my mere stop'ling, above three thousand pound,
Within that term; by googing of them out
Just to the size of my bottles, and not slicing:
There's infinite loss in that.[1]

All the projects, moreover, are said to be carried through
in a way that keeps close to reality. The method, of course,
is to keep the audience shifting uneasily from fantastic
caricature to sober truth, and back, until reality itself is seen
in the same critical light as the caricature. Here is Meercraft's introduction of himself on his first appearance:

Sir, money's a whore, a bawd, a drudge;
Fit to run out on errands: let her go.
Via, pecunia! when she's run and gone,
And fled, and dead; then will I fetch her again
With *aqua vitae*, out of an old hogshead!
While there are lees of wine, or dregs of beer,
I'll never want her! Coin her out of cobwebs,
Dust, but I'll have her! raise wool upon egg shells,
Sir, and make grass grow out of marrow-bones,
To make her come.[2]

Some of Meercraft's projects rank with those of Sir Politick
Would-be,[3] and the end of his speech suggests that we are to
be transported to a cloud-cuckoo land of projectors. But
the *aqua vitae* patent, with its abuses, was taken direct from
life,[4] and the ironic play generates a critical attitude which
allows the main point to have its full effect.

For the intention is not, of course, to raise prejudice
against invention itself. The scheme on which Meercraft

[1] II, i (V, 44).   [2] II, i (V, 38).
[3] *Volpone*, IV, i (III, 262-265).
[4] See Scott, I, p. 116. Cf. T. and P., II, pp. 271, 281: 'Beer-eager,
Vinegar, aqua-vitae, be it never so bad, if the patentee hath his imposition, it passeth for good' (1601). See also *The Alchemist*, I, i
(IV, 14)—'sell the dole beer to aqua vitae men'—which suggests how
the aqua vitae was made.

persuades Fitzdottrel to embark, the reclaiming of 'drowned land', was both feasible and (abuses in the execution apart) something that could be honestly approved.[1] The audience therefore had no excuse for missing the point: it is the greed that prompts this and the other schemes which is aimed at.

> *Meercraft.*   Sir, there's not place
> To give you demonstration of these things,
> They are a little too subtle.   But I could show you
> Such a necessity in it, as you must be
> But what you please; against the received heresy,
> That England bears no dukes.   Keep you the land, sir,
> The greatness of the estate shall throw't upon you.
> If you like better turning it to money,
> What may not you, sir, purchase with that wealth?
> Say you should part with two of your millions,
> To be the thing you would, who would not do't?
> As I protest I will, out of my dividend,
> Lay for some pretty principality
> In Italy, from the church: now you, perhaps,
> Fancy the smoke of England rather?   But—
> Have you no private room, sir, to draw to,
> To enlarge ourselves more upon?[2]

[1] The main fen drainage schemes belong to the reign of Charles I, but various undertakers had been busy under Elizabeth, and in 1605 Sir John Popham and others had attempted to drain the 'Great Level'.—See Scott, II, pp. 352-357.   There was, of course, justification for the popular hostility towards the drainage companies.   'The first notorious undertaker was the Earl of Lincoln, in Queen Elizabeth's days.   His covetous Lordship by bribes to some Courtiers, and mis-information by pretending what a glorious work draining would be to the public, and that he had the consent of the Country (which indeed were but an inconsiderable party of his own faction) procured a patent or commission for the draining of the Fens.   But his private ends were to drain his own surrounded foul lands at the public charges; and he so packed his commissioners by making them Judges and Parties, that they made a Level and took away the poor country-men's lands (which were never drowned, or bettered by overflowing) for melioration' (*Anti-Projector* (1651), p. 2, quoted by Cunningham, II, p. 113, note 8).—See also, *ibid.*, pp. 114-119.
[2] II, i (V, 45).

If Fitzdottrel's response is a caricature, it is a caricature in which the reality is easily recognizable.

> He will make me a duke!
> No less, by heaven! Six mares to your coach, wife!
>
> . . . All Crowland
> Is ours, wife; and the fens, from us, in Norfolk,
> To the utmost bounds in Lincolnshire! we have view'd it,
> And measur'd it within all, by the scale:
> The richest tract of land, love, in the kingdom!
> There will be made seventeen or eighteen millions,
> Or more, as't may be handled! [1]

This, then, is the impulse behind the projects of the time—'Advantageous to the country, not burdensome to those affected, profitable to the Crown, and a source of some slight profit to the petitioner'!

Purely economic considerations contribute to *The Devil is an Ass*, but the play goes beyond economics and questions of expediency. Since it is the work of a great artist it cuts beneath the superficial follies, the accidental forms, and goes to the root of the disease, shaping the material in the light of an humane ideal that is implicit throughout.

The Staple of News was produced by the King's Men, first on the public stage then at Court, early in 1626, at the time, that is, when the country was beginning to recover from the depression in which the reign of James I had ended.[2] It

[1] II, i (V, 55).
[2] The Shopkeepers
> have had a pitiful hard time on't,
> A long vacation from their cozening.
>> (I, i (V, 170))
Thomas the Barber's patent
> for aid of our trade,
> Whereof there is a manifest decay
>> (III, i (V, 232))
may glance at projects designed to foster commercial activity.

is a curious mixture. In the first place it is a revue of social and economic topicalities, making its appeal by satiric references to commonplaces of the hour. There is satire on litigious country gentlemen,[1] on the 'golden heir' whose arrival in town is 'news indeed, and of importance' for the fortune hunters,[2] on the usurer, worried that money has 'fallen off two in the hundred',[3] on puritans,[4] on 'jeerers', followers of a fashionable craze[5] and on the unpopular Gondomar.[6] The pedigree of Lady Pecunia is deduced 'from all the Spanish mines in the West-Indies',[7] and the opportunities open to native gold-miners are mentioned together with a thinly veiled reference to Sir Bevis Bulmer:

> *Pennyboy Junior.* Dost thou want any money, founder?
> *Pennyboy Canter.* Who, sir, I?
> Did I not tell you I was bred in the mines,
> Under Sir Bevis Bullion.
> *Pennyboy Junior.* That is true,
> I quite forgot, you mine-men want no money,
> Your streets are pav'd with't: there the molten silver
> Runs out like cream on cakes of gold.[8]

And of course there are mock patents,[9] and the courtier is castigated for his 'fly-blown projects';[10] he is

[1] *Pennyboy Junior.* Here is domine Picklock,
My man of law, solicits all my causes,
Follows my business, makes and compounds my quarrels
Between my tenants and me; sows all my strifes,
And reaps them too; troubles the country for me,
And vexes any neighbour that I please. (II, i (V, 209).)
[2] I, ii (V, 172).
[3] II, i (V, 189). The legal rate of interest had been reduced to eight per cent. by a statute of 1624. [4] III, i (V, 227 ff.).
[5] IV, i (V, 248 ff.). [6] III, i (V, 233).
[7] II, i (V, 192). Her 'line' also includes the mines of Hungary, and of Barbary, besides 'the Welsh mine'. IV, i (V, 263).
[8] I, i (V, 171). See above, pp. 89 ff., for Bulmer.
[9] A precept for the wearing of long hair,
To run to seed, to sow bald pates withal. (III, i (V, 232).)
[10] IV, i (V, 265).

a moth, a rascal, a court-rat,
That gnaws the commonwealth with broking suits,
And eating grievances.[1]

The best of the merely topical satire is found in the Staple scenes (I, i; I, ii; III, i) where Jonson exposes contemporary newsmongers and their credulous customers.[2] The news vented at the Staple is 'made like the time's news (a weekly cheat to draw money) and could not be fitter reprehended, than in raising this ridiculous office of the Staple, wherein the age may see her own folly, or hunger and thirst after published pamphlets of news, set out every Saturday, but made all at home, and no syllable of truth in them'.[3]

But the play is also a morality play on the power of money.[4] The symbolism is, in fact, too obvious. Pennyboy Junior (Prodigality) comes into his estate on the supposed death of his father, Pennyboy Canter. He courts the Lady Pecunia,

[1] IV, i (V, 268).

[2] For an account of the early newspaper enterprises in the sixteen-twenties see the Introduction to this play by Herford and Simpson, II, pp. 171-177. The earliest English newspapers were printed in Holland, but in 1622 London had at least two news-sheets of its own, *Weekly News from Italy, Germany, Hungaria. . . . Translated out of the Low Dutch Copy*, printed by Bourne and Archer, and *News from most parts of Christendom*, printed by Nathaniel Butter. Cf. Jonson's references to 'buttered news', etc. Another may have been run by one Captain Gainford, to whom Jonson refers as 'the Captain' (*ibid.*, pp. 172-173). Judging by the 'Low Dutch' sheets, the early news vendors had the same tastes as their successors in preferring the sensational and the pathetic. See the account of some executions at Prague (1621), *The First Newspapers of England*, ed. W. P. Van Stockum, p. 10. Jonson had previously attacked the news-mongers in the masque, *News from the New World Discovered in the Moon* (1620).

[3] III, i, 'To the Reader' (V, 219).

[4] Jonson is explicit: '. . . the allegory and purpose of the author', III, i, 'To the Reader' (V, 219). The characters 'are attired like men and women of the time, the vices male and female. Prodigality, like a young heir, and his mistress Money (whose favours he scatters like counters), pranked up like a prime lady, the Infanta of the mines' (II, i (V, 216-217)).

who is staying in the house of his uncle Pennyboy (Miser) Senior with her train—Broker, her usher, Mortgage, her nurse, her women Statute and Band, and Wax, the chambermaid. The young heir, however, distributes Pecunia's favours too freely to his parasites, and Pecunia falls into a consumption. At the end Pennyboy Canter, who has been following his son in the disguise of a beggar, declares himself, and Miser and Prodigal are alike reclaimed from their vices. Pecunia speaks the moral at the end:

> And so Pecunia herself doth wish,
> That she may still be aid unto their uses,
> Not slave unto their pleasures, or a tyrant
> Over their fair desires; but teach them all
> The golden mean; the prodigal how to live;
> The sordid and the covetous how to die:
> That with sound mind: this, safe frugality.[1]

It is a flat conclusion, but the money theme had given Jonson an opportunity for some characteristic satire. Pecunia is

> The talk o' the time! the adventure of the age!
>   .   .   .   .   .
> All the world are suitors to her.
> All sorts of men, and all professions.
> You shall have stall-fed doctors, cramm'd divines,
> Make love to her, and with those studied
> And perfumed flatteries, as no room can stink
> More elegant, than where they are.[2]

The Miser praises 'The Venus of the time and state, Pecunia':[3]

---

[1] V, ii (V, 291). The Prodigal and his money had formed part of that earlier theatrical medley, *Cynthia's Revels, or The Fountain of Self-Love* (1601). There Asotus, the citizen's son turned pseudo-gallant, had been similarly careless of Argurion (money), who had wasted away under his foolish treatment. 'Cupid strikes Money in love with the Prodigal, makes her dote upon him, give him jewels, bracelets, carcanets, etc. All which he most ingeniously departs withal to be made known to the other ladies and gallants . . .' (Induction (II, 208)).

[2] I, ii (V, 183-184).   [3] II, i (V, 210).

> All this nether world
> Is yours, you command it, and do sway it;
> The honour of it, and the honesty,
> The reputation, ay, and the religion,
> (I was about to say, and had not err'd,)
> Is Queen Pecunia's.[1]

The poet, Madrigal, makes a saraband in her honour:

> She makes good cheer, she keeps full boards,
> She holds a fair of knights and lords,
> A market of all offices,
> And shops of honours, more or less.
>
> According to Pecunia's grace,
> The bride hath beauty, blood, and place;
> The bridegroom virtue, valour, wit,
> And wisdom, as he stands for it.[2]

The quotations that have been given show how the verse varies from tame moralizing to brisk sardonic satire. There is a good deal that is merely boring—as when Jonson relies solely on symbolic action.[3]   But the money theme does not

---

[1] II, i (V, 191).

[2] IV, i (V, 255-256). Cf.
> . . . my most noble Money . . .
> My princess here; she that, had you but kept
> And treated kindly, would have made you noble,
> And wise too: nay, perhaps have done that for you,
> An act of Parliament could not, made you honest.
> > (IV, i (V, 260).)

Apparently the only thing money cannot do is to instil a taste for literature.   Broker tells Madrigal,
> your hope
> Of Helicon will never carry it here,
> With our fat family; we have the dullest,
> Most unbored ears for verse among our females!
> > (II, i (V, 204).)

[3] E.g. II, i (V, 213), where Pennyboy Junior is allowed to have Pecunia on condition that he returns Mortgage, Band, etc., to his uncle; or IV, i (V, 256), where he makes Pecunia kiss each of his hangers-on.

222

only provide an opportunity for moralistic comments, the best parts of the play (and they are both finer and more numerous than the common verdict seems to allow) still exhibit Jonson's firm grasp of an humane scheme of values, values which are potently *there*.

> *Pennyboy Senior.* Your grace is sad, methinks, and
>   melancholy,
> You do not look upon me with that face
> As you were wont, my goddess, bright Pecunia!
> Altho' your grace be fallen off two in the hundred,
> In vulgar estimation; yet am I
> Your grace's servant still; and teach this body
> To bend, and these my aged knees to buckle,
> In adoration, and just worship of you.
> Indeed, I do confess, I have no shape
> To make a minion of, but I am your martyr,
> Your grace's martyr. I can hear the rogues,
> As I do walk the streets, whisper and point,
> 'There goes old Pennyboy, the slave of money,
> Rich Pennyboy, lady Pecunia's drudge,
> A sordid rascal, one that never made
> Good meal in his sleep, but sells the acates are sent him,
> Fish, fowl, and venison, and preserves himself,
> Like an old hoary rat, with mouldy pie-crust!'
> This I do hear, rejoicing I can suffer
> This, and much more for your good grace's sake.[1]

Besides this caricature, done with the old skill, we can place the bitter comment of Pennyboy Canter,

> I am a wretch, a beggar: She the fortunate,
> Can want no kindred; we the poor know none.[2]

The Magnetic Lady (1632), Jonson's last completed play, is one of the only two that can properly be classed as a

---

[1] II, i (V, 189). Compare the fine passage beginning 'Who can endure to see the fury of men's gullets . . .? quoted on p. 191 above.
[2] IV, i (V, 256).

'dotage'.[1]   The uncertainty of purpose that had prevented *The Staple of News* from achieving greatness now results in complete dissipation.   Here are 'fine fancies, figures, humours, characters, ideas, definitions of lords and ladies',[2] everything, in fact, but inspiration.

An exhibition of 'humours' of the old kind is combined with a morality element similar to that of *The Staple of News*.   Placentia Steel is an orphan in the charge of the rich Lady Loadstone, and she has been 'brought up' by Polish, with 'the nurse Keep that tended her'.[3]   Her dowry, however, is in the hands of Sir Moth Interest, a usurer, brother of Lady Loadstone; and various suitors—a prelate, a doctor, a 'vi-politic or sub-secretary' and a lawyer—attempt to marry her and get her dowry from Sir Moth.   Finally she (or rather the real Placentia, for the supposed ward turns out to be a changeling) marries Compass, whose function it is to 'reconcile' the various humours.   Lady Loadstone and her niece share the attributes of the Lady Pecunia—

> Your ladyship is still the Lady Loadstone,
> That draws, and draws unto you, guests of all sorts;
> The courtiers, and the soldiers, and the scholars,
> The travellers, physicians, and divines,[4]

and there is a good deal of unrealized symbolism.   The only parts of the play that are of any interest are those that deal with money and business methods.

In *The Staple of News* Pennyboy Senior is an obvious caricature of the new type of business man.   It is not merely

[1] The other being *The New Inn* (1629).
[2] Induction (VI, 5).   The 'characters' of course are pithy character sketches of the kind that had long been popular in the pages of Overbury, Earle, Breton, etc.
[3] I, i (VI, 19).
[4] I, i (VI, 18).   Lady Loadstone's husband had been Governor of the East India Company, and had left her 'the wealth of six East-Indian fleets at least' (II, i (VI, 40)).

that he has an unquenchable thirst for money, he flaunts those virtues that are not incompatible with the pursuit of gain.

> *Pennyboy Senior.*   I'd keep my word, sure;
> I hate that man that will not keep his word.
> When did I break my word?
> *Lickfinger.*   Or I, till now?
> And 'tis but half an hour.
> *Pennyboy Senior.*   Half a year,
> To me that stand upon a minute of time:
> I am a just man, I love still to be just.

He shuns gluttony, 'gross gluttony, that will undo our land', and he has a righteous hatred of government interference in business: the act which reduced interest to eight per cent. not only 'bound our hands... shorten'd our arms', it defrauded the poor by lessening the opportunity for philanthropy!

> ... they that made that law,
> To take away the poor's inheritance!
> It was their portion, I will stand to it;
> And they have robb'd them of it, plainly robb'd them.
> I still am a just man, I tell the truth.[1]

Similarly, in *The Magnetic Lady* Sir Moth Interest displays a methodical business thrift:

> *Compass.*   There's within
> Sir Interest, as able a philosopher,
> In buying and selling! has reduced his thrift
> To certain principles, and in that method,
> As he will tell you instantly, by logarithms,
> The utmost profit of a stock employed;
> Be the commodity what it will: the place,
> Or time, but causing very little,
> Or, I may say, no parallax at all,
> In his pecuniary observations![2]

----

[1] *The Staple of News*, II, i (V, 194-197).
[2] *The Magnetic Lady*, I, i (VI, 24).

Since, as Compass observes, 'all men are philosophers, to their inches',[1] he rationalizes his greed, and believes that he is a necessary member of the commonwealth:

> *Sir Moth.* The portion left was sixteen thousand pound,
>   I do confess it, as a just man should.
>   And call here Master Compass, with these gentlemen,
>   To the relation; I will still be just.
>   Now for the profits every way arising,
>   It was the donor's wisdom, those should pay
>   Me for my watch, and breaking of my sleeps;
>   It is no petty charge, you know, that sum,
>   To keep a man awake for fourteen year.
> *Practice.* But, as you knew to use it in that time,
>   It would reward your waking.
> *Sir Moth.*   That's my industry,
>   As it might be your reading, study, and counsel,
>   And now your pleading; who denies it you?
>   I have my calling too.[2]

Sir Moth's monies are

>   my blood, my parents, kindred;
> And he that loves not these, he is unnatural,

and the best satire in the play is found in his defence of wealth:

> I am persuaded that the love of money
> Is not a virtue only in a subject,
> But might befit a prince. . . .
>   .   .   .   .   .
>   Wealth gives a man the leading voice
> At all conventions; and displaceth worth,
> With general allowance to all parties:
> It makes a trade to take the wall of virtue,
> And the mere issue of a shop right honourable.
> . . . It doth enable him that hath it,
> To the performance of all real actions,
> Referring him to himself still, and not binding

---

[1] *The Magnetic Lady*, I, i (VI, 24).   [2] II, i (VI, 40-41).

His will to any circumstance, without him.
It gives him precise knowledge of himself;
For, be he rich, he straight with evidence knows
Whether he have any compassion,
Or inclination unto virtue, or no;
Where the poor knave erroneously believes,
If he were rich, he would build churches, or
Do such mad things.[1]

Unfortunately a few passages do not make a play, and *The Magnetic Lady* has been included here merely for the purpose of illustration. From first to last one of Jonson's main preoccupations was acquisition. In his last play we have the anti-acquisitive attitude expressed as bare moral statement. In his earlier and greater plays, it is a part of a rich and complex organization. But we cannot appreciate the greatness of Jonson's art until we are fully aware of that attitude, an attitude which informs *Volpone* and which stirs a few flickers of genius even in *The Magnetic Lady*.

[1] II, i (VI, 41-43).

227

CHAPTER EIGHT

DEKKER, HEYWOOD AND CITIZEN MORALITY

To turn from Jonson to Dekker is to be jolted into recognition of the gulf between the higher and the lower ranges of Jacobean dramatic literature. With a few exceptions Dekker's plays are uniformly dull, and the effort of attention they require—the sheer effort to keep one's eyes on the page —is out of all proportion to the reward. They were, however, 'best sellers'—most of them were acted 'with great applause' by the Admiral's (afterwards the Prince's) Men, the Queen's Men or the Children of Paul's—and as an index of contemporary taste and opinion they provide some information that is relevant to this study.

Dekker was one of the neediest of the journeymen of letters at a time when authorship was one of the most precarious trades.[1] He had neither a share in a fellowship of players, nor aristocratic patronage, and he was forced to follow the taste of the moment as closely and as quickly as possible, either in play or pamphlet. It is usual to think of him as primarily a playwright, but his essentially journalistic talent is best brought out if we approach him through

[1] He began by hack-writing for Henslowe, and between 1598 and 1602 he is said to have had a hand in thirty-nine plays for the Admiral's Men.—Chambers, *Elizabethan Stage*, III, pp. 302-304. And Henslowe 'made money by shrewd dealing, by an often slavish following of the popular taste of the moment, and by the active competition of authors in an age when nearly anybody could write an acceptable play' (Schelling, *Elizabethan Drama*, I, p. 318).

his non-dramatic works; many of his plays are little more than dramatized versions of these.

As a journalist Dekker addressed the lower levels of the London reading public. His journalism was not, of course, the newsmongering of a Nathaniel Butter. A representative pamphlet such as *The Wonderful Year* (1603) consists of desultory gossip together with rhetorical accounts of events that were known to everybody, larded with 'tales cut out in sundry fashions, of purpose to shorten the lives of long winter nights'.[1] His accounts of wonders and marvels are all homely and commonplace,[2] and the descriptions are matched by the moralizing. Dekker's purpose was not solely to amuse. The majority of the pamphlets contain accounts of 'an Army of insufferable abuses, detestable vices, most damnable villainies, abominable pollutions, inexplicable mischiefs, sordid iniquinations, horrible and hellhound-like perpetrated flagitious enormities',[3] so 'that thou and all the world shall see their ugliness, for by seeing them, thou mayst avoid them'.[4] There is no need to doubt Dekker's moral purpose in his description of damnable villainies, but the quality of the description is fairly indicated by the tautological introduction that I have quoted. In the pamphlets mainly designed to show up abuses we learn little of the peculiar quality of contemporary social life; or rather, such evidence as they present is incidental.

In *The Seven Deadly Sins of London* (1606) the seven

[1] For the gossip and its significance see Appendix A, 'Elizabethan Prose', p. 305 A representative example of his rhetoric is the account of the plague quoted below, p. 322.

[2] *E.g.* the history of Charing Cross, or the account of the kings buried at Westminster, *The Dead Term*, *Non-Dramatic Works*, IV, pp. 11, 39-40, 152 ff. And cf. his frequent accounts of gipsies, thieves, etc.

[3] *The Belman of London*, *ibid.*, III, p. 168.

[4] *The Seven Deadly Sins of London*, *ibid.*, II, pp. 14-15.

sins are 'Politick Bankruptism', Lying, 'The Nocturnal Triumph', Sloth, Apishness, 'Shaving' and Cruelty. There are the usual puns and forced rhetoric, but what distinguishes the pamphlet is its humanitarianism. In the section on cruelty Dekker denounces parents who drive their children into unwilling marriages, cruel creditors, and unconscionable masters, and he pleads for the provision of hospitals and decent burial grounds. The approach to economic problems is entirely moralistic. In his denunciation of the 'politic bankrupt' he appeals to the Commandments, and shows the sin as a combination of covetousness and theft,[1] whilst the practice of imprisonment for debt is described as both useless and inhuman: 'We are most like to God that made us when we show love one to another, and do most look like the Devil that would destroy us, when we are one another's tormentors'.[2] So too he complains of the members of the London Companies who try to limit their numbers, and who will not allow apprentices, their seven years expired, to become masters,

> as if Trades, that were ordained to be communities, had lost their first privileges, and were now turned Monopolies. . . . Remember, O you rich men, that your servants are your adopted children; they are naturalized into your blood, and if you hurt theirs, you are guilty of letting out your own, than which, what cruelty can be greater? [3]

Dekker, in short, is following the traditions of the Church in regarding 'buying and selling, lending and borrowing, as a simple case of neighbourly or unneighbourly conduct'.[4] It is on these grounds that he judges landlords who rack rents, cheating tradesmen, brewers and bakers who give false measure, fraudulent executors, and usurers,

---

[1] *The Seven Deadly Sins of London, ibid.*, II, p. 17 ff.
[2] *Ibid.*, II, p. 72.　　　　　[3] *Ibid.*, II, p. 74.
[4] Tawney, *Religion and the Rise of Capitalism*, p. 54.

who for a little money and a great deal of trash (as fire-shovels, brown paper, motley cloak-bags, etc.) bring young novices into a fool's paradise till they have sealed the mortgage of their lands, and then like pedlars go they (or some familiar spirit for them, raised by the usurer) up and down to cry *Commodities*, which scarce yield the third part of the sum for which they take them up.[1]

A summary of the admirably humane proposals scattered throughout Dekker's pamphlets would suggest that I had done him an injustice. But what I am complaining of is the lack of something that can only be called the artistic conscience. Dekker is never sure of what he wants to do. The moral drive is dissipated by the constant striving after obvious 'effects', by the recurring introduction of irrelevancies, by the failure to maintain a consistent tone, so that although Dekker is never guilty of tickling his readers' palates with descriptions of vice, one often suspects the journalistic intention. One thing at least is proved by the blemishes themselves: Dekker was completely at one with his London audience.[2] He does not draw on popular thought and refine it, like Jonson, his thoughts *are* the thoughts of the average Londoner.

Dekker's social morality is a morality that the average decent citizen would find acceptable. He does not despise or

---

[1] *The Seven Deadly Sins of London, Non-Dramatic Works*, II, p. 64. Cf. *ibid.*, II, p. 135 ff. (usury), III, p. 367 (monopolies). Miss Gregg points out that 'The intimate relationship between personal sin and national calamity had a first place in all of Dekker's muck-raking pamphlets, and probably had a considerable part in making him one of the popular writers of his day'. He was, she adds, as thoroughgoing a conservative as Spenser, Shakespeare, Bacon or Jonson.— *Thomas Dekker, A Study in Economic and Social Backgrounds*, pp. 96-97.

[2] Cf. The address to the City in the Induction to *The Seven Deadly Sins of London*: 'From thy womb received I my being, from thy breasts my nourishment' (*ibid.*, II, p. 10 ff.; and *The Dead Term* (1608), *ibid.*, IV, pp. 9-10).

distrust riches so long as they are used conscionably. Virtue itself is rewarded by earthly prosperity—

> England shall ne'er be poor, if England strive
> Rather by virtue than by wealth to thrive.[1]

The rich should be fair and charitable; the poor should aim at content; the honest workman should maintain himself decently in his calling, and if he rises it must only be within the limits of his own order. One cannot classify this morality as either 'medieval' or 'modern'. Dekker accepts the traditional social ethic, but his Protestant Christianity is that of the seventeenth-century middle class.[2] It is significant that in *A Strange Horse Race* (1613) the first virtue that he mentions is Humility, the second, Thrift. Thrift, running a race with Prodigality, is 'vigilant in his course, subtle in laying his wager, provident in not venturing too much, honest to pay his losses, industrious to get more (twenty sundry ways) if he should happen to be cheated of all'.[3] It is a citizen morality, but it is neither entirely individualistic nor out of touch with tradition.

The plays, like the pamphlets, gave the public—Alleyn's public—what it wanted and what it could digest easily: amusement, naïvely 'dramatic' situations, moral 'sentences' and pictures of contemporary virtues and vices, eked out occasionally by fireworks.[4] Shakespeare took popular ele-

---

[1] *Old Fortunatus*, V, ii.

[2] Decidedly anti-Catholic. See *The Double PP* (1606), directed against the Catholics after the Gunpowder Plot, and *The Whore of Babylon* (1605–1607).

[3] *Ibid.*, III, p. 334. Cf. 'London . . . being ravished with unutterable joys . . . puts off her formal habit of Trade and Commerce, treading *even Thrift itself* underfoot' (*The Magnificent Entertainment given to King James* (1603), *Dramatic Works*, I, p. 303).

[4] *Old Fortunatus* (1599)—generally considered one of Dekker's best plays—is chiefly remarkable for the number of popular elements which he has contrived to work in. There is a morality framework

ments and transformed them to his own purposes; Dekker gives us an amalgam of all that popular taste demanded. His dramatic satire is usually directed against fairly obvious abuses:

> *1st Devil.* I have with this fist beat upon rich men's hearts,
> To make 'em harder: and these two thumbs thrust,
> (In open churches) into brave dames' ears,
> Damming up attention; whilst the loose eye peers
> For fashions of gown-wings, laces, purles, ruffs,
> Falls, cauls, tires, wires, caps, hats, and muffs and puffs.
> For so the face be smug, and carcase gay,
> That's all their pride.[1]

His satire, that is, either deals in generalities, or else it presents particulars drawn from the life of the time without grasping their full significance and implications. It does not penetrate far below the surface.

It is for this reason that Dekker's comedies, although far less 'universal' than Jonson's, tell us comparatively little about the economic and social changes that can be discerned behind *The Alchemist*. There are, of course, scattered references. *Westward Ho!* (1604), in particular, gives some interesting thumbnail sketches. There are needy courtiers [2] and luxurious citizens;[3] there is satire on the buying of

containing a romantic story and a satirical sub-plot; there is music, song and dance, together with pageantry, jewels and fine dresses; there is a quibbling clown, and there are scraps of foreign languages and broken English, such as might be heard on the quay side or at the Exchange; but there really isn't much else.

[1] *If it be not Good, the Devil is in It* (1610–1612) (III, 328-329). (Unless otherwise stated the references in brackets are to the volume and page of Dekker's Plays, edited by R. H. Shepherd, in the Pearson Reprints.)

[2] *Monopoly* (the courtier). 'O no sir. I must disburse instantly: we that be courtiers have more places to send money to, than the devil hath to send his spirits' (I, i (II, 289)).

[3] *Merchant's Wife* (to her husband). 'Your prodigality, your dicing, your riding abroad, your consorting yourself with noblemen, your building a summer house hath undone us' (I, i (II, 287)).

knighthoods,[1] and on monopolies;[2] and farmers are described as 'grinding the jaw-bones of the poor'.[3] But in this play Dekker collaborated with Webster, and I think that it is to Webster that the most effective satire belongs. In *If It be not Good, the Devil is in It* (1610–1612), it is true, there is a straightforward attack on commercial wiles. Pluto sends to earth three devils, one to corrupt a court, another a monastery, and a third is given these instructions:

> Be thou a city-devil. Make thy hands
> Of Harpy's claws, which being on courtiers' lands
> Once fasten'd, ne'er let loose. The Merchant play,
> And on the Burse, see thou thy flag display,
> Of politic bankruptism: train up as many
> To fight under it, as thou canst, for now's not any
> That break, (They'll break their necks first). If beside,
> Thou canst not through the whole city meet with pride,
> Riot, lechery, envy, avarice, and such stuff,
> Bring 'em all in coach'd, the gates are wide enough.
> The spirit of gold instruct thee.[4]

[1] *Clare* (a merchant's wife). 'Fabian Scarecrow us'd to frequent me and my husband divers times. And at last comes he out one morning to my husband, and says, master Tenterhook, says he, I must trouble you to lend me 200 pound about a commodity which I am to deal in, and what was that commodity but his knighthood' (V, i (II, 342)).

[2] *Monopoly* (promising to reward Birdlime, a bawd). '. . . I'll stick wool upon thy back.' *Birdlime*. 'Thanks sir, I know you will, for all the kindred of the Monopolies are held to be great fleecers' (II, ii (II, 309)). Cf. *Match me in London*, Act I (IV, 149): 'A flat-cap, pish! If he storm, give him a court-loaf, stop's mouth with a monopoly.'

[3] *Justiniano*. 'Why there's no minute, no thought of time passes, but some villainy or other is brewing: why, even now, now, at holding up of this finger, and before the turning down of this, some are murdering, some lying with their maids, some picking of pockets, some cutting purses, some cheating, some weighing out bribes. In this city some wives are cuckolding some husbands. In yonder village some farmers are now-now grinding the jaw-bones of the poor' (II, i (II, 299)). I have quoted the passage to show how unlike Dekker a good deal of the satire is.   [4] (III, 270.)

234

Bartervile, the merchant with whom the city-devil takes service, does not need much instruction. He gets the lands of a gentleman who owes him money by pretending that the hour for repayment is passed;[1] he loses the farm of some royal imposts, but obtains it again because the King needs to borrow money ('Who bids most, he buys it').[2] He devises a variation on 'Politic bankruptism',[3] and boasts that he has the royal protection:

> *Bartervile.* A merchant, and yet know'st not
> What a protection is? I'll tell thee. . . .
> It is a buckler of a large fair compass,
> Quilted with fox-skins; in the midst
> A pike sticks out, (sometimes of two years long,
> And sometimes longer). And this pike keeps off
> Sergeants and bailiffs, actions, and arrests:
> 'Tis a strong charm 'gainst all the noisome smells
> Of Counters, Jailors, garnishes, and such hells;
> By this, a debtor craz'd, so lusty grows,
> He may walk by, and play with his creditor's nose.
> Under this buckler, here I'll lie and fence.[4]

Above all, he lives solely for his immediate gain:

> *Lurchall.* But pray sir, what is't turns you into a Turk?
> *Bartervile.* That, for which many their Religion,
> Most men their Faith, all change their honesty,
> Profit, (that gilded god) Commodity,
> He that would grow damn'd rich, yet live secure,
> Must keep a case of faces. . . .[5]

Dekker, however, is not often so consistently explicit. Generally he is content to denounce gold, 'the world's saint',[6] in general terms. Old Fortunatus, given the choice

---

[1] (III, 296-301.)   [2] (III, 297, 317, 320-321.)
[3] (III, 323.) Compare *The Seven Deadly Sins of London, Non-Dramatic* Works, II, p. 17 ff.
[4] (III, 324.) The play also shows Church revenues farmed out to a courtier. (III, 319.)   [5] (III, 322.)   [6] (III, 271.)

of wisdom, strength, health, beauty, long life, and riches, chooses riches:

> My choice is store of gold; the rich are wise.
> He that upon his back rich garments wears,
> Is wise, though on his head grow Midas' ears.
> Gold is the strength, the sinews of the world,
> The health, the soul, the beauty most divine,
> A mask of gold hides all deformities;
> Gold is Heaven's physic, life's restorative,
> Oh therefore make me rich.[1]

But it is obvious that Dekker's acceptance of citizen thrift and industry is severely qualified by the traditional distrust.

> 'Twas never merry world with us, since purses and bags were invented, for now men set lime-twigs to catch wealth: and gold, which riseth like the sun out of the East Indies, to shine upon everyone, is like a cony taken napping in a purse-net, and suffers his glistering yellow-face deity to be lapped up in lambskins, as if the innocency of those leather prisons should dispense with the cheveril consciences of the iron-hearted gaolers.[2]

Dekker never manages to work up this theme into an effective play (the effect of a single play is very different from the effect of these assembled extracts); but what we have to notice is that even in giving the public what it wanted, even in praising the citizen virtues, he is far nearer to the medieval moralists than to the new economic rationalists.

Dekker's best known play—a favourite with his contemporary audience—is *The Shoemaker's Holiday*.[3] There is no doubt that its success was largely due to the way in which it appealed to the pride of the citizen-craftsman in his

[1] *Old Fortunatus* (1599), I, i (Mermaid Edition, 303).
[2] *Ibid.*, I, ii (Mermaid Edition, 307).
[3] Acted by the Admiral's Men in 1599 at the Fortune and at Court. There are extant editions dated 1600, 1610, 1618, 1624, 1631, 1657.

craft and status.[1] It called for no effort of readjustment or reorganization, but—like the long line of patriotic chronicle plays [2]—simply reinforced a prevalent social attitude. In the first place, the citizens had the pleasure of familiar recognition. Simon Eyre, celebrated by Stow as well as by Deloney, was a figure of traditional legend, and the account of the building and naming of the Leadenhall [3] appealed to the taste which produced such things as *If You Know not Me You Know Nobody, With the Building of the Royal Exchange.* Eyre's progress from master craftsman to Sheriff and finally Lord Mayor of London (not, significantly, to a house in the country) represented a dream which a good many apprentices must have cherished.[4] And Eyre's relations with his workmen are presented in the most attractive light. He drinks and jests with them, listens to their advice, and protects them from the tongue of his wife; 'By the Lord of Ludgate', he swears, 'I love my men as my life'. The relationship, although obviously idealized, had, as we have seen, a basis in fact, and its presentation would be particularly appreciated since it depicted a state of affairs that was rapidly vanishing as business became more impersonal. Moreover, the pride, the ambition, the prejudices of Eyre and his men are limited by the city. Not only does the Earl of Lincoln oppose the marriage of Lacy, his nephew, to

---

[1] Like Deloney's *Gentle Craft* (1598), on which the play is based.
[2] See below, pp. 243 ff.   [3] V, ii.
[4] Dr Robertson points out that Eyre made his fortune 'by a sharp practice of which the modern equivalent would be obtaining credit by false trade references' (*Economic Individualism*, pp. 190-191). Certainly the bargain by which Eyre gains 'full three thousand pound' (III, i, iii) is not very reputable, but there is no need to make much of it, or to connect it, as Dr Robertson does, with 'the wave of speculation' which was then affecting all classes. Dekker merely intends to show that fortune is on the side of the good-hearted tradesman; it is characteristic that he slurs over the issues without thinking very hard about them.

237

Rose, a citizen's daughter, her father the Lord Mayor 'scorns to call Lacy son-in-law',[1] and Eyre advises her:

> A courtier, wash, go by, stand not upon pishery-pashery: those silken fellows are but painted images, outsides, outsides, Rose; their inner linings are torn. No, my fine mouse, marry me with a gentleman grocer like my lord mayor, your father; a grocer is a sweet trade: plums, plums. Had I a son or daughter should marry out of the generation and blood of the shoemakers, he should pack; what, the gentle trade is a living for a man through Europe, through the world.[2]

Rose, it is true, marries Lacy in the end, but Lacy has proved himself a good fellow and has not scorned the gentle craft; besides, romance demanded it. It is the citizen's independence, however, that is most applauded. Even the surly attitude of the shoemakers when they demand the journeyman's wife, Jane, from the wealthy and inoffensive Hammon (V, ii) is presented for approval; and Eyre, though proud of his civic dignities, has none of those ambitions to step outside the limits of his order which were already providing material for the comic dramatists.

> Am I not Simon Eyre? Are not these my brave men, brave shoemakers, all gentlemen of the gentle craft? Prince am I none, yet am I nobly born.[3]

It is impossible, however, merely to dismiss Dekker by saying that *The Shoemaker's Holiday* is an appeal to prejudice (in any case its appeal was wider than my account may

---

[1] I, i (Mermaid Edition, 8).   [2] III, v (Mermaid Edition, 47).
[3] III, i (Mermaid Edition, 30). Cf. Candido's defence of the flat cap in *The Honest Whore, Part II*, I, iii (Mermaid Edition, 208):

> It is a citizen's badge, and first was worn
> By th' Romans. . . .
> Flat caps as proper are to city gowns,
> As to armours helmets, or to king's their crowns.
> Let then the city-cap by none be scorned,
> Since with it princes' heads have been adorned.

suggest) or that his work in general is a mere reflection of popular taste. What we have to ask ourselves, with the twentieth-century reading public in mind, is what that taste demanded besides easy amusement. For in spite of Dekker's feeble grasp of tradition, his narrow moral scope, his work does embody, or reflect, however fragmentarily, a decent traditional morality. I am not thinking of the stilted moralism of *The Honest Whore* but of the shrewd, caustic comments on social ambition, wealth and luxury that are scattered throughout his plays. His approval of Eyre does not prevent him from laughing at the naïve assumption of dignity by Eyre's wife,[1] and I have shown something of his attitude towards mere acquisition. But the point is best made by a comparison with a modern novel. There is no need to draw on the fiction that caters for the needs of a class corresponding to 'the original civility of the Red Bull'. The standards behind Arnold Bennett's popular *Imperial Palace* are fairly indicated by extracts such as these:

> And he liked her expensive stylishness. The sight of a really smart woman always gave him pleasure. In his restaurant, when he occasionally inspected it as a spy from a corner behind a screen, he always looked first for the fashionable, costly frocks, and the more there were the better he was pleased. . . . Only half an hour ago she had probably been steering a big car at a mile a minute on a dark curving road. And here with delicate hands she was finishing the minute renewal of her delicate face.[2]

> Gracie, stared at by a hundred eyes until she sat down, was just as much at her ease as a bride at a wedding. Created by

---

[1] III, iv (Mermaid Edition, 40 ff.). *Margery.* 'Art thou acquainted with never a farthingale-maker, nor a French hood-maker? I must enlarge my bum, ha, ha! How shall I look in a hood, I wonder? . . . It is very hot, I must get me a fan or else a mask. . . . But, Ralph, get thee in, call for some meat and drink, thou shalt find me worshipful towards thee,' etc.

[2] *The Imperial Palace*, p. 9.

heaven to be a cynosure, rightly convinced that she was the best-dressed woman in the great, glittering, humming room, her spirit floated on waves of admiration as naturally as a goldfish in water. Evelyn, impressed, watched her surreptitiously as she dropped on to the table an inlaid vanity-case which had cost her father a couple of hundred pounds. . . . Surely in the wide world that night there could not be anything to beat her! Idle, luxurious rich, but a master-piece! Maintained in splendour by the highly skilled and expensive labour of others, materially useless to society, she yet justified herself by her mere appearance. And she knew it, and her conscience was clear.[1]

Throughout the book—there is a little, uneasy, irony—the reader is invited to admire, or to accept with complacence, the monstrous material standards symbolized by a modern luxury hotel. Dekker and his audience had another set of values.

Lord, Lord, to see what good raiment doth. . . . O sweet wares! Prunes, almonds, sugar-candy, carrot-roots, turnips, O brave fatting meat![2]

Whenever Dekker dwells on luxury there is no doubt of the expected response: here, for example:

Birdlime. O the entertainment my Lord will make you. Sweet wines, lusty diet, perfumed linen, soft beds, O most fortunate gentlewoman![3]

Or here, where the devil, disguised as a novice, is told to say grace:

Prior. Stand forth, and render thanks.
Rush. Hum, hum:
For our bread, wine, ale and beer,
For the piping hot meats here:
For broths of sundry tastes and sort,

---

[1] *The Imperial Palace*, p. 81. For comment, see Q. D. Leavis, *Fiction and the Reading Public*, p. 199.
[2] *Shoemaker's Holiday*, III, i.   [3] *Westward Ho!* I, i (II, 285).

> For beef, veal, mutton, lamb, and pork:
> Green-sauce with calve's head and bacon,
> Pig and goose, and cramm'd-up capon:
> For pastries rais'd stiff with curious art,
> Pie, custard, florentine and tart.
> Bak'd rumps, fried kidneys, and lamb-stones,
> Fat sweet-breads, luscious marrowbones,
> Artichoke, and oyster pies,
> Butter'd crab, prawns, lobsters' thighs,
> Thanks be given for flesh and fishes,
> With this choice of tempting dishes:
> To which preface, with blithe looks sit ye,
> Rush bids this Convent, much good do't ye.[1]

It is not merely that Dekker, without Jonson's poise, is nevertheless insistent on 'the rotten strength of proud mortality'[2]—

> And though mine arm should conquer twenty worlds,
> There's a lean fellow beats all conquerors[3]—

he had been taught by religion, by the traditional morality, that there were other standards than those implied by 'the high standard of living' of the Imperial Palace.

And, finally, Dekker's conception of the ordered state is, in general, the traditional conception that lies behind Ulysses' speech on 'Degree',[4] on the one hand, and the acts

---

[1] *If It be not Good, the Devil is in It* (III, 281).
[2] *Old Fortunatus*, II, ii.
[3] *Ibid.*, I, i.
[4] *Troilus and Cressida*, I, iii. It is perhaps worth noticing that Dekker imitates this speech in *The Double PP, Non-Dramatic Works*, II, p. 185, on the Judge:

> The fourth that stands this quarrel, is more strong
> In scarlet than in steel: look how the moon
> Between the day, so he twixt right and wrong
> Sits equal umpire: like the orbed moon
> Empires by him swell high, or fall as soon;
> For when Law alights, uproars on foot-cloths ride. . .

of the Elizabethan Privy Council on the other. So far as one can piece together a coherent social attitude behind the plays, it is approval of a scheme in which each man has his proper place, the whole being bound together by justice. The King in *If It be not a Good Play*, planning his reign, gives first place to equity.

> That day, from morn till night, I'll execute
> The office of a judge, and weigh out laws
> With even scales. . . .
> The poor and rich man's cause
> I'll poise alike: it shall be my chief care
> That bribes and wrangling be pitch'd o'er the bar. . . .
> Tuesdays we'll sit to hear the poor man's cries,
> Orphans and widows: our own princely eyes
> Shall their petitions read: our progress then
> Shall be to hospitals which good minded men
> Have built to pious use, for lame, sick, and poor.
> We'll see what's given, what spent, and what flows o'er.
> Churls (with God's money) shall not feast, swill wine,
> And fat their rank guts whilst poor wretches pine.[1]

Dekker praises thrift, industry, and the citizen virtues, but his description of the artisan is significant:

> The rear-ward last advanced up, being led
> By the industrious, thriving Artisan:
> The ways of science needs he well must tread,
> For seven years go to make him up a man.
> And then by all the lawful steps he can,

---

[4] *Foot-note continued from p. 241:*
> The regal chair would down be thrown: religion
> Take sanctuary: no man durst be good,
> Nor could be safe being bad: confusion
> Would be held order: and (as in the Flood
> The world was covered) so would all in blood
> If Justice eyes were closed: No man sleeps, speaks,
> Nor eats but by her.

[1] (III, 274.)

> Climbs he to wealth. Enough is his he vaunts,
> If though he hoard not much, he feels not wants.[1]

The 'lawful steps' are insisted upon, and Dekker sets his face against the 'doctrineless individualism' represented by the merchant, Bartervile:

> Nature sent man into the world, alone,
> Without all company, but to care for one,
> And that I'll do.[2]

It is the devil who insists that this is 'True City doctrine, sir'.

—

The Knight of the Burning Pestle was first acted in 1607. Most of its genial ridicule was directed against the absurdities of Heywood's *Four Prentices of London*, and similar plays, which made London citizens the heroes of romantic adventures in exotic settings. But Beaumont's Citizen stands for popular taste in general:

> Why could you not be contented (he asks the speaker of the Prologue) . . . with 'The Legend of Whittington', or 'The Life and Death of Sir Thomas Gresham, with The Building of the Royal Exchange', or 'The Story of Queen Eleanor, with the rearing of London Bridge upon Woolsacks'.[3]

The class of plays indicated here was large, varied and extremely popular. It included histories, biographies, plays of adventure and of domestic life, the common element being that they all presented 'something notable in honour of the commons of the city'[4]—or of the countryside. They appealed to local, as well as to national, patriotism, and they exalted familiar types and familiar virtues. Since

[1] *The Double PP, Non-Dramatic Works*, II, p. 190.
[2] *If It be not Good, the Devil is in It* (III, 324).
[3] Induction to *The Knight of the Burning Pestle*.   [4] *Ibid.*

they formed a natural development of the chronicle plays they are best approached through these.

The increased intensity of national feeling, particularly in the years immediately before and after 1588, was accompanied by a new interest in England's past. But although the chronicle play, as such, dates from about 1580, it sprang, as Schelling points out, from a deep-rooted popular interest —something attested by the historical and familiar elements in the mystery and morality plays, the plays and ballads about Robin Hood and St. George, as well as by the chronicles of Hall, Stow, Fox, and Holinshed, and versified chronicles such as Warner's *Albion's England*.[1] The popularity of the chronicle plays reached its height in the last decade of the sixteenth century, when political circumstances made it inevitable that they should not be disinterested dramatic accounts of past times, but direct incitements to patriotic feeling, propaganda designed to make one Englishman feel that he really was as good as three Spaniards.[2]

[1] F. L. Schelling, *The English Chronicle Play*, chaps. i and ii. Schelling shows the popularity of the chronicles; Stow's *Summary*, for example, went into a tenth edition in 1604.

[2] Between 1562 (*Gorboduc*) and 1642 there is record of more than 150 chronicle plays, about half of which are extant; some eighty of them were produced in the years 1590 to 1600. *Ibid.*, p. 51. Cf. Schelling, *Elizabethan Drama*, I, pp. 251-252. Schelling refers to the 'Mystères Patriotiques', 'which the misfortunes of the Hundred Years' War caused to flourish in France', *e.g. La Mystère du siège d'Orléans, La Déconfiture de Talbot advenu en Bordelais* (1453). See G. Bapst, *Essai sur l'histoire du théâtre*, chap. iii:

'Le jour même de la délivrance de l'Orléans, le 8 mai 1429, les habitants encore tout émus de la lutte acharnée de la journée, organisèrent spontannément une grande procession, qui parcourut les principales voies de la ville, en " faisant pose" sur les places. . . . Au milieu de la procession, marchaient la Pucelle, le Bâtard, d'Orléans, plus connu sous le nom de Dunois, Gilles de Raiz et d'autres capitaines. Tous les ans, à la même date, la même cérémonie se renouvelle. . . . La municipalité fait construire sur son

In these plays the effects are simple and obvious. There is, said Puttenham, 'no one thing in the world with more delectation reviving our spirits than to behold as it were in a glass the lively image of our dear forefathers',[1] and it did not matter whether the 'dear forefathers' were the mythical sons of Brutus, King of Britain, popular figures from history such as Henry V or Sir Thomas More, or semi-historical worthies like Robin Hood, Earl of Huntingdon. The truly *Lamentable Tragedy of Locrine* (c. 1591, by Peele?) may, as Schelling thinks, have contained 'a take-off of the Senecan excesses of the moment',[2] but it is unlikely that the patriotic speeches were received as parody. The overthrow of a barbarian invading force must have been received with cheers,[3] and the proof that God is on the side of his Englishmen would certainly be acceptable.[4] 'What a glorious thing it is', said Nashe, ironically, 'to have Henry the Fifth represented on the stage leading the French king prisoner, and forcing both him and the Dauphin swear fealty'.[5] We can at least imagine the thrill with which, in the year of the Armada, the audience received the more resounding lines

parcours des tréteaux, sur lesquels on représente des pantomimes relatives aux événements du siège'.

[1] *The Art of English Poesy* (1589), *Elizabethan Critical Essays* (ed. Gregory Smith), II, p. 41.

[2] *Elizabethan Drama*, I, p. 256.

[3]
        Lo, here the harms that wait upon all those
        That do intrude themselves in other lands
        Which are not under their dominions.
                      (II, ii.)
The Britons defy Troglodytes, Æthiopians, Amazons and 'all the hosts of Barbarian lands', if these 'should dare to enter in our little world' (IV, i).

[4]
        Mighty Jove the supreme king of heaven,
        That guides the concourse of the meteors
        And rules the motions of the azure sky,
        Fights always for the Briton's safety.
                      (IV, i.)

[5] *Pierce Penilesse* (1592).

from *The Famous Victories of Henry the Fifth*,[1] or even, later, those from Shakespeare's histories.[2]

But I am not concerned with the cruder forms of patriotic propaganda, the point to notice is that the chronicle play was one of the earliest forms of drama drawing upon and reinforcing group sanctions. The historical plays were recognized as containing direct topical references, and they led naturally to such plays as *George a Green, The Pinner of Wakefield* (1588–1592), *The Shoemaker's Holiday* (1599) and Haughton's *Englishmen for my Money* (1598), pseudo-histories and biographies such as *Thomas, Lord Cromwell* (1592) and *Sir Thomas More* (*c.* 1596)—the plays, in short, of the kind that Beaumont's citizen demanded.

In plays of this kind the dramatist is concerned to stabilize or invigorate a mode of feeling that is generally considered desirable amongst the group addressed: to provide his audience with a sense of well-being that comes from seeing slightly idealized copies of themselves upon the stage. The historical and biographical plays, and the plays that had for subject national or local types, appealed in various ways. They provided information (more or less reliable), they showed picaresque adventures, and they gave opportunity for miscellaneous pageantry, devices and clowning; but all of them fostered, in some way, what Schelling calls the 'sense

[1]   Tell the French King
      That Harry of England hath sent for the crown,
      And Harry of England will have it.
                              (*Famous Victories*, Scene ix.)
[2]   This is the English, not the Turkish court;
      Not Amurath an Amurath succeeds,
      But Harry Harry.
                              (*2 Henry IV*, V, ii.)
Cf. Gaunt's eulogy of 'This happy breed of men, this little world'; the defiance of the Pope and the Bastard's final speech in *King John*; and Cranmer's prophecy in *Henry VIII*.

of community'.[1] Often the method consists of crudely
derogatory remarks about foreigners and foreign countries:

> Pigs and Frenchmen speak one language, *awee, awee*,[2]

or

> My Lord, no court with England may compare
> Neither for state nor civil government:
> Lust dwells in France, in Italy, and Spain,
> From the poor peasant to the Prince's train.
> In Germany and Holland riot serves,
> And he that most can drink, most he deserves:
> England I praise not, for I here was born,
> But that she laugheth the others unto scorn.[3]

But other effects were possible. Sometimes historical plays
provided moral instances,[4] and the plays on various worthies
held up examples of the accepted virtues of the different

---

[1] *The English Chronicle Play*, p. 5.

[2] *Englishmen for my Money* (1598, Admiral's Men), I, i. In this
play Pisario, a usurer, wishes to marry his three daughters to a
Frenchman, a Dutchman and an Italian, respectively. These, however, love three Englishmen, who have mortgaged their lands to
Pisario. These flout the foreigners, outwit them and Pisario, and
finally marry the daughters.

[3] *Thomas, Lord Cromwell* (not later than 1602, Chamberlain's
Men), III, iii. Cromwell, says Schelling, 'stands for the glorification,
the very apotheosis of citizen virtue. It is Cromwell's honourable
thrift and capacity in trade, his temperance, piety and staunch
Protestantism which are dwelt on and extolled. He befriends the
broken debtor and outwits the wrong-doer. He is mindful of others'
favours to him, forgetful of his own' (*English Chronicle Play*, p. 217).
That is as good a summary as one can make of a very bad play.

[4] The general approach to history was moral, as can be seen from
the school text-books in use at the time. Reusner's *Symbola
Heroica*, for instance, was 'a collection of character sketches . . .
treated symbolically "so as to portray from the concrete instance
some instruction, by way of example or warning, helpful towards the
inculcation of prudence, wisdom and morality"' (Foster Watson,
English Grammar Schools to 1660, chap. xxvi). And the plays were
explicit: *Gorboduc*

> A mirror shall become to princes all
> To learn to shun the cause of such a fall.

247

classes. George a Greene, the Pinner of Wakefield, for example, stands for the yeoman class 'that in times past made all France afraid',[1] and the play makes much the same kind of appeal as Deloney's *Jack of Newbery*.[2]

But it is not enough to say that 'community' plays stabilized accepted social attitudes; so does *Punch*. Most of the popular plays representing English types are bad enough as poetry and as drama; an attempt at evaluation can only be an attempt to answer the question, What sanctions are appealed to, what kind of prejudices are played upon? With this question in mind, a short study of those of Heywood's plays that fall within the category will do more than suggest a profitable approach to the class in general.

Heywood, like Dekker, was 'a typical literary Jack-of-all-trades of the epoch'.[3] Unlike Dekker he wrote at least two plays that have some life in them and do not consist of assembled parts, and the best of his verse is at least dramatically effective. But he was no poet; and to say this is to say that he was incapable of exploring, modifying or making effectively his own the morality of the age: 'his sensibility is merely that of ordinary people in ordinary life'.[4] It is this

---

[1] Harrison, *Description of England*, Book II (ed. Furnivall), p. 133.

[2] See the Dedication 'To all the famous clothworkers of England': '. . . those for whose sake I took pains to compile it, that is, for the well minded clothiers; that herein they may behold the great worship and credit which men of this trade have in former times come unto'. In *George a Green* (before 1593) the hero, after repulsing the Scots invaders, refuses knighthood at the hands of the king:

> Then let me live and die a yeoman still.
> So was my father, so must live his son.

[3] T. S. Eliot, *Elizabethan Essays*, p. 102.

[4] *Ibid.*, p. 107. Since the literary judgement is relevant to one's opinion of Heywood as a representative of popular taste it may be reinforced here. Consider the imagery of *A Woman Killed with Kindness*, for example:

indeed that gives him his significance here. Just as *A Woman Killed with Kindness* is based on conventional ethics, so his plays of London life reflect prevailing attitudes and sentiments.

The immensely popular *Edward IV* and *If You Know Not Me, You Know Nobody* are the most interesting in this connexion.[1] Each of them appeals to national and local pride.

> (*a*) My God! what have I done? what have I done?
> My rage hath plunged into a sea of blood,
> In which my soul lies drowned.
> (I, iii.)
> (*b*) A song! ha, ha: a song! as if, fond man,
> Thy eyes could swim in laughter, when thy soul
> Lies drenched and drowned in red tears of blood.
> (II, iii.)
> (*c*) Drops of cold sweat sit dangling on my hairs
> Like morning's dew upon the golden flowers.
> (III, ii.)

Where the imagery is not inept, as in (*c*), it is commonplace, as in (*a*) and (*b*); there is nothing highly charged or potently evocative. In Heywood's general dramatic technique statement takes the place of evocation: Mrs Frankford is *stated* to be the model wife, and the moral of the play is stated, not implicit; in other words Heywood's drama is sentimental rather than ethical. And sentimental drama is made by exploiting situations provided by conventional morality rather than by exploring the full significance of those situations.

Heywood's quality as moralist and journalist is brought out by his *Gynaikeion, or Nine Books of Various History Concerning Women* (1624), in which one forgets the essential purpose in working through the mixture of anecdotal, historical and moralistic fiction ('For variety of history, intermixt with discourse of times, makes the argument less tedious to the reader', as he remarks in *A Curtain Lecture* (1637), p. 49).

[1] The two parts of *Edward IV* were probably acted towards the end of the sixteenth century, and were published in editions dated 1600, 1605, 1613, 1619 and 1626. There is some dispute about the authorship, but I cannot doubt that the greater part of the play is by Heywood. *If You Know Not Me, You Know Nobody* was produced in 1605. Part I, or *The Troubles of Queen Elizabeth*, was published in 1605 (it was pirated), and reprinted in 1606, 1608, 1610, 1613, 1623,

The early part of *Edward IV* shows the siege of London by the rebel Falconbridge and his repulse by the citizens. The events are acted in familiar places:

The Mint is ours, Cheap, Lombard Street our own[1]—

and the Lord Mayor and Aldermen with their 'Velvet coats and gorgets, and leading staves', the citizens in their flat caps, 'the whole companies of Mercers, Grocers, Drapers, and the rest' are represented on the stage.[2] The rebels are finally beaten off by the true citizens and 'the prentices do great service'[3]—

> Nay, scorn us not that we are prentices.
> The Chronicles of England can report
> What memorable actions we have done,
> To which this day's achievements shall be knit,
> To make the volume larger than it is.[4]

The second part of *If You Know Not Me* makes a similar appeal to London pride, and provides the pleasure which comes from a recognition of the familiar. We see the planning, building and naming of the Royal Exchange, which is declared peerless:

> *1 Lord.* Trust me, it is the goodliest thing I have seen:
> England affords none such.
> *2 Lord.* Nor Christendom;
> I might say all the world has not his fellow.[5]

But Heywood demands the sympathy of his audience in

1632 and 1639. Part II, *With the Building of the Royal Exchange: And the Famous Victory of Queen Elizabeth, in the Year 1588*, was published in editions dated 1606, 1609, 1623 (?) and 1632. According to *Eastward Ho!* (III, ii) the actors called it 'their get-penny'.

[1] I, 26. (The references are to the volume and page of Heywood's *Dramatic Works* in the Pearson Reprints.)

[2] I, 11-13.   [3] I, 20.   [4] I, 18.

[5] I, 295. Gresham also speaks of Gresham College: 'my school of the seven learned liberal sciences' (I, 301).

more important ways than these. In the first place, we notice the faithful representation of homely wisdom.

> *King* (in disguise). Prithee tell me, how love they King
> Edward?
> *Hobs* (the Tanner of Tamworth). Faith, as poor folks love
> holidays, glad to have them now and then; but to have
> them come too often will undo them. So, to see the king
> now and then 'tis comfort; but every day would beggar us;
> and I may say to thee, we fear we shall be troubled to lend
> him money; for we doubt he's but needy.[1]
>
> *King.* King Henry is dead . . . How will the Commons take it?
> *Hobs.* Well, God be with good King Henry.
> Faith, the Commons will take it as a common thing.
> Death's an honest man; for he spares not the King.
> For as one comes, another's ta'en away;
> And seldom comes the better, that's all we say.[2]

The homeliness is significant. Heywood may appeal to prejudice, he may occasionally reinforce undesirable attitudes (as in the scene of vulgar ostentation where Gresham boasts of his wealth and drinks a priceless pearl[3]), but neither he nor any of his fellows encouraged the audience to indulge in enervating fantasy. The plays of romantic adventure, such as *The Four Prentices* and *The Fair Maid of the West*, are frankly romantic and extravagant,—fairy tales, although their characters are taken from everyday life. In Heywood's realistic plays, as in Dekker's, there is the usual insistence on the happiness of humble life:

> *King.* Farewell, John Hobs, the honest true tanner!
> I see plain men, by observation
> Of things that alter in the change of times,
> Do gather knowledge; and the meanest life
> Proportion'd with content sufficiency,
> Is merrier than the mighty state of kings.[4]

---

[1] *Edward IV*, Part I; I, 45. [2] *Ibid.*, I, 51.
[3] *The Second Part of If You Know Not Me*, I, 301.
[4] *Edward IV*, Part I; I, 47.

251

And although citizen advancement to wealth and dignity is frequently represented [1] it is almost always shown as advancement within one's order, a result of honest dealing; and it involves corresponding duties. In *Edward IV* the Lord Mayor, Sir John Crosbie, 'in his scarlet gown', tells how as a castaway he was found by a shoemaker, and later apprenticed to the Grocer's trade:

> Wherein God pleased to bless my poor endeavours,
> That, by his blessing, I am come to this.
> The man that found me I have well requited,
> And to the Hospital, my fostering place,
> An hundred pound a year I give for ever.
> Likewise, in memory of me, John Crosbie,
> In Bishopsgate Street, a poor-house have I built,
> And as my name have called it Crosbie House. [2]

Honest thrift is, of course, applauded; thus one of Gresham's factors describes his master:

> He is a merchant of good estimate:
> Care how to get, and forecast to increase,
> (If so they be accounted) be his faults.
> *Merchant*. They are especial virtues, being clear
> From avarice and base extortion. [3]

---

[1] *Lord Mayor*. And, prentices, stick to your officers,
   For you may come to be as we are now.
                                        (*Edward IV*, Part I; I, 17.)

[2] I, 57. Compare the 'increase of wealth and advancement' brought by 'honest and orderly industry' to the goldsmith's apprentice Goulding, in *Eastward Ho!* (1605). There is an obvious element of parody in this play, written by Jonson, Chapman and Marston, acted at the Blackfriars, and dedicated 'to the City'—but it shows what the citizens liked. At the Blackfriars Touchstone's tags— 'Keep thy shop and thy shop will keep thee', etc.—the sudden rise of the honest apprentice and the equally sudden repentance of the prodigal were probably not received in the same spirit as they would have been at the Fortune.

[3] *The Second Part of If You Know Not Me*, I, 251.

But descriptions of advancement are usually made the occasion for moral homilies. When the Dean of St. Paul's has reconciled the merchants, Gresham and Ramsie, he shows them portraits of London worthies and their wives, and recounts their civic fame:

> This, Ave Gibson, who in her husband's life,
> Being a Grocer, and a Sheriff of London,
> Founded a Free School at Ratcliff,
> There to instruct three score poor children;
> Built fourteen alms-houses for fourteen poor,
> Leaving for Tutors 50 pound a year,
> And quarterly for every one a noble.[1]

The merchants are moved to emulation:

> *Gresham.* And we may be ashamed,
> For in their deeds we see our own disgrace.
> We that are citizens, are rich as they were,
> Behold their charity in every street,
> Churches for prayer, alms-houses for the poor,
> Conduits which brings us water; all which good
> We do see, and are relieved withal,
> And yet we live like beasts, spend time and die,
> Leaving no good to be remembered by.[2]

The Dean replies with a little sermon obviously addressed to the audience:

> If you will follow the religious path
> That these have beat before you, you shall win Heaven.
> Even in the mid-day walks you shall not walk the street,
> But widows' orisons, lazars' prayers, orphans' thanks,
> Will fly into your ears, and with a joyful blush
> Make you thank God that you have done for them;
> When, otherwise, they'll fill your ears with curses,
> Crying, We feed on woe, you are our nurses,
> O is't not better than young couples say,
> You rais'd us up, than, You were our decay?[3]

---

[1] *Ibid.*, I, 278.   [2] I, 277.   [3] I, 278.

The charitable ideal expressed here was not, of course, by itself sufficient to meet the new economic problems of the age, of which Heywood, like Dekker, was imperfectly aware. But it represents the medieval tradition of neighbourliness, and on the few occasions that Heywood mentions specific economic diseases of the time he treats them in the same spirit. Enclosers of commons are 'greedy cormorants' [1]— the usual phrase—and usurers' claws are more cruel than those of the devil.[2] An interesting passage occurs where Edward IV offers the Tanner of Tamworth a boon:

> *King.* Hast thou no suit touching thy trade, to transport hides or sell leather only in a certain circuit; or about bark, or such like, to have letters patent?
>
> *Hobs.* By the mass and the matins, I like not those patents. Sirrah, they that have them do as the priests did in old time, buy and sell the sins of the people. So they make the King believe they mend what's amiss, and for money they make the thing worse than it is. There's another thing in too, the more is the pity . . . that one subject should have in his hand that might do good throughout the land.[3]

Economic individualism is met by arguments based on considerations of the common good. One of the petitioners of Jane Shore complains that she has forgotten his suit:

[1] *Edward IV*, Part I; I, 9.

[2]
> Thou wretch, thou miser, thou vile slave
> And drudge to money, bondman to thy wealth,
> Apprentice to a penny, thou that hoards up
> The fry of silver pence and half-pennies,
> With show of charity to give the poor,
> But put'st them to increase. . . .
> Thou that invent'st new clauses for a bond
> To cozen simple plainness: O not a dragon
> No, nor the devil's fangs are half so cruel
> As are thy claws.
> (*The Fair Maid of the Exchange*, II, 29.)

[3] I, 46.

Jane. Oh, 'tis for a licence to transport corn
From this land, and lead, to foreign realms.
I had your bill; but I have torn your bill;
And 'twere no shame, I think, to tear your ears,
That care not how you wound the commonwealth.
The poor must starve for food, to fill your purse,
And the enemy bandy bullets of our lead!
No, Master Rufford, I'll not speak for you,
Except it be to have you punished.[1]

It is not, however, in isolated instances of this kind that we find the main social significance of these plays, but in the kind of conduct that they extol. Most of them contain examples of neighbourly dealing; debts are forgiven, the poor and unfortunate are relieved.[2] 'Impersonal' economic processes, that is, are not accepted with complacency; they are seen in terms of human suffering and happiness. However bad the plays of the category we have been discussing may be, most of them fostered that 'sense of community' that was a legacy from the Middle Ages, and helped to stabilize decent social attitudes on which the greater dramatists could build.

[1] *Edward IV*, Part I; I, 83.
[2] Cf. *The Life and Death of Thomas, Lord Cromwell*, II, i, IV, ii, and IV, iv, and *The Second Part of If You Know Not Me*, I, 304-307.

CHAPTER NINE

MIDDLETON AND THE NEW SOCIAL CLASSES

THE assimilation of what is valuable in the literary past—the reminder is relevant at this point—is impossible without the ability to discriminate and to reject. Everyone would admit this, in a general way, but there are few to undertake the essential effort—the redistribution of stress, the attempt to put into currency evaluations based more firmly on living needs than are the conventional judgements. To disestablish certain reputations that have 'stood the test of time', to see to it that the epithet 'great' does not spill over from undeniable achievement to a bulk of inferior matter in the work of any one author, is not incompatible with a proper humility.

Sharp discrimination is nowhere more necessary than in the Elizabethan and post-Elizabethan period. It is not—emphatically—a minor nuisance that young men who are capable of an interest in literature should be stimulated to work up a feeling of enjoyment when reading the plays of Dekker and Heywood, or *A King and No King*. There is of course such a thing as an historical interest, but it is as well we should know when it is that we are pursuing and when we are engaged in a completely different activity. It is as well that we should realize—to come to the subject of this chapter—that our 'appreciation' of *The Changeling* is something different in kind from our 'appreciation' of *The Roaring Girl, A Trick to Catch the Old One, The Phoenix, Michaelmas Term* and all those plays which have led Mr Eliot to assert that Middleton is 'a great comic writer'.

The reference to Mr Eliot is deliberate. His essay on Middleton is, it seems to me, a good deal nearer to Lamb than Mr Eliot would care to admit. It does not of course show the exuberant idolatry of Romantic criticism, but it encourages idolatry (see the unusually generous provision of 'great's' in the final paragraphs) and—what is the same thing—inertia. Now that *The Sacred Wood* and its successors are academically 'safe' it is all the more necessary to suggest that certain of Mr Eliot's Elizabethan Essays (those, I would say, on Middleton, Marston, Heywood and Ford) are in quite a different class from, say, the essay on Massinger, and that to ignore the lapses [1] from that usually taut and distinguished critical prose is not the best way of registering respect for the critic. Middleton, then, is an interesting case—for various reasons.

As the author of *The Changeling*, perhaps the greatest tragedy of the period outside Shakespeare, Middleton deserves to be approached with respect. It is, however, as a comic writer that I wish to consider him here, and a careful re-reading of the dozen comedies by which he is remembered suggests that the conventional estimate of him—the estimate that Mr Eliot has countenanced—needs to be severely qualified.

In the first place, it is usually held that Middleton is a great realist. 'He is the most absolute realist in the Eliza-

---

[1] 'The words in which Middleton expresses his tragedy are as great as the tragedy' (*Elizabethan Essays*, p. 91). 'In poetry, in dramatic technique, *The Changeling* is inferior to the best plays of Webster. But in the moral essence of tragedy it is safe to say that in this play Middleton is surpassed by one Elizabethan alone, and that is Shakespeare' (*ibid.*, p. 93). 'There is better *poetry* in these two plays [of Marston's], both in several passages, quotable and quoted, and in the general atmosphere, than there is in the *Satires* . . .' (*ibid.*, pp. 180-181).

bethan drama, vying with the greatest of his fellows in fidelity to life'—that is the text-book account.[1] Miss Lynch remarks that, 'As the greatest realist in Elizabethan drama, Middleton is a hearty observer of life at first hand',[2] and Mr Eliot, endorsing her verdict, says: 'There is little doubt . . . that Middleton's comedy was "photographic", that it introduces us to the low life of the time far better than anything in the comedy of Shakespeare or the comedy of Jonson, better than anything except the pamphlets of Dekker and Greene and Nashe'.[3]

'Realist', of course, means many things, but what these critics are asserting is that Middleton accurately reflects the life of a certain section of Jacobean London, of gallants and shopkeepers, of lawyers, brokers, cheats and prostitutes. But, reading his comedies as carefully as we can, we find— exciting discovery!—that gallants are likely to be in debt, that they make love to citizens' wives, that lawyers are concerned more for their profits than for justice, and that cutpurses are thieves. Middleton tells us nothing at all about these *as individuals* in a particular place and period. (Turn up any of his brothel scenes—in *Your Five Gallants*, say—for examples of completely generalized conventionality: *The Honest Whore* does it better.) And the obvious reason, it seems to me, is that he was not interested in doing so.[4]

[1] Schelling, *Elizabethan Drama*, I, p. 516.

[2] Kathleen M. Lynch, *The Social Mode of Restoration Comedy*, p. 25.

[3] *Elizabethan Essays*, pp. 97, 99.

[4] An interesting test for Middleton's 'realism' is, a few weeks after reading the comedies, to attempt to recall where the various characters belong; with the exception of Moll, the Roaring Girl, not one of them can be easily allocated, and no trait, no aspect of human nature revealed by Middleton makes a permanent impression on the mind. In comparing Middleton's scenes of low life, to their advantage, with those of Shakespeare and Jonson, Mr Eliot must have completely forgotten Cade, Pompey and Mrs Overdone, Subtle, Drugger and Dapperwit, etc.

If we take *A Chaste Maid in Cheapside*, a typical comedy, neither one of Middleton's worst nor his best, we find after a second or third reading that all that remains with us is the plot. That certainly is complicated and ingenious. The only fortune of Sir Walter Whorehound, a decayed Welsh knight, lies in his expectations from his relative, the childless Lady Kix. He plans to better his fortunes by marrying Moll, the daughter of Yellowhammer, a goldsmith, and he brings to town a cast-off mistress whom he represents as an heiress and a fit match for Tim, the goldsmith's son. Moll, however, is in love with Touchwood Junior, whose lusty elder brother has had to part from his wife since he begets more children than he can maintain. In London Sir Walter visits the Allwit household, where the husband, Master Allwit (= Wittol—the joke is characteristic) is well paid to father the illegitimate children of Sir Walter and Mistress Allwit. Alarmed lest the knight's marriage should cut off his livelihood Allwit reveals the existence of Sir Walter's children to Yellowhammer, just as the news arrives that Touchwood Senior has procured an heir for Lady Kix, and Sir Walter's creditors are ready to foreclose. The true lovers are united by the well-worn device of feigning death and going to church in their coffins, and the only unfortunates are Sir Walter and Tim, now married to the Welshwoman.

I have summarized the plot since it may be evident even from this where the interest centres; it centres on the intrigue. Swinburne's praise is significant:

> The merit does not indeed consist in any new or subtle study of character, any Shakespearean creation or Jonsonian invention of humours or of men: the spendthrifts and the misers, the courtesans and the dotards, are figures borrowed from the common stock of stage tradition: it is the vivid variety of incident and intrigue, the freshness and ease and

vigour of the style, the clear straightforward energy and vivacity of the action, that the reader finds most praiseworthy.[1]

The style is certainly easy and, for its purpose, vigorous enough, but incident, intrigue and action do not make literature, nor are they capable of presenting a full-bodied, particular impression of any kind. Some of Jonson's comedies are the best of farces, but in each of them it is what is *said* that remains in the memory rather than what is *done*. *A Chaste Maid*, however, is thoroughly representative. Middleton's comedies are comedies of intrigue (in spite of the occasional professions of moral intention [2]), and they yield little more than the pleasure of a well-contrived marionette show. One need hardly say that the charge is not that they fail to present full-bodied, three dimensional 'characters' (neither does *Volpone* or *The Alchemist*), nor that they suffer from the 'invraisemblance choquante' of which M. Castelain once found Jonson guilty (the impressionistic scenes are often very good [3]), it is simply that they present neither thought, nor an emotional attitude to experience, nor vividly realized perceptions. They stake all on the

[1] Introduction to *The Best Plays of Middleton* (Mermaid Edition), p. xiii.

[2] See the plays *passim*, and compare *The Black Book*, by T. M. (probably Middleton), 1604; the dedication—'to all those that are truly virtuous, and can touch pitch and yet never defile themselves'—declares that the author will expose vices to 'sober and continent livers, who thereby may shun those two devouring gulfs, to wit, of deceit and luxury'; but the book is merely a rattling satire on the various knaves of contemporary London, a journalistic exhibition, rather than an exposure, of vice.

My description of 'intrigue comedy' applies equally to such things as *The Phoenix* and *Your Five Gallants*. These have little plot, and representatives of various vices are exposed in turn, but it is only the merry-go-round of the action that one gets interested in.

[3] E.g. *The Phoenix*, IV, i, where the lawyer, Tangle, interviews his clients to the accompaniment of 'voices within', the shouting of legal jargon in the Law Courts.

action, and that which made them successful on the stage makes them rank low as literature.

To say this is to suggest their limited usefulness as 'social documents'—and it is as social documents 'introducing us to the low life of the time' that they are often praised.   They do not embody the thought and opinion of the time, since that is irrelevant to the intrigue.   They do not seize on, clarify and explore particular aspects of the social scene, since general counters are all that the action demands. Their value in this connexion lies almost entirely in what Middleton takes for granted, in the indications provided by the situations—situations to which he thought the audience would respond sufficiently for the action to be got under way.

Indirectly, then, but only indirectly and within these limitations, Middleton does reflect some important aspects of the social scene, and we should be grateful to Miss Lynch for telling us where to look.   The background that he implicitly asks his audience to accept is a world of thriving citizens, needy gallants and landed gentlemen, and fortune-hunters of all kinds—a world that had sufficient basis in actuality to provide some theatrical verisimilitude for his thoroughly improbable plots.

His shopkeepers and merchants are all of the kind described in *The Roaring Girl*—'coached velvet caps' and 'tuftaffety jackets' who 'keep a vild swaggering in coaches now-a-days; the highways are stopt with them';[1] who have 'barns and houses yonder at Hockley-hole',[2] and throughout Surrey, Essex and the neighbouring counties.   The gallants, on the other hand,

are people most uncertain; they use great words, but little

---

[1] *The Roaring Girl* (*c*. 1610), III, i (IV, 59).—The references in brackets are to Bullen's edition of the *Works*.
[2] *Ibid.*, III, ii (IV, 71).

sense; great beards, but little wit; great breeches but no money,[1]

and most of the country gentlemen in Town are like Laxton of *The Roaring Girl*:

> All my land's sold;
> I praise heav'n for't, 't has rid me of much trouble.[2]

For all of this class a wealthy widow or a citizen's daughter is an irresistible bait, and if they cannot manage a 'good' marriage they intrigue with citizens' wives for maintenance.

The numerous kindred of Sir Walter Whorehound are all fortune hunters, and a good deal of the amusement they provided, when their intrigues were successful, must have been due to their showing the tables turned; the underlying assumption is that as a rule the city preys on the country:

> Alas, poor birds that cannot keep the sweet country, where they fly at pleasure, but must needs come to London to have their wings clipt, and are fain to go hopping home again! [3]

It is not merely that the city is the home of the usurer, or that individual merchants 'die their conscience in the blood of prodigal heirs',[4] Middleton assumes a major social movement—the transference of land from the older gentry to the citizen middle class.

> You merchants were wont to be merchant staplers; but now gentlemen have gotten up the trade, for there is not one gentleman amongst twenty but his land be engaged in twenty statutes staple.[5]

In *A Trick to Catch the Old One* (*c.* 1605?) Witgood,

---

[1] *The Family of Love* (*c.* 1604), I, iii (III, 22).
[2] *The Roaring Girl*, III, i (IV, 60).
[3] *Michaelmas Term* (1606?), III, ii (I, 279).
[4] *A Chaste Maid in Cheapside* (1611), I, ii (V, 18).
[5] *The Family of Love*, I, iii (III, 25). Compare the description of Lussurioso and Infesto in *The Phoenix*, V, i, and of Lady Goldenfleece in *No Wit, No Help Like a Woman's*, I, i.

having sunk all his 'goodly uplands and downlands . . . into that little pit, lechery', resolves to mend his fortunes. He takes a former mistress to London, introducing her to his uncle, Lucre, as a wealthy widow whom he is about to marry. The trick succeeds as only the tricks of comedy prodigals can. Lucre holds the mortgage of Witgood's lands, and to improve his nephew's prospects with the 'widow' temporarily—as he intends—hands over the papers. Hoard, another usurer and Lucre's lifelong enemy, also pays court to the widow, finally marrying her. Both Lucre and Hoard realize that they have been duped, whilst Witgood, freed from his debts, marries Hoard's niece.

The fun that Middleton gets out of this is dependent upon three assumptions. The first is that a widow reputed to have land worth £400 a year will be 'mightily followed'; [1] the second, that the gulling of usurers, lawyers and creditors is intrinsically comic; the third, that the bait of a country estate will catch any citizen.

Michaelmas Term has a similar basis of reference. Easy, a gentleman of Essex, comes to London at the beginning of the Michaelmas Term. Quomodo, a grasping woollen-draper, has seen and coveted Easy's lands, and sets one of his 'familiar spirits', Shortyard, to bring about his ruin. Easy is soon gulled; he enters into bond for the disguised Short-yard, standing surety for a supply of cloth worth less than a third of its nominal value, and finally forfeits his estate to Quomodo. The latter, however, overreaches himself. He spreads a false report of his death (so that he can enjoy the

[1] Cf. III, ii (II, 298):
Witgood. O she's mightily followed.
Lucre. And yet so little rumoured!
Witgood. Mightily: here comes one old gentleman, and he'll make her a jointure of three hundred a year, forsooth . . . here a merchant's son will possess her with no less than three goodly lordships at once, which were all pawns to his father.

spectacle of his sorrowing widow), and so prepares the way for a stage trick by which Easy both regains his estates and marries Quomodo's wife. As usual there are subordinate figures who illustrate various 'foul mysteries'.

Here too the merchants and shopkeepers form part of a flourishing economy:

> You've happened upon the money-men, sir; they and some of their brethren, I can tell you, will not stick to offer thirty thousand pound to be cursed still: great monied men, their stocks lie in the poor's throats.[1]

The source of their gains is indicated—'Gentry is the chief fish we tradesmen catch', 'We undo gentlemen daily'—and Easy, Salewood, Rearage, as their names show, belong to the class whose incomes have failed to rise in proportion to prices.

In both these plays it is the manner in which citizen ambition is presented that is significant. Hoard, rejoicing at having obtained the widow, soliloquizes:

> What a sweet blessing hast thou, Master Hoard, above a multitude! . . . Not only a wife large in possessions, but spacious in content. . . . When I wake, I think of her lands—that revives me; when I go to bed, I dream of her beauty. . . . She's worth four hundred a year in her very smock. . . . But the journey will be all, in troth, into the country; to ride to her lands in state and order following; my brother, and other worshipful gentlemen, whose companies I ha' sent down for already, to ride along with us in their goodly decorum beards, their broad velvet cassocks, and chains of gold twice or thrice double; against which time I'll entertain some ten men of mine own into liveries, all of occupations or qualities; I will not keep an idle man about me: the sight of which will so

---

[1] II, iii (I, 256). Cf. 'There's no merchant in town but will be greedy upon't [a supply of woollen cloth], and pay down money upo' th' nail; they'll despatch it over to Middleburgh presently, and raise double commodity by exchange' (*ibid.* (I, 254)).

vex my adversary Lucre—for we'll pass by his door of purpose, make a little stand for the nonce, and have our horses curvet before the window—certainly he will never endure it, but run up and hang himself presently. . . . To see ten men ride after me in watchet liveries, with orange-tawny capes,— 'twill cut his comb i' faith.[1]

Quomodo's ambition is the same as Hoard's; it is 'land, fair neat land' that he desires.

O that sweet, neat, comely, proper, delicate, parcel of land! like a fine gentlewoman i' th' waist, not so great as pretty, pretty; the trees in summer whistling, the silver waters by the banks harmoniously gliding. I should have been a scholar; an excellent place for a student; fit for my son that lately commenced at Cambridge, whom now I have placed at Inns of Court. Thus we that seldom get lands honestly, must leave our heirs to inherit our knavery. . . . Now I begin to set one foot upon the land: methinks I am felling of trees already; we shall have some Essex logs yet to keep Christmas with, and that's a comfort.[2]

Now shall I be divulg'd a landed man
Throughout the livery: one points, another whispers,
A third frets inwardly; let him fret and hang!
. . . Now come my golden days in. Whither is the worshipful Master Quomodo and his fair bed-fellow rid forth? To his land in Essex. Whence come those goodly loads of logs? From his land in Essex. Where grows this pleasant fruit, says one citizen's wife in the Row? At master Quomodo's orchard in Essex. O, O, does it so? I thank you for that good news, i' faith.[3]

A fine journey in the Whitsun holydays, i' faith, to ride down with a number of citizens and their wives, some upon pillions, some upon side-saddles, I and little Thomasine i' th' middle, our son and heir, Sim Quomodo, in a peach-colour taffeta jacket, some horse-length, or a long yard before us;— there will be a fine show on's, I can tell you.[4]

[1] *A Trick*, IV, iv (II, 322-323).
[2] *Michaelmas Term*, II, iii (I, 249-250, 260).
[3] *Ibid.*, III, iv (I, 282).   [4] *Ibid.*, IV, i (I, 299).

There is an obvious difference between the tone and manner of these soliloquies and the handling of similar themes by Jonson or Massinger, and it is this difference that places Middleton as a social dramatist. The ambition of Hoard and Quomodo is not set in the light of a positive ideal of citizen conduct (something that we find, though fitfully, in the work of Dekker and Heywood, dramatists inferior to Middleton), its implications are not grasped and presented. (Contrast the way in which we are made to feel the full significance of Volpone's lusts, of the City Madam's ambitions.) Middleton is, I think, relying on what was almost a stock response, making a gesture in the direction of a familiar scene where those goodly decorum beards wagged in real life as their owners journeyed to their newly acquired manors in the country.

To say this is to say that the attitude presented at a given point does not emerge from the interplay of different pressures *within* the drama, and that it does not engage with other elements in the reader's response to form a new whole. In each case it is a purely local effect that is obtained (it is significant that prose, not verse, is the medium), and Hoard's meditation could appear equally well in any one of half a dozen plays. Middleton's satire, in short, is related to the non-dramatic prose satire of the period; more particularly, it has affinities with the 'Character', in which the sole end proposed is the exhibition of witty 'sentences' and ingenious comparisons, of a general self-conscious dexterity.

> How many there be in the world of his fortunes, that prick their own calves with briars, to make an easy passage for others; or, like a toiling usurer, sets his son a-horseback, while he himself goes to the devil a-foot in a pair of old strossers.[1]

What a fortunate elder brother is he, whose father being a

[1] *No Wit, No Help Like a Woman's*, II, i (IV, 320).

rammish ploughman, himself a perfumed gentleman spending the labouring reek from his father's nostrils in tobacco, the sweat of his father's body in monthly physic for his pretty queasy harlot! he sows apace i' th' country; the tailor o'ertakes him i' th' city, so that oftentimes before the corn comes to earing, 'tis up to the ears in high collars, and so at every harvest the reapers take pains for the mercers: ha! why, this is stirring happiness indeed.[1]

. . . Then came they [gallants] to their gentility, and swore *as they were gentlemen*; and their gentility they swore away so fast, that they had almost sworn away all the ancient gentry out of the land; which, indeed, are scarce missed, for that yeomen and farmers' sons, with the help of a few Welshmen, have undertook to supply their places.[2]

Middleton constantly gives us such glimpses of a society in the process of rapid reorganization.[3] Most of his characters assume that social advancement is a major preoccupation of the citizen class,[4] and certainly the passages that I have quoted are amongst the most vivid in his plays; but Miss Lynch is, I think, wrong when she says that 'his comic intrigue is directed by the psychology of class relationships'.[5] That would imply a far different distribution of emphasis within the plays themselves, and a far keener penetration; for Middleton only seizes on a few external characteristics—the velvet cassocks and gold chains of the citizens galloping into the country in their holiday clothes—and these, lively as the descriptions sometimes are, are merely

[1] *The Phoenix*, I, ii (I, 112).
[2] *The Family of Love*, I, iii (III, 23).
[3] A society, too, in which there is plenty of work for lawyers. Cf. the Induction to *Michaelmas Term*.
[4] Merchants not only acquire land, they send their sons to the university to make them gentlemen,—Tim, the goldsmith's son in *A Chaste Maid in Cheapside*, and Sim, the woollen-draper's son in *Michaelmas Term*. And there are the usual gibes at the newly created knights of James I's reign.
[5] *The Social Mode of Restoration Comedy*, p. 25.

incidental to the main intention. It is possible, that is, to assemble 'evidence' of a limited kind from Middleton's plays, but it is no use looking for the more important kind of illustration of the life of the period, for the kind of fact that is inseparable from interpretation and criticism of the fact. The isolated passages are not, in fact, unified by a dominant attitude, and one can only regret that the profound understanding of an essential human morality that one finds in *The Changeling* is nowhere displayed in the comedies.[1]

That Middleton was a 'transitional' writer, not merely because he reflected social change, a single comparison may show. If we read, first, Jonson's satire on 'the godly brethren' in *The Alchemist*,[2] then Dryden's description of Shimei, we shall be in a position to judge the quality of Middleton's satire on 'puritan' hypocrisy.

> *Dryfat.* I do love to stand to anything I do, though I lose by it: in truth, I deal but too truly for this world. You shall hear how far I am entered in the right way already. First, I live in charity, and give small alms to such as be not of the right sect; I take under twenty i' th' hundred, nor no forfeiture of bonds unless the law tell my conscience I may do't; I set no pot on a' Sundays, but feed on cold meat drest a' Saturdays; I keep no holydays nor fasts, but eat most flesh o' Fridays of all days i' th' week; I do use to say inspired graces, able to starve a wicked man with length; I have Aminadabs and Abrahams to my godsons, and I chide them when they ask me blessing: and I do hate the red letter more than I follow the written verity.[3]

[1] Mr Eliot thinks that *The Roaring Girl* 'more than any Elizabethan comedy realizes a free and noble womanhood', and that Moll herself 'remains a type of the sort of woman who has renounced all happiness for herself and who lives only for a principle'. These are claims which seem to demand some evidence or explanation, but Mr Eliot points to nothing in the play that might justify them.

[2] *The Alchemist*, III, i, ii.

[3] *The Family of Love*, III, iii (III, 59).

The Middleton passage is good fooling, but it has neither the drive and assurance of Jonson, on the one hand, nor of Dryden on the other.   I have tried to indicate the source of Jonson's power; he is able to enlist the common interests of a heterogeneous audience, and to build on common attitudes; in the satire directed against Ananias the idiom and the method of caricature are alike 'popular'.   Dryden provides an obvious contrast.   The tone of the Shimei passage is one of cool superiority, and the manner is, characteristically, urbane.   Dryden, that is, is sure of his code; it is the code of a homogeneous, though limited, society—'the Town'.   Middleton has neither of these sources of strength. At times he betrays something like a positive animus against the citizens,[1] but he has nothing to set against their standards, neither an aristocratic code nor a popular tradition.   That he was an almost exact contemporary of Jonson warns us against a rigid interpretation of any period, and suggests the limits to which an enquiry into the effects of environment on personality can be profitably pursued.   And we should do well, I think, to reserve the description 'great comedy' for plays of the quality of *Volpone* and *The Alchemist*—when we can find them.

[1] See especially *A Chaste Maid in Cheapside*, III, ii, where the gathering of city wives for a christening is presented with an imperfectly controlled disgust.   I am convinced that Act IV, scene ii of *The Roaring Girl*, exhibiting honest citizen virtues, is by Dekker.

CHAPTER TEN

THE SIGNIFICANCE OF MASSINGER'S SOCIAL COMEDIES

WITH A NOTE ON 'DECADENCE'

THE first symptom of decadence that we notice in Massinger is his dependence on Shakespeare. Canon Cruickshank gives a close-packed page to 'a few examples of the imitation of incidents', and over seven pages to 'parallels in thought and diction'.[1] The nature of this indebtedness is discussed by Mr Eliot, who concludes that,

> Massinger's feeling for language had outstripped his feeling for things; that his eye and his vocabulary were not in co-operation. . . . Every vital development in language is a development of feeling as well. The verse of Shakespeare and the major Shakespearian dramatists is an innovation of this kind, a true mutation of species. The verse practised by Massinger is a different verse from that of his predecessors; but it is not a development based on, or resulting from, a new way of feeling. On the contrary it seems to lead us away from feeling altogether.[2]

Massinger not only imitates Shakespeare, he repeats his imitations and he repeats himself. There is not only dilution, there is a tendency towards stereotyped feelings and perceptions. And besides the influence of Shakespeare there is the influence of Jonson, most potent in *The City Madam*.
      In by-corners of
This sacred room, silver in bags, heap'd up

[1] A. H. Cruickshank, *Philip Massinger*, pp. 77-81, 163-168.
[2] *Elizabethan Essays*, pp. 159-160.

Like billets saw'd and ready for the fire,
Unworthy to hold fellowship with bright gold
That flow'd about the room, conceal'd itself.
There needs no artificial light; the splendour
Makes a perpetual day there, night and darkness
By that still-burning lamp for ever banish'd!
But when, guided by that, my eyes had made
Discovery of the caskets, and they open'd,
Each sparkling diamond from itself shot forth
A pyramid of flames, and in the roof
Fix'd it a glorious star, and made the place
Heaven's abstract, or epitome!—rubies, sapphires,
And ropes of orient pearl, these seen, I could not
But look on with contempt. And yet I found
What weak credulity could have no faith in,
A treasure far exceeding these: here lay
A manor bound fast in a skin of parchment,
The wax continuing hard, the acres melting;
Here a sure deed of gift for a market-town,
If not redeem'd this day, which is not in
The unthrift's power: there being scarce one shire
In Wales or England, where my monies are not
Lent out at usury, the certain hook
To draw in more. I am sublimed! gross earth
Supports me not; I walk on air.[1]

There is no need to quote Volpone's address to his gold;[2] it is clear where the central inspiration comes from. There is, besides, a minor borrowing from *Epicoene*,[3] and the speech ends with a reminiscence of *Sejanus*.[4] The play reveals other direct borrowings,[5] but what this speech shows

[1] *The City Madam*, III, iii (Gifford's edition of the *Plays*, IV, 65).
[2] *Volpone*, I, i.
[3] *Epicoene*, II, i ('she feels not how the land drops away, nor the acres melt').
[4] 'My roof receives me not; 'tis air I tread' (*Sejanus*, V, i).
[5] *E.g.*   And when you appear
            Like Juno in full majesty, and my nieces
            Like Iris, Hebe, or what deities else

also is that Massinger is not a mere unconscious plagiarist. The passage has a life of its own, and it forms a genuinely original variation on the Jonsonian mode. Much more could be said about Massinger's verse. It is capable of sudden vividness—

> Think of the basket, wretches,
> And a coal-sack for a winding-sheet,[1]

and it is almost always a serviceable dramatic medium. It is, however, 'the nearest approach to the language of real life at all compatible with a fixed metre',[2] and its virtues—perspicuity and a freedom from 'poeticisms'—too easily become vices.

> Now to you we'll discover
> The close design that brought us, with assurance,
> If you lend your aids to furnish us with that
> Which in the colony was not to be purchased,
> No merchant ever made such a return
> For his most precious venture, as you shall
> Receive from us.[3]

This is not verse at all, and passages of this kind reinforce Mr Eliot's verdict that 'if Massinger's age, "without being exactly corrupt, lacks moral fibre", Massinger's verse, without being exactly corrupt, suffers from cerebral anaemia'[4]—

> Old poets fancy, (your cramm'd wardrobes richer
> Than various natures,) and draw down the envy
> Of our western world upon you
> > (III, ii (IV, 63).)

Cf. *Volpone*, III, vi (to Celia) and, more particularly, *The Alchemist*, IV, i ('Thy wardrobe Richer than nature's', etc.). Cf. 'A perpetuity of being'—*City Madam*, V, iii (IV, 108)—and 'a perpetuity of life and lust'—*The Alchemist*, IV, i. (Repeated as 'A perpetuity of pride and pleasure' in *The Bondman*, I, iii.)

[1] *The City Madam*, IV, iii (IV, 86). The basket is the basket of food provided by charity for the poorest prisoners.
[2] Coleridge, *Lectures on Shakespeare* (Bohn Edition), p. 404.
[3] *The City Madam*, V, i (IV, 95).
[4] *Elizabethan Essays*, p. 162.

though one has to add that it is far from being consistently anaemic.

Comment of this kind was a necessary preliminary to a consideration of Massinger's handling of social themes in his two admirable comedies, *A New Way to Pay Old Debts* and *The City Madam*. Here, as the verse tells us to expect, we find that Massinger is derivative, but not, like Shirley, entirely dependent upon a literary common-stock. His themes are drawn from the Jonsonian field, he breaks no fresh ground, and his manner of approach and presentation is obviously dependent upon Jonson's. But each of the plays lives; neither is a mere *repetition* of work that had been done better. That is to say that there is fresh perception of a contemporary world, and the treatment shows that the tradition on which Jonson drew is active in Massinger, not a matter of inert convention.

In *A New Way to Pay Old Debts* (1621) Wellborn, ruined by his own prodigality and by the extortion of his uncle, Sir Giles Overreach, persuades Lady Allworth, whose late husband he had once helped in similar circumstances, to countenance a plot, and she allows it to be understood that he is about to marry her. His credit immediately rises; to those who had turned on him in his degradation he is now 'worthy Master Wellborn'. Even Sir Giles insists on lending him a thousand pounds and protests his affection—while plotting to gain his lands when he shall have married the widow. Meanwhile Sir Giles has planned to marry his daughter, Margaret, to Lord Lovell, whose page, Tom Allworth, is in love with the girl. Lord Lovell helps the lovers, and Tom, instead of his lord, is secretly married to Margaret. By this time Overreach has been deprived of the lands extorted from Wellborn and the double disappointment drives him mad. Lord Lovell

273

marries the widow, and Wellborn, determined to regain his reputation as well as his estate, goes abroad to fight in the wars.

The relationship between this play and Middleton's *A Trick to Catch the Old One* has been made too much of. Massinger borrows the central device of the plot—the hero's supposed engagement to a rich widow—but the scope and method are entirely different from Middleton's. In his comedies Middleton's inspiration derives from nothing more profound than the desire to make a play; Massinger does at least feel indignation at a contemporary enormity. It is commonly recognized that Sir Giles Overreach— 'Cormorant Overreach'[1]—is Sir Giles Mompesson. The play was produced shortly after his impeachment,[2] and the Christian name was probably sufficient indication for the first audience. As Gifford points out, Massinger refers to Mompesson's gold and silver thread monopoly in *The Bondman* (II, iii—1623).

> Here's another,
> Observe but what a cozening look he has!
> Hold up thy head, man; if, for drawing gallants
> Into mortgages for commodities, cheating heirs
> *With your new counterfeit gold thread*, and gumm'd velvets,
> He does not transcend all that went before him,
> *Call in his patent.*

Overreach, moreover, like Mompesson, has power over tavern keepers:

> For, from the tavern to the taphouse, all,
> On forfeiture of their licences, stand bound

---

[1] *A New Way*, I, i (III, 488). See p. 84 and note, above.

[2] Schelling says that 'the play was certainly on the stage by 1625', and quotes Fleay's opinion that the first performance took place in 1622 (*Elizabethan Drama*, II, p. 253). The Shakespeare Association's *Chart of Plays* (ed. W. P. Barrett), p. 38, places it in 1621, the year of the impeachment.

Ne'er to remember who their best guests were,
If they grow poor,[1]

and Tapwell and Froth are represented as creatures of Sir Giles. Mompesson, it will be remembered, issued licences solely with an eye to his profit, ignoring his functions as a guardian of public order.[2]

But just as Dryden's Achitophel stands independently of

---

[1] I, i (III, 485).

[2] Gifford gives a quotation from Wilson's *Life and Reign of James I* (Fol. 155), which may be reproduced here:

'They [Mompesson and Michell] found out a new alchemistical way to make gold and silver lace with copper and other sophistical materials, to cozen and deceive the people. And so poisonous were the drugs that made up this deceitful composition, that they rotted the hands and arms, and brought lameness upon those that wrought it; some losing their eyes, and many their lives, by the venom of the vapours that came from it. . . . Sir Giles Mompesson had fortune enough in the country to make him happy, if that sphere could have contained him, but the vulgar and universal error of satiety with present enjoyments, made him too big for a rustical condition, and when he came at court he was too little for that, so that some novelty must be taken up to set him in *aequilibrio* to the place he was in, no matter what it was, let it be never so pestilent and mischievous to others, he cared not, so he found benefit by it. To him Michell is made compartner; a poor sneaking justice, that lived among the brothels near Clarton-well, whose clerk and he picked a livelihood out of those corners, giving warrants for what they did, besides anniversary stipends (the frequent revenue of some justices of those times) for conniving. This thing was a poisonous plant in its own nature, and the fitter to be an ingredient to such a composition—whereby he took liberty to be more ravenous upon poor people, to the grating of the bones, and sucking out the very marrow of their substance.'

'From this apposite extract', says Gifford, 'it will be sufficiently apparent not only from whence Massinger derived his principal character, but also where he found Marrall and Greedy. The "sneaking justice", Michell, undoubtedly sat for the latter, and his clerk for the "term-driving" Marrall; whose hopeful education will now enable the reader to account for his knowledge of the "minerals, which he incorporated with the ink and wax" of Wellborn's bond' (III, pp. 505-506).

the historic Shaftesbury, so Overreach is very much more than a portrait of a living person. *A New Way to Pay Old Debts* is a play—something made, not a mirror of persons and events. Overreach is created, though not quite consistently, on Jonsonian lines.

> *Marrall.*　　　　I wonder,
> Still with your license, why, your worship having
> The power to put this thin-gut in commission,
> You are not in't yourself?
> *Overreach.*　　　　Thou art a fool:
> In being out of office I am out of danger;
> Where, if I were a justice, besides the trouble,
> I might or out of wilfulness, or error,
> Run myself finely into a praemunire,
> And so become a prey to the informer.
> No, I'll have none of't; 'tis enough I keep
> Greedy at my devotion: so he serve
> My purposes, let him hang, or damn, I care not;
> Friendship is but a word.[1]

Those lines are spoken by a descendant of Barabas; other passages clearly relate Overreach to Volpone and Sir Epicure Mammon,[2] though as each example shows, Massinger is a creator inspired by his predecessors, not a mere imitator.

---

[1] II, i (III, 503-504). Mr Eliot has pointed out the inconsistencies in the mode in which Overreach is presented. Massinger, that is, has not Jonson's complete sureness of purpose. A minor example is provided by the Justice, Greedy; he is admirably comic, but he has no part in the main design, as Jonson's minor figures have, and his exhibition of greed tends to become merely extraneous fooling.

[2] *E.g.* Spare for no cost; let my dressers crack with the weight
　　　Of curious viands. . . .
　　　And let no plate be seen but what's pure gold,
　　　Or such whose workmanship exceeds the matter
　　　That it is made of; let my choicest linen
　　　Perfume the room, and, when we wash, the water,

Throughout the play there is a sure grasp of the actual. Massinger, that is, observes the significant economic activities of the time, and sees their significance.[1]

Marrall. What course take you,
    With your good patience, to hedge in the manor
    Of your neighbour, master Frugal? as 'tis said
    He will nor sell, nor borrow, nor exchange;
    And his land lying in the midst of your many lordships
    Is a foul blemish.
Overreach. I have thought on't, Marrall,
    And it shall take. I must have all men sellers,
    And I the only purchaser. . . .
    I'll therefore buy some cottage near his manor,
    Which done, I'll make my men break ope his fences,
    Ride o'er his standing corn, and in the night
    Set fire on his barns, or break his cattle's legs:
    These trespasses draw on suits, and suits expenses,
    Which I can spare, but soon will beggar him.
    When I have harried him thus two or three year,
    Though he sue *in forma pauperis*, in spite
    Of all his thrift and care, he'll grow behind hand. . . .
    Then, with the favour of my man of law,
    I will pretend some title: want will force him
    To put it to arbitrement; then, if he sell
    For half the value, he shall have ready money,
    And I possess his land.[2]

Elsewhere Overreach describes himself as

Extortioner, tyrant, cormorant, or intruder

> With precious powders mix'd, so please my lord,
> That he may with envy wish to bathe so ever.
>   (III, ii (III, 529-530).)

—A good example of the poetic force that is generated by Massinger's carefully managed, cumulative constructions.

[1] Cf. The Projector scenes in *The Emperor of the East*, and Timoleon's speeches to the senate in *The Bondman*, I, iii. Massinger also had keener *political* interests than most of his fellows. Cf. S. R. Gardiner, 'The Political Element in Massinger', *The Contemporary Review*, August 1876.   [2] II, i (III, 504-506).

> On my poor neighbour's right, or grand encloser
> Of what was common, to my private use,[1]

and his relationship with Greedy typifies the power of
money over justice.[2]   The reflection (if we call it that) is of
course magnified—

> To have a usurer that starves himself. . . .
> To grow rich, and then purchase, is too common:
> But this Sir Giles feeds high, keeps many servants,
> Who must at his command do any outrage;
> Rich in his habit, vast in his expenses;
> Yet he to admiration still increases
> In wealth and lordships. . . .
> . . . No man dares reprove him.
> Such a spirit to dare, and power to do, were never
> Lodged so unluckily [3]

—but Overreach certainly represents the new aristocracy of
wealth.   It is not merely that he plans to marry his daughter
to a lord, so that she may 'write honourable, right honourable' and have the wives 'of errant knights' to tie her shoes—
in spite of the

> strange antipathy
> Between us and true gentry [4]

—he is also conscious of his own social power:

[1] IV, i (III, 553).

[2]
. . . And yet
The chapfall'n justice did his part, returning,
For your advantage, the certificate,
Against his conscience, and his knowledge too,
With your good favour, to the utter ruin
Of the poor farmer.

(II, i (III, 503).)

He frights men out of their estates,
And breaks through all law-nets, made to curb ill men,
As they were cobwebs.

(II, ii (III, 517).)

[3] II, ii (III, 517).   [4] II, i (III, 508).

> In birth! why art thou not my daughter,
> The blest child of my industry and wealth?
>
> .   .   .   .   .
>
> Be thou no enemy to thyself; my wealth
> Shall weigh his titles down, and make you equals.[1]

But more goes to the making of Overreach than typical traits. I do not think it is too much to say that he represents the traditional figure of Avarice—one of the Seven Deadly Sins. He is explicitly anti-Christian:

> I would be worldly wise; for the other wisdom
> That does prescribe us a well-govern'd life,
> And to do right to others, as ourselves,
> I value not an atom.[2]

He instructs his daughter, Margaret,

> Learn any thing,
> And from any creature that may make thee great;
> From the devil himself,[3]

and her reply, 'This is but devilish doctrine', both echoes Welborn's retort to Marrall, 'Thy religion! The devil's creed!'[4] and foreshadows the 'atheistical assertions' that Overreach makes to Lord Lovell when he expects the latter to become his son-in-law:

> Then rest secure; not the hate of all mankind here,
> Nor fear of what can fall on me hereafter,
> Shall make me study aught but your advancement
> One story higher: an earl! if gold can do it.
> Dispute not my religion, nor my faith;
> Though I am born thus headlong by my will,
> You may make choice of what belief you please,
> To me they are equal.[5]

It would be foolish to make too much of isolated passages of this kind, but they help to bring out the theological-moral

---

[1] III, ii (III, 532-534). [2] II, i (III, 504).
[3] III, ii (III, 535).   [4] II, i (III, 509).   [5] IV, i (III, 553-554).

aspect of a scene such as that where Marrall—following the instructions of Overreach, 'this blasphemous beast'[1]—attempts to drive Wellborn 'to despair'.[2] 'Despair' had fairly definite religious connotations, and when Marrall fails to persuade Wellborn to hang himself—

> Will you stay till you die in a ditch, or lice devour you?
> . . . If you like not hanging, drown yourself; take some course
> For your reputation,

the religious theme is made explicit:

> 'Twill not do, dear tempter,
> With all the rhetoric the fiend hath taught you.
> I am as far as thou art from despair.[3]

A New Way to Pay Old Debts is a comedy, not a morality play, but that it is so much more than mere amusement is largely due to the way in which Massinger has drawn on and made his own the traditional attitude towards avarice and worldly ambition.

In *The City Madam*[4] the traditional social morality is even more potently present. The intrigue is of much less importance than that of *A New Way*; the whole effect lies in the presentation of two major social themes.

The wife and two daughters of Sir John Frugal, a City merchant, ape the manners of Court, and their stupid haughtiness drives away two suitors. Sir John's younger

[1] IV, i (III, 554).
[2] The second half of II, i—

> Do anything to work him to despair,
> And 'tis thy masterpiece.

Miss Bradbrook has pointed out the references to religious 'despair' in *The Duchess of Malfi.—Themes and Conventions of Elizabethan Tragedy*, pp. 195-212.   [3] II, i (III, 510).
[4] Licensed in 1632, but probably first produced some considerable time before that date, perhaps as early as 1619.

brother, Luke, after a career of dissipation, lives in the house as a humble pensioner—a model of patience and piety. Sir John, wishing to test his brother, and tired of his wife's extravagance, leaves his home, giving out that he is retiring to a monastery abroad and that his estate is to be managed by Luke. The women receive the news complacently since Luke ironically promises to increase their splendours. Then follows an exhibition of 'miserly grasping'. Luke humbles the City Madams, attempts to ruin two apprentices whom he had previously encouraged in extravagance and dishonesty, and shows no mercy to his debtors. Finally he bargains with three 'Indians', agreeing to ship Lady Frugal and her daughters to Virginia as human sacrifices in return for 'a mine of gold'. The Indians, of course, are Sir John and the two suitors in disguise; Luke's villainy is unmasked, and the women are reclaimed from their folly.

The impossibilities of the plot can be disregarded. The self-made Sir John is a representative member of the thriving merchant class. In the first scene we learn that he has made 500 per cent. profit on a single voyage, that he is buying up manors in the country, and that one of his daughters is to marry the son of Lord Lacy.[1] Lord Lacy stands for the older aristocracy; his land is mortgaged to Sir John,[2] and he

> needs my master's money
> As his [Sir John's] daughter does his honour.[3]

Indeed, throughout the play, there is sufficient verisimilitude in the general setting to link the 'improbable fiction' to a contemporary world. What is more important, the emotions dealt with are real emotions.

---

[1] I, i (IV, 5-8).
[2] *Luke.* I find in my counting-house a manor pawn'd,
　　Pawn'd, my good lord; Lacy manor, and that manor
　　From which you have the title of a lord.
　　　　　　　　　　　　　　　　　　　　(V, ii (IV, 105).)
[3] I, i (IV, 8).

The theme that gives the title to the play is similar to that of *Eastward Ho!* (1605). Like Gertrude in that play the City Madam and her daughters 'must be ladified forsooth, and be attir'd just to the court-cut and long tail'.[1] In the first scene one apprentice tells another:

The want of one [male heir],
Swells my young mistresses, and their madam-mother,
With hopes above their birth, and scale: their dreams are
Of being made countesses, and they take state
As they were such already. When you went
To the Indies, there was some shape and proportion
Of a merchant's house in our family; but since
My master, to gain precedency for my mistress
Above some elder merchants' wives, was knighted,
'Tis grown a little court in bravery,
Variety of fashions, and those rich ones:
There are few ladies going to a mask
That do outshine ours in their every-day habits.[2]

This short speech not only shows Massinger's variations on the Jonsonian mode, it suggests the standards by which the City Madam is judged ('hopes above their birth and scale', 'shape and proportion', 'bravery'). Throughout the play the women exhibit a purely material ambition, scaring away the suitors by their extravagant demands for an idle and undisputed luxury after marriage. But the worthlessness of that ambition is best exposed by Luke when, becoming for the occasion 'a new satirist'—significantly—'to scourge a general vice', he denounces Lady Frugal:

Your father was
An honest country farmer, goodman Humble,
By his neighbours ne'er called Master. Did your pride
Descend from him? but let that pass: your fortune,
Or rather your husband's industry, advanced you
To the rank of a merchant's wife. He made a knight,
And your sweet mistress-ship ladyfied, you wore

---

[1] *Eastward Ho!* I, i.   [2] *City Madam*, I, i (IV, 6).

Satin on solemn days, a chain of gold,
A velvet hood, rich borders, and sometimes
A dainty miniver cap, a silver pin
Headed with a pearl worth three-pence, and thus far
You were privileged, and no man envied it;
It being for the city's honour that
There should be a distinction between
The wife of a patrician, and plebeian. . . .
     . . . But when the height
And dignity of London's blessings grew
Contemptible, and the name lady mayoress
Became a by-word, and you scorn'd the means
By which you were raised, my brother's fond indulgence,
Giving the reins to it; and no object pleased you
But the glittering pomp and bravery of the court;
What a strange, nay monstrous, metamorphosis follow'd!
No English workman then could please your fancy,
The French and Tuscan dress your whole discourse;
This bawd to prodigality entertain'd
To buzz into your ears what shape this countess
Appear'd in the last mask, and how it drew
The young lord's eyes upon her; and this usher
Succeeded in the eldest prentice' place
To walk before you. . . .
The reverend hood cast off, your borrow'd hair,
Powder'd and curl'd, was by your dresser's art
Form'd like a coronet, hang'd with diamonds,
And the richest orient pearl. . . .
Great lords and ladies feasted to survey
Embroider'd petticoats; and sickness feign'd
That your night-rails of forty pounds a piece
Might be seen with envy of the visitants.
     . . . You were served in plate,
Stirr'd not a foot without your coach, and going
To church, not for devotion, but to shew
Your pomp, you were tickled when the beggars cried,
Heaven save your honour! this idolatry
Paid to a painted room.[1]

       [1] IV, iv (IV, 90-93).

As I have indicated, in the presentation of this theme there are implicit standards of judgement. The most obvious is the conception of decorum, of degree, which was then almost universally accepted,[1] and which had provided the authors of *Eastward Ho!* with the platitudinous moralizing of Mildred, the goldsmith's 'good' daughter, who opposed the social ambitions of her sister, engaged to Sir Petronel Flash.

Where ambition of place goes before fitness of birth, contempt and disgrace follow. I heard a scholar once say that Ulysses, when he counterfeited himself mad, yoked cats and foxes and dogs together to draw his plough, whilst he followed and sowed salt; but sure I judge them truly mad, that yoke citizens and courtiers, tradesmen and soldiers, a goldsmith's daughter and a knight.[2]

I had rather make up the garment of my affections in some of the same piece, than, like a fool, wear gowns of two colours, or mix sackcloth with satin. . . . These hasty advancements are not natural. Nature hath given us legs to go to our objects; not wings to fly to them.[3]

In *The City Madam* the women do not observe decorum:

> A fit decorum must be kept, the court
> Distinguish'd from the city.[4]

---

[1] See pp. 144–148, above.   [2] *Eastward Ho!* I, ii.

[3] *Ibid.*, II, i. I have said that there is obvious burlesque in this story of the prodigal and the good apprentice and of the ambitious and the dutiful daughter—written by Marston, Chapman and Jonson for the Blackfriars, not by Dekker for the Fortune. (Cf. Touchstone's 'thrifty sentences', I, i; Goulding's sudden promotion to civic dignity, III, ii; Quicksilver's no less sudden and edifying repentance in the last act, etc.) But the play is not entirely parody. In any case it provides 'evidence' of the current notions of citizen propriety; the burlesque is not directed against these but against their easy exploitation for stage purposes—and the ambitious daughter is the chief butt.

[4] *City Madam*, III, ii (IV, 62).

Luke's satire is meant to 'cry up this *decency* and neatness', and to provide

> examples for our proud city dames,
> And their proud brood to imitate.[1]

The play closes with Sir John's exhortation:

> Make you good
> Your promised reformation, and instruct
> Our city dames, whom wealth makes proud, to move
> In their own spheres; and willingly to confess,
> In their habits, manners, and their highest port,
> A distance 'twixt the city and the court.[2]

But the theme, as presented, is based on a finer human code than this; if it were merely an argument in favour of sumptuary legislation we should not find it interesting and important to-day. The conception of a 'proper sphere' is allied with—is part of—a Jonsonian sense of limitations, something founded on religion, common sense and decency. The vanity that accompanies Lady Frugal's ambition is perennial:

> Why should you talk of years? Time hath not ploughed
> One furrow in your face; and were you not known
> The mother of my young ladies, you might pass
> For a virgin of fifteen.[3]

So is her superstition.[4] But the implicit condemnation is

---

[1] IV, iv (IV, 90).   [2] V, iii (IV, 114).   [3] I, i (IV, 10).
[4] Cf. her dealings with Stargaze:

> —parcel physician,
> And as such prescribes my diet, and foretells
> My dreams when I eat potatoes; parcel poet,
> And sings encomiums to my virtues sweetly;
> My antecedent, or my gentleman-usher,
> . . . an absolute master
> In the calculation of nativities;
> Guided by that ne'er-erring science call'd
> Judicial astrology
>
> (II, ii (IV, 36-37).)

285

sharpest in Mary's objection to ordinary household duties:

Mary. And can you, in your wisdom,
   Or rustic simplicity, imagine
   You have met some innocent country girl, that never
   Look'd further than her father's farm, nor knew more
   Than the price of corn in the market; or at what rate
   Beef went a stone? that would survey your dairy,
   And bring in mutton out of cheese and butter?
   That could give directions at what time of the moon
   To cut her cocks for capons against Christmas,
   Or when to raise up goslings?
Plenty. These are arts
   Would not misbecome you, though you should put in
   Obedience and duty [1]

[1] II, ii (IV, 41-42). That these 'arts' were not considered beneath the dignity of a born lady is clear from the records of the Verney family, from Smyth's description of Lady Anne Berkeley (p. 112, note 2, above), and from any contemporary book of household management.

The moralists, echoing common opinion, are all emphatic on this point. Thus Becon: 'Let them [wives] be no delicate minions, nor no white-fingered housewives, which can do nothing else but trick up themselves like puppets, and prick upon a clout without any gain, swift to command, but ready to do nothing, except it be to eat and drink, to keep company with some he-saint, to play at the dice and cards, to dance, to play upon a lute . . . but rather let them be such as will lay their hands to work, help to get the penny, save such things as the man bringeth in, dress meat and drink, spin and card, look to her family, nurse her own children, suffer nothing to perish, and in fine, even such one as Soloman describeth in the thirty-first chapter of his Proverbs.' Becon (*d. c.* 1570), *A New Catechism, Works,* II, p. 356. The popular Barnabe Rich describes the marks of a virtuous woman: 'She seeketh wool and flax, and laboureth, she putteth her hands to the wheel. . . . Soloman pointed her a housework it should seem, she must not be a gadder about the streets but a Home house-wife. And although her degree be such that she putteth not herself to bodily labour, yet she over seeth the ways of her household, she must see to her children, her servants and her family. . . . A dishonest woman is hardly kept within her own house, but she must be a-ramping, and a-roistering about to make herself known' (*The Excellency of Good Women* (1613), pp. 23-24).

and in the presentation of Anne's petty, egocentric vanities:

> *Sir Maurice.* Is there aught else
>   To be demanded?
> *Anne.* Yes, sir, mine our doctor,
>   French and Italian cooks, musicians, songsters,
>   And a chaplain that must preach to please my fancy:
>   A friend at court to place me at a mask;
>   The private box ta'en up at a new play,
>   For me and my retinue; a fresh habit,
>   Of a fashion never seen before, to draw
>   The gallants' eyes, that sit on the stage, upon me;
>   Some decayed lady for my parasite,
>   To flatter me, and rail at other madams;
>   And there ends my ambition.[1]

Direct observation of this kind merges into a Jonsonian mode in which the essential impulses are isolated and magnified.

> *Luke*   You are wide,
>   Wide the whole region, in what I purpose.
>   Since all the titles, honours, long descents,
>   Borrow their gloss from wealth, the rich with reason
>   May challenge their prerogatives: and it shall be
>   My glory, nay a triumph, to revive,
>   In the pomp that these shall shine, the memory
>   Of the Roman matrons, who kept captive queens
>   To be their handmaids.   And when you appear
>   Like Juno in full majesty, and my nieces
>   Like Iris, Hebe, or what deities else
>   Old poets fancy, (your cramm'd wardrobes richer
>   Than various nature's,) and draw down the envy
>   Of our western world upon you; only hold me
>   Your vigilant Hermes with aerial wings,
>   (My caduceus, my strong zeal to serve you,)
>   Prest to fetch in all rarities may delight you,
>   And I am made immortal.[2]

The dramatic heightening of Luke's promise to the women (it doesn't matter that it is a false promise) is followed by the

[1] II, ii (IV, 40).   [2] III, ii (IV, 63).

magnificent impressionism of the forty lines in which Lady
Frugal, Anne and Mary are rapt into a dream of greatness.

> *Lord Lacy.* Are we all turned statues? have his strange words
> charm'd us? What muse you on, lady?
> *L. Frugal.* Do not trouble me.
> *Lord Lacy.* Sleep you too, young ones?
> *Anne.* Swift-wing'd time till now
> Was never tedious to me. Would 'twere night!
> *Mary.* Nay, morning rather.
> *Lord Lacy.* Can you ground your faith,
> On such impossibilities? have you so soon
> Forgot your good husband?
> *L. Frugal.* He was a vanity
> I must no more remember.[1]

But 'impressionism' is not the word; we can see and hear
the women in their day-dream, and Luke's speech only
serves to underline the author's attitude towards the more
'normal' ambitions of the City Madam and her daughters
that have already been illustrated.

Luke Frugal in his character, first as slave, then as seeming
pander, then as the agent of the women's humiliation, is the
connecting link between the two themes of the play. The
women stand for greed and social ambition, he for avarice.
Luke's exultation over his treasure has already been quoted
(p. 270, above). He exclaims before his gold,

> to possess
> What wise men wish and toil for! Hermes' moly,
> Sibylla's golden bough, the great elixir,
> Imagined only by the alchymist,
> Compared with thee are shadows,—thou the substance
> And guardian of felicity.[2]

His avarice, like that of Sir Epicure Mammon (who is clearly
echoed in these lines), is infinite:

[1] III, ii (IV, 64).   [2] III, iii (IV, 65).

> Increase of wealth
> Is the rich man's ambition, and mine
> Shall know no bounds.[1]

But (a parallel with the treatment of the ambition theme) his greed is not merely a caricature of reality. Luke represents the attitude that was becoming common of acquisitiveness basing itself on legality. In the first act he describes his brother:

> He is a citizen,
> And would increase his heap, and will not lose
> What the law gives him: such as are worldly wise
> Pursue that track, or they will ne'er wear scarlet,[2]

and Sir John Frugal stands on his strict legal rights with his debtors until dissuaded by his hypocritical piety.[3] But when in power—'honester now by a hundred thousand pound'[4]—Luke takes all that he can get from the debtors—which seems to have been rather more than a fair return for the money lent.[5]

> Conscience! no, no; so it may be done with safety,
> And without danger of the law.[6]

Asked to show mercy to the apprentices whom he had ruined, he tells them,

> Conscience, my friends,
> And wealth, are not always neighbours. Should I part
> With what the law gives me, I should suffer mainly
> In my reputation; for it would convince me
> Of indiscretion: nor will you, I hope, move me

---

[1] IV, ii (IV, 82).   [2] I, ii (IV, 20).   [3] I, iii.   [4] V, ii (IV, 104).
[5] *Luke.* I have got into my hands
> Your bargain from the sailor, 'twas a good one
> For such a petty sum.   I will likewise take
> The extremity of your mortgage, and the forfeit
> Of your several bonds; the use and principal
> Shall not serve.
>   (IV, iii (IV, 86).)
[6] V, i (IV, 96).

> To do myself such prejudice.
> *Lord Lacy.* No moderation?
> *Luke.* They cannot look for't, and preserve in me
>   A thriving citizen's credit.[1]

We are left in no doubt concerning Massinger's attitude towards avarice, even when it works within the bounds of strict legality. In this play, as in *A New Way to Pay Old Debts*, the anti-acquisitive attitude is explicitly related to religious teaching.

> The devil—why start you at his name? if you
> Desire to wallow in wealth and worldly honours,
> You must make haste to be familiar with him.[2]

So says the disguised Sir John, and Luke had already bidden

> Religion, conscience, charity, farewell!
> To me you are words only, and no more;
> All human happiness consists in store.[3]

Massinger's is not a merely formal piety; it is related to the living conception of community, and neighbourly dealing within that community, that we have seen in Dekker and Heywood.
>   Such
> As are born only for themselves, and live so,
> Though prosperous in worldly understandings,
> Are but like beasts of rapine, that, by odds
> Of strength, usurp, and tyrannize o'er others
> Brought under their subjection.[4]

This is the 'reformed' Luke of the early scenes; in prosperity he regards hospitality to his 'poor neighbours' as 'a virtue grown obsolete, and useless', and expresses the same feelings as Dekker's merchant, Bartervile:

---

[1] V, ii (IV, 104).   Cf. Sir John Frugal:
>   I shall be laugh'd at for my foolish pity,
>   Which money-men hate deadly.
>   (I, iii (IV, 26).)
[2] V, i (IV, 96).   [3] IV, ii (IV, 83).   [4] I, iii (IV, 24).

> I will sit
> Alone, and surfeit in my store, while others
> With envy pine at it; my genius pamper'd
> With the thought of what I am, and what they suffer
> I have mark'd out to misery.[1]

In the essay from which I have already quoted Mr Eliot has this paragraph:

> What may be considered corrupt or decadent in the morals of Massinger is not an alteration or diminution of morals; it is simply the disappearance of all those personal and real emotions which this morality supported and into which it introduced a kind of order. As soon as the emotions disappear the morality which ordered it appears hideous. Puritanism itself became repulsive only when it appeared as the survival of a restraint after the feelings which it restrained had gone. . . . The Elizabethan morality was an important convention; important because it was not consciously of one social class alone, because it provided a framework for emotions to which all classes could respond, and it hindered no feeling. . . . Fletcher and Massinger rendered it ridiculous; not by believing it, but because they were men of great talents who could not vivify it; because they could not fit into it passionate, complete human characters.[2]

This account is admirably stimulating; it may, perhaps, apply to Massinger's tragedies and tragi-comedies,[3] and it certainly applies to Fletcher's. It does not apply to Mas-

---

[1] V, i (IV, 102). Contrast the description of Wellborn's father, a country gentleman of the old style:

> a man of worship,
> Old Sir John Wellborn, justice of peace and quorum. . . .
> Bore the whole sway of the shire, *kept a great house,*
> *Relieved the poor,* and so forth.
>
> (*A New Way,* I, i (III, 483).)

[2] *Elizabethan Essays,* pp. 165-166.

[3] 'When Massinger's ladies resist temptation they do not appear to undergo any important emotion; they merely know what is expected of them; they manifest themselves to us as lubricious prudes' (*ibid.*).

singer's two fine comedies. In one sense *A New Way to Pay Old Debts* and *The City Madam* are derivative; they sometimes seem to approach the tradition through Jonson rather than directly, and their content is correspondingly less rich and full. But in the figures of Sir Giles Overreach, Luke Frugal and the City Madam and her daughters the Elizabethan social morality is certainly 'vivified'. Coming at such a time, and from an author who was only too susceptible to new influences, the two plays witness to the strength of the tradition that has been explored in these pages.

The problem that criticism still has to solve is the problem of 'decadence'; the contrast between the richness of 'Elizabethan' drama and the poverty of Caroline and Restoration drama is not due *merely* to the different amount of talent available in each period. In tackling this problem there are three points to start from, none of which can be treated in isolation from the others. The first, and most important, is the handling of the verse or, more generally, the dramatic medium. The second is found in the kind and quality of the interests enlisted in each play, or group of plays. The third concerns the constitution, the literary and general interests, of the theatre audience.

The completeness with which Fletcher represents (and fosters) a changing taste deserves to be more fully realized than it is. If Massinger's verse tends towards the dilution of feeling, the emotions which Fletcher presents are faked: they are worked up, and the purpose is impure. Fletcher's serious mode is fairly represented by this passage from *A King and No King* (1611):

> Good lady, be not fearful: though he should not
> Give you your present end in this, believe it,
> You shall feel, if your virtue can induce you

> To labour out this tempest (which I know,
> Is but a poor proof 'gainst your patience),
> All these contents your spirit will arrive at,
> Newer and sweeter to you. Your royal brother,
> When he shall once collect himself, and see
> How far he has been asunder from himself,
> What a mere stranger to his golden temper,
> Must, from those roots of virtue, never dying,
> Though somewhat stopt with humour, shoot again
> Into a thousand glories, bearing his fair branches
> High as our hopes can look at, straight as justice,
> Loaden with ripe contents.[1]

Everything is vague, general, and unrealized ('these contents
... newer and sweeter to you', 'a mere stranger to his golden
temper'); the final metaphor is particularly betraying—one
can grasp nothing particular in those 'roots of virtue . . .
stopt with humour', and the metaphorical tree is loaded with
abstractions, 'a thousand glories' and 'ripe contents'. But
Fletcher's metaphors are invariably unrealized or commonplace. Love, as in the Restoration heroic plays, is always
a 'flame',[2] frozen souls 'melt',[3] and here is a description of
inconstancy:

[1] *A King and No King*, IV, i (Variorum Edition of Beaumont and
Fletcher, I, p. 308).   The play is a Beaumont and Fletcher collabora-
tion, but there is 'practical unanimity' in assigning this scene, together with IV, ii, iii and V, i, iii to Fletcher.—Chambers, *Elizabethan
Stage*, III, p. 225.

[2] *Tigranes*. I feel my old fire flame again, and burn
   So strong and violent.
>   (*Ibid.*, IV, ii (I, 311)—Fletcher.)

Cf. *Arbaces*. If you above love not such sins as these,
   Circle my heart with thoughts as cold as snow,
   To quench these rising flames that harbour here.
>   (*Ibid.*, IV, iv (I, 324).)

[3] *Amintor*. I am now dissolved;
   My frozen soul melts.
>   (*Maid's Tragedy*, IV, i (Fletcher) (I, 82).)

She lives to tell thee thou art more unconstant
Than all ill women ever were together;
Thy faith as firm as raging overflows,
That no bank can command; and as lasting
As boys' gay bubbles, blown i' the air and broken:
The wind is fix'd to thee. . . .[1]

If Shakespeare is not a fair test ('Heaven stops the nose at it, and the moon winks'), we have only to put beside this any example of imagery from, say, *The Changeling* ('Let the common sewer take it from distinction') or *The Revenger's Tragedy* ('Does the silkworm expend her yellow labours for thee?') to expose its essential falsity.

The reason for the vagueness and generality, the commonplace figures and unrealized imagery, is that there is no informing emotion, no pressure from within. 'The blossoms of Beaumont and Fletcher's imagination draw no sustenance from the soil, but are cut and slightly withered flowers stuck into sand.'[2] Since there is no firm pressure of emotion behind the verse of, say, *A King and No King*, the play itself is not a coherent emotional development: there is no emotion to develop. Everything, therefore, is sacrificed to the immediate effect; we have merely a succession of emotional high spots,[3] and the comedy is merely 'comic relief'.

---

[1] *A King and No King*, IV, ii (Fletcher) (I, 312).

[2] T. S. Eliot, 'Ben Jonson', *Elizabethan Essays*, p. 78.

[3] *Gobrias.*   Know,
    You kill your father.
    Arbaces.   How!
    Gobrias. You kill your father.
    Arbaces. My father! Though I know it for a lie,
        Made out of fear, to save thy stained life,
        The very reverence of the word comes 'cross me,
        And ties my arm down.
                            A King and No King, V, iv (I, 346).
    Compare: *Evadne.* Why, 'tis the King.
             Amintor.   The King!

294

A further consideration leads directly to the domain of morals, and therefore approaches the subject of this book. R. P. Blackmur says that for Henry James, 'art was the viable representation of moral value; in the degree that the report was intelligent and intense the morals were sound'.[1] In the Beaumont and Fletcher 'serious' plays the report (of human emotions) is not 'intelligent and intense', and in consequence the moral issues which they profess to raise—incest in *A King and No King*, conflicting loyalties and revenge in *The Maid's Tragedy*—are not squarely faced. The moral problem merely gives an additional fillip to the emotions, and provides the maximum number of piquant situations. In these plays tragedy becomes pathos, and pathos an indulgence, not part of a larger organization.[2] Each of the tragedies and tragi-comedies of Beaumont and Fletcher is a series of cunningly contrived situations to exploit, not to explore and express, emotions; and that is decadence.

A similar judgement is enforced by Fletcher's comedies. Maybe Fletcher 'understood and imitated the conversation of gentlemen much better (than Shakespeare); whose wild debaucheries and quickness of wit in repartees, no poet

> Evadne.　　What will you do now?
> Amintor. It is not the King!
> 　. . . Oh, thou hast named a word, that wipes away
> 　All thoughts revengeful! etc.
> 　　　　　(*The Maid's Tragedy*, II, i (I, 42-43).)

These scenes are probably by Beaumont, but they are relevant here.

[1] 'The Critical Prefaces', *Hound and Horn*, April–June 1934, VII, No. 3, p. 452.

[2] Contrast Aspatia's song, 'Lay a garland on my hearse' (*Maid's Tragedy*, II, i) with Desdemona's Willow song (*Othello*, IV, iii). The song occurs in a Beaumont scene; for a corresponding effect by Fletcher see Evadne's speech:

> I was once fair,
> Once I was lovely; not a blowing rose
> More chastely sweet. . . .
> 　　　　　(*The Maid's Tragedy*, V, ii (I, 98).)

before him could paint as he has done',[1] and certainly his
comedies are amusing. But gaiety and gentlemanly re-
partee are not enough. To write great comedy one has to
be serious about something; and the only thing that Fletcher
took at all seriously—that at least is to his credit—was the
question of a decent freedom for women.[2] In *The Elder
Brother* (completed by Massinger) there is some mild satire
on the way in which 'virgins of wealthy family waste their
youth'—which goes no deeper than Addison's 'Diary of a
Young Lady of Fashion'—and a glance at the vanities of
court, where one learns 'to speak a tedious piece of nothing'.
But satirical effects of this kind are quite unrelated to the
central purpose of the play, which is to exhibit the romantic
adventures of the studious Charles. As a rule, indeed, it is
hard to tell what central purpose there is. In *The Scornful
Lady* (with Beaumont) the skits on Shakespeare (' "To
sleep, to die; to die, to sleep", a very figure, sir'[3]), the light-
hearted use of popular sententiousness ('Let thy chimneys
smoke'; 'Hang it, dirt!'—contrast the implications of
'spacious in the possession of dirt'), the superficial wit (*e.g.*
about Abigail's age) and the buffoonery, all indicate the

---

[1] Dryden, *Essay of Dramatic Poesy*. Dryden has 'they'. The
passage precedes the famous sentence which describes Beaumont and
Fletcher's popularity in the Restoration period: 'Their plays are now
the most pleasant and frequent entertainments of the stage; two of
theirs being acted through the year for one of Shakespeare's or
Jonson's: the reason is, because there is a certain gaiety in their
comedies and pathos in their more serious plays, which suits generally with all men's humours'.

[2] See especially *The Little French Lawyer* (with Massinger, 1619–
1622) and *The Wild Goose Chase* (1621). In the latter Rosalura
wishes

> to maintain good women's honours,
> Their freedoms, and their fames.

Cf. Lillia Bianca: 'A merry and a free wench, give her liberty'.

[3] Cf. I will run mad first, and, if that get not pity,
I'll drown myself to a most dismal ditty.—III, ii.

quality of the amusement that is offered. The usurer, Morecraft, is a stock figure whose practices are forgotten as soon as mentioned, and it is not only in the skirmishings round sex [1] that we are reminded of the Restoration stage. In *Wit Without Money* (1614), *The Humorous Lieutenant* (*c*. 1619), *Rule a Wife and Have a Wife* (*c*. 1624) and the rest, everything is subordinate to the intrigue, to amusing dialogue, to the immediate comic effect [2] (the most notorious instance being the Lieutenant's venereal disease in *The Humorous Lieutenant*). There is of course incidental satire, but it remains incidental. The major interests of a diverse audience are not aroused.

Shirley and Brome are even nearer to the later Comedy of Manners. Different as they are, they are alike in practising in a narrower field than any of their predecessors. Fashionable society, or the imitation of fashionable society, provides their themes. Brome 'habitually regards from the outside the manners of fashionable society, gaining his comic effects through their caricature and distortion when aped by curious citizens who perceive them only as mannerisms'.[3] Shirley has perhaps an even narrower range. His comedy is the comedy of polite society,[4] and when wider issues are men-

[1] For the tone of
    You that be coming on, make much of fifteen (IV, i)
compare
        At twenty-five in women's eyes
        Beauty does fade, at thirty dies (1674).
[2] 'An incurable zest for random adventure and farcical intrigue' (K. M. Lynch, *op. cit.*, p, 24).
[3] K. M. Lynch, *op. cit.*, p. 29. The projector scenes of *The Court Beggar* are merely rather dull imitations of Jonson.
[4] A typical effect from *The Lady of Pleasure* (1635):
    Frederick. My most loved aunt.
    Lady Bornwell. Support me, I shall faint.
    Littleworth. What ails your ladyship?
    Lady B. Is that Frederick? In black?
    Kickshaw. Yes, madam; but the doublet's satin.

tioned they seem to have a literary ancestry rather than to be the result of direct observation.[1]

In comedy Massinger is the last of the Elizabethans, whilst Fletcher is the first of the direct line that runs through Shirley and Brome (although Brome was a 'son of Ben') to the comic writers of the post-Restoration period.[2] The comedies of these three are indeed best discussed in conjunction with the later comedy of manners. One touches here on a subject that cannot be treated summarily—the changing taste of the theatre audiences and of the reading public points directly to the shifts in national culture which form one of the major changes of our history—and discussion is best deferred. But once the truth of this alignment is accepted one important point becomes clear. For the significance of the Restoration theatre as a functional unit in the national life is seen in the account that M. Beljame has given of its audience:

> Ces spectateurs . . . étaient peu nombreux. La Cité, restée puritaine, choquée des mœurs du jour et de l'audace des pièces, ne venait pas aux représentations, ou fort peu. 'Tous

Lady B. The boy's undone.—II, i.
Or,
    Little. Your French tailor
    Has made you a perfect gentleman; I may
    Converse now with you, and preserve my credit.
(IV, ii.)

[1] *E.g.* With lordships, but no manors! one that has
    But newly cast his country skin, come up
    To see the fashions of the town, has crept
    Into a knighthood, which he paid for heartily;
    And in his best clothes is suspected for
    A gentleman.
(*Changes, or Love in a Maze* (1632), I, i.)
This adds nothing to the similar satire of the early part of the century. Compare the passage on the decline of hospitality, *The Lady of Pleasure*, II, i.

[2] For some important lines of communication, see K. M. Lynch, *op. cit.*, chap. ii.

ceux qui tenaient à passer pour des gens sérieux et estimables se gardaient de paraître au théâtre.   Un jeune homme de loi respectable aurait compromis sa dignité; un jeune commerçant aurait fait tort à son crédit en se montrant dans ces cercles de la licence effrénée.' . . . C'était une partie nombreuse de l'auditoire qui se trouvait supprimée, et peut-être la meilleure, celle qui est assez instruite pour apprécier, et en même temps assez simple, assez naïve encore pour connaître les rires francs et les émotions sincères, pour se laisser prendre par les entrailles.   Les spectateurs se réduisaient donc à la cour et à ce monde de fonctionnaires et de désœuvrés qui gravite autour du roi.[1]

The Restoration theatre, that is, catered for a small group whose interests were notoriously limited,[2] and its writers had nothing to correspond to the major interests of the Elizabethan-Jacobean dramatists.

The great break, of course, occurred with the closing of the theatres and the Civil War.   Before then there was no positive bar to the participation of the 'respectable' middle

[1] Beljame, *Le Public et les hommes de lettres en Angleterre au dix-huitième siècle, 1660–1744*, pp. 56-57.   The quotation is from Johnson's Life of Dryden.   Cf. C. V. Deane, *Dramatic Theory and the Rhymed Heroic Play*, p. 58.   Mr A. M. Clark notes the signs in the reign of James I: 'The theatre both gained and lost by the direct patronage of the crown and the extended authority of the Master of the Revels; for while on the one hand the wealthier citizens and still more their wives looked with a favourable eye on the now fashionable and therefore respectable theatres, the stage was ceasing to be a national institution and was becoming more and more dependent on the court, more restricted in its appeal, and in reality no more acceptable to an ever-increasing body of puritans' (*Thomas Heywood*, p. 70).   Chambers notes 'some development of censorial practice' when Buck succeeded Tilney as Master of the Revels in 1610 (*Elizabethan Stage*, I, p. 322), and this was increased under Sir Henry Herbert in the next reign.   But much more is involved here than censorship.
[2] For the tastes of the Restoration audience see Beljame, *op. cit.*, pp. 56-70, and Deane, *op. cit.*, pp. 58-62.   But the Restoration plays themselves are sufficient evidence on this point.

classes. But an increasing puritanism was already turning many away from the theatres, and there was already a wide gap between the tastes that were catered for at the private houses in Drury Lane, at Salisbury Court or the Blackfriars and 'the original civility of the Red Bull'.[1] And in Fletcher, Brome and Shirley we can see that progressive narrowing of the scope of drama that leads from *Lear* to *Aureng-Zebe*, from *The Alchemist* to *Love for Love*. Fletcher, we may say, had nothing in common with Heywood and Dekker, whereas Jonson, and to a less extent Massinger, shared many of the more important interests and attitudes of these popular writers, as well as those of lay and ecclesiastical moralists.

[1] Dryden, *Essay of Dramatic Poesy.*

APPENDIX A

ELIZABETHAN PROSE

MR ROBERTS' useful anthology [1] should do more than remind the general reader that Elizabethan Prose is not confined to a few patches of fine writing. A careful reading of his extracts from journalists alone is sufficient to increase our understanding of Elizabethan verse and to suggest an important approach to the culture of the period.

We can learn a good deal merely by comparing a few sentences by an Elizabethan and by a modern journalist. The first of the following extracts is from *The Unfortunate Traveller*, the second from *The World Crisis*.

> So it fel out, that it being a vehement hot summer when I was a sojourner there, there entered such a hotspurd plague as hath not bin heard of: why it was but a word and a blowe, Lord have mercie upon us and he was gone. Within three quarters of a yeere in that one citie there died of it a hundred thousand looke in Lanquets chronicle and you shall finde it. To smell of a nosegay that was poisond, and turne your nose to a house that had the plague, it was all one. The clouds like a number of cormorants that keepe their corne til it stinke and is mustie, kept in their stinking exhalations till they had almost stifeled all Romes inhabitants.

> When the great organizations of this world are strained beyond breaking point, their structure often collapses at all points simultaneously. There is nothing on which policy, however wise, can build; no foothold can be found for virtue or valour, no authority or impetus for a rescuing genius. The mighty framework of German Imperial Power, which a few days before had overshadowed the nations, shivered suddenly into a thousand individually disintegrating fragments. All her Allies whom she had so long sustained, fell

[1] *Elizabethan Prose*, selected and prefaced by Michael Roberts.

down broken and ruined, begging separately for peace. The faithful armies were beaten at the front and demoralized from the rear. The proud efficient Navy mutinied. Revolution-exploded in the most disciplined of States. The Supreme War Lord fled.

Such a spectacle appals mankind; and a knell rang in the ear of the victors, even in their hour of triumph.

I shall speak later of the characteristics of Nashe's prose. Here it is sufficient to remark that if his comparison of the clouds to contemporary capitalists is too highly charged with vitality (for it has a life of its own independent of the rest of the sentence) Mr Churchill's metaphors are ghosts. 'Organizations' are never, in fact, 'strained beyond breaking point'—but throughout the second extract the relation of word to thing is so tenuous that the reader is baffled whenever he attempts to find more than the minimum of content in any of the glib phrases: in such a diluted style it is fitting that a 'framework' should 'overshadow the nations' in pretended solidity. The passage is in fact fraudulent, claiming a response which it does nothing to justify. I do not, of course, suppose that Nashe and Mr Churchill are trying to do the same kind of thing, but they are both engaged in exploiting their medium for a particular end, and Nashe is the more conscious of what he is doing and his method is the more honest. Now the point that the difference is something more than a personal difference between two writers seems best enforceable by saying that if a book were to be written on the kinds of verbal exploitation that have been possible in different periods it would have to begin by considering the relation of the written and the spoken word. Except on a political platform none of Mr Churchill's sentences could be spoken. The paragraph from Nashe, like the bulk of Elizabethan prose, is based on living idiomatic speech.

This is probably one of the most important clues to a

proper understanding of Elizabethan literature; but, unqualified, the same remark might be applied to the prose of
very different writers in a different age—to the following
passage from Dryden's Preface to *All for Love*, for example:

> Dionysius and Nero had the same longings, but with all
> their power they could never bring the business well about.
> 'Tis true, they proclaimed themselves poets by sound of
> trumpet; and poets they were, upon pain of death to any man
> who durst call them otherwise. The audience had a fine
> time on't, you may imagine; they sat in bodily fear, and
> looked as demurely as they could: for it was a hanging matter
> to laugh unseasonably; and the tyrants were suspicious, as
> they had reason, that their subjects had 'em in the wind; so,
> every man, in his own defence, set as good a face upon the
> business as he could. 'Twas known beforehand that the
> monarchs were to be crowned laureates; but when the show
> was over, and an honest man was suffered to depart quietly,
> he took out his laughter which he had stifled, with a firm
> resolution never more to see an Emperor's play, though he
> had been ten years a-making it.

The most striking difference between this and anything
by Nashe, 'Marprelate' or Gosson is, I suppose, one of tone
and manner. Dryden's words contain an implicit assurance that the reader will not be asked to respond in certain
ways; there will be no attack on the heart or liver. But it
is not merely that the audience, and therefore literary
manners, had changed. The staple of Dryden's prose is a
language more select and refined, more Polite, than that of
the Elizabethans. Elizabethan prose—since the argument
requires the obvious—is closer to folk speech, to the English
of ploughing, carting, selling and small town gossip. And
if it was possible to say many things in Augustan prose
that could not be said in the prose of Nashe, Nashe and
his contemporaries had a source of strength denied to the
Augustans: 'Here is your husband; like a mildewed ear,

Blasting his wholesome brother'. 'Money is like muck, not good except it be spread.' Bunyan alone of Dryden's contemporaries had such resources: 'Thou talkest like one on whose head is the shell to this very day'.—A low phrase, Dr Johnson would say, debased by vulgar mouths.

It is only too easy, when discussing the vigour of Elizabethan prose, to divagate into sociological generalizations. But the mind of an age is best studied in its literature— Elizabethan prose reflects a way of living not merely because there are prose accounts of Elizabethan habits— and the social background can only be profitably discussed when a start has been made from criticism. The few simple facts about 'conditions' that are necessary to give the right perspective may be conveniently summarized here.

Elizabethan England consisted mainly of agricultural communities, each with a vigorous local life and tradition; and the town dweller shared most of the mental habits of the countryman. London was obviously exceptional, but in many ways its ethos was that of the market town. It was still comparatively small, and its inhabitants were familiar with the processes necessary for growing, making and selling most of its commodities. It had a genuine community of interests, reflected even in a common stock of objects of derision: a reference to a local eccentric ('he that is knowne by wearing a cloake of tuftaffatie eighteene yeare', for example) was expected to be immediately recognizable. And its gossip was that of the small town: familiar jests, proverbial sayings ('Farewell Bowe, have over the Bridge, where I heard say honest Conscience was once drown'd'), accounts of traditional wonders and stories of familiar places. Popular interests are reflected clearly enough in the titles of plays and pamphlets: 'The Famous Chronicle of king Edwarde the first sirnamed Edwarde Longshankes. . . . Lastly, the sinking of Queene Elinor, who sunck at Charingcrosse, and rose again at Potters-hith now named Queen-hith'; 'The Second Part of, If you know not me, you know no bodie. With the building of the Royall Exchange: And the famous Victorie of Queene Elizabeth, in the Yeare 1588.' The popularity of Dekker's pamphlets, *The Dead Term* and *The Wonderful Year* for example, was largely due to the way in which he exploited this kind of interest:

> Such was the fashion of this Land, when the great Land-Lady thereof left it: Shee came in with the fall of the leafe, and went away in the Spring: her life (which was dedicated to Virginitie), both beginning and closing up a miraculous Mayden circle: for she was borne upon a Lady Eve, and died upon a Lady Eve: her Nativitie and death being memorable by this wonder: the first and last yeares of her Raigne by this, that a *Lee* was Lorde Maior when she came to the Crowne, and a *Lee* Lorde Maior when she departed from it. Three places are made famous by her for three things, *Greenewich* for her birth, *Richmount* for her death, *White-Hall* for her Funerall.

Gossip of this kind has obvious affinities with Malinowski's 'phatic communion'. Its nearest modern equivalent is the desultory talk of the bar-parlour in the more remote villages.

The point that I wish to make is that, in a certain sense, Elizabethan society was 'primitive' (no one need suppose that I am comparing the Elizabethans to Trobriand Islanders), and its language retained many more of the primitive functions of speech than are to be found after the seventeenth century. Not only was the relation of word and thing, of word and action, far more intimate than in a society that obtains most of its more permanent impressions from books and newspapers, a large number of Elizabethan words and phrases are the direct equivalent of action— gestures of sociability, contempt or offence (the Eliza-

bethans had a particularly rich vocabulary of abuse).
Moreover, the muscular content of Elizabethan English
is an important part of its 'meaning', and it was this, together with the reading habits fostered by speaking such a
language, that enabled physical states to be portrayed with
such immediacy:

> O so I was tickled in the spleene with that word, my hart
> hopt and danst, my elbowes icht, my fingers friskt, I wist not
> what should become of my feete, nor knewe what I did for
> joy.

Poets, as well as prose writers, could rely on their readers to
do more than attach a bare referential meaning to each
word. 'When Shakespeare describes a thing', said Dryden,
'you more than see it, you feel it too.' And it was not only
things that could be evoked in concrete immediacy.

> What shalt thou expect,
> To be depender on a thing that leans?
> Who cannot be new built, nor has no friends
> So much as but to prop him.

One has only to attempt to read these lines with the eye
alone to realize what is meant by 'the body and movement
of the language'.

The social and linguistic factors referred to are sufficient
to account for the strength and the limitations of Elizabethan prose. Judging by achievement we may say that
it is an admirable medium for vivid and fanciful description and narrative, but not for exact description; for
folk humour, not for wit; for satire and invective (often
more violent than the occasion demands—'Pappe with an
Hatchet'), not for analysis or logical argument. Its virtue
is vigour not perspicuity. It misses effects depending upon
tone, subtlety, and an exact control of tempo and movement. Its significant limitations are particularly noticeable in two fields, those of argument and literary criticism.

306

I shall return to the question of dialectic. As for the second point, a careful reading of Gregory Smith's two volumes can only confirm the opinion that, if the chief function of criticism is clarification, there is no Elizabethan criticism worth the name. Nor was it possible to use Elizabethan prose in the lucid explication of a mature attitude. A comparison of Florio with Montaigne does more than make this clear; the habits of the language may be seen merely by putting a few sentences of the original and the translation side by side.

On a raison de descrier l'hipocrisie qui se trouve en la guerre: car qu'est il plus aisé à un homme practic que de gauchir aux dangers et de *contrefaire le mauvais, ayant le cœur plein de mollesse?*

There is great reason the hipocrisie that is found in war should be discovered: For, what is more easie in a man of practise then to flinch in dangers and *to counterfeit a gallant and a boaster when his heart is full of faintnesse, and ready to droope for feare?*

Il faut trier de toute une nation une douzaine d'hommes pour juger d'un arpent de terre; et le jugement de nos inclinations et de nos actions, la plus difficile matière et la plus importante, qui soit, nous la remettons *à la voix de la commune et de la tourbe,* mère d'ignorance, d'injustice et d'inconstance.

We are often driven to empanell and select a jury of twelve men out of a whole countrie to determine of an acre of land: And the judgement of our inclinations and actions (the weightiest and hardest matter that is) we referre it *to the idle breath of the vaine voice of the common sort and base raskalitie,* which is the mother of ignorance, of injustice, and inconstancie.

Peu de gens ont espousé *des amies qui ne s'en soyent repentis.*

Few men have wedded *their sweet hearts, their paramours or mistresses, but have come home by weeping Crosse, and ere long repented their bargaine.*

307

If the English is more diffuse than the French this is not because Florio was a bad translator; the diffuseness was essential in an attempt to convey the full meaning of the original. It is not merely that there was frequently no exact verbal equivalence between the two languages ('Those which are called honest, vertuous and sufficient' is the nearest that Florio can get to 'ceux qu'on appelle honnestes et habiles hommes'): the *tone* of the second passage allows Montaigne's short phrase to convey all that is contained in Florio's expanded description. In the third example not only is the English version longer than the French, the folk idiom ('weeping Crosse') and the word 'bargaine' (with its associations drawn from the popular Woman Controversy—'filthy bargain', etc.) completely transform the sentence. It is no longer a detached *observation* but a misogynist commonplace of the tavern, with an emotional fringe entirely lacking in the French. The two sentences require an entirely different kind of acceptance from the reader. Further comparison is impossible here, but the extracts are typical. Florio's difficulties (his unusually heavy stopping seems to be an attempt to reproduce the logical ordonnance of the French) are due to the fact that the language which he had to use did not allow precisely those qualities which distinguish the prose of Montaigne— lucidity, compactness, flexibility and submission to control.[1]

To say this is to explain why, although there are scores of written works whose object is, ostensibly, to explain or to persuade, there is no Elizabethan prose which is *intellectually* persuasive. Hooker's prose is admirable, but it is

[1] This is not to say that some of these qualities are not sometimes found separately in Elizabethan prose; the superiority of Montaigne's prose lies in the combination. Bacon's prose is compact ('His hearers could not cough, or look aside from him, without loss') but no one could call it flexible; his sentences lie stiffly side by side like logs.

not, strictly speaking, an intellectual prose. He is at his best not when he is arguing a case, but when he is expressing a conviction emotionally held, as in the following passage (the effect depends entirely upon the rhythm and the metaphors), where he is expressing his feelings about order:

> Now if nature should intermit her course, and leave altogether though it were but for a while the observation of her own laws; if those principal and mother elements of the world, whereof all things in this lower world are made, should lose the qualities which now they have; if the frame of that heavenly arch erected over our heads should loosen and dissolve itself; if celestial spheres should forget their wonted motions, and by irregular volubility turn themselves any way as it might happen; if the prince of the lights of heaven, which now as a giant doth run his unwearied course, should as it were through a languishing faintness begin to stand and to rest himself; if the moon should wander from her beaten way, the times and seasons of the year blend themselves by disordered and confused mixture, the winds breathe out their last gasp, the clouds yield no rain, the earth be defeated of heavenly influence, the fruits of the earth pine away as children at the withered breasts of their mother no longer able to yield them relief: what would become of man himself, whom these things do now serve? See we not plainly that obedience of creatures unto the law of nature is the stay of the whole world? [1]

In Elizabethan sermons the method of the public disputation is the usual one adopted: opposition points are put up and knocked down in order; there are appeals to

[1] Contrast the use of metaphor in, say, the *Leviathan* (1651). For example: 'All men are by nature provided of notable multiplying glasses (that is their Passions and Selfe-love), through which, every little payment appeareth a great grievance; but are destitute of those prospective glasses (namely Morall and Civil Science), to see a farre off the miseries that hang over them, and cannot without such payments be avoyded'.

authority and custom; there is a large amount of verbal quibbling;[1] there is rarely an attempt to deploy a consistent argument. Much the same might be said of the early economic tracts, to take another example. Clearly the deficiency cannot be explained *merely* by a reference to vocabulary and idiom: many other factors must be taken into account, such as the Elizabethan fondness for rhetoric on the one hand, and the absence of the 'scientific spirit' and the lack of adequate information on the other. But if factors such as these helped to shape the language, they were themselves, in part, determined by it.[2] Anyone who has looked at Gresham's letters on the foreign exchange or blown the dust off the volumes of the Parker Society will understand what is meant by saying that the strictly intellectual elucidation of a proposition was impossible, that there were limitations inherent in the language.

The controversial pamphlets were not called in evidence in the last two paragraphs for obvious reasons; they often contain a show of formal logic, but it is the merest bluff, hardly meant to deceive. But there is no need to point out their importance, and a very brief account of some characteristics of the pamphleteering method will help to correct the emphasis placed on the limitations of Elizabethan prose.

In popular controversy, such as that of Nashe or Marprelate, one of the more obvious devices is to start with a

[1] 'Even the works of God are not equally excellent; this (the making of woman) is but *faciam*, it is not *faciamus*; in the creation of man, there is intimated a Consultation, a Deliberation of the whole *Trinity*; in the making of *woman*, it is not expressed so; it is but *faciam*' (John Donne, *Fifty Sermons* (1649), Sermon II). The remark is repeated and expanded later.

[2] In any society habits and language form a complex interacting whole, of which the parts cannot be studied in artificial isolation. This is admirably brought out by Malinowski in *The Sexual Life of Savages* and in his Supplementary Essay in *The Meaning of Meaning*.

crude or simple feeling, cast about for the first suitable metaphor, and then to let the metaphor develop of its own momentum in the general direction indicated by the feeling:

> They call the Bishops butchers, I like the Metaphore wel, such calves must be knockt on the head, and who fitter than the Fathers of the Church, to cut the throates of heresies in the Church. Nay, when they have no propertie of sheepe but baa, their fleece for flockes, not cloath, their rotten flesh for no dish, but ditches: I thinke them woorth neither the tarring nor the telling, but for their scabbedness to be thrust from the pinfolde to the scaffold, and with an *Habeas Corpus* to remoove them from the Shepheards tarre-boxe, to the hangmans budget.

The argument is conducted by invective and ridicule, by parable and metaphor, by alliteration and puns: 'I but he hath sillogismes in pike sauce, and arguments that have been these twentie yeres in pickle. I, picke hell, you shall not find such reasons.' Often, as here, an interlocutor is imagined as present, and there are pages which can only be understood if we realize that certain sentences—there is no typographical distinction—come from the opposition side. The pamphleteering method is, in short, the method of spoken dialectic. Popular writing is largely, like verbal fencing, an exhibition of skill, and the writer, like an improvisator on the stage, takes care to call attention to a particular display of agility: 'Now comes a biting speech, let mee stroake my beard thrice like a German, before I speak a wise word'; 'O sweetlie brought in, at least three figures in that line, besides the wit on't.'

For a proper appreciation of Elizabethan prose, as the pamphlets make plain, we need to understand both the close relation of the written to the spoken word (words had not—to adapt a remark of Mr Empson's—a mere newspaper meaning, intended to be mechanically snapped up by the eye), and the Elizabethan love of verbal ingenuity. It is the latter which accounts for the vogue of Euphuism, for the popularity of sermons and the pervasive interest in rhetoric, and which explains the bulk of Elizabethan journalism. There is a book to be written on the significance of Thomas Nashe, who besides being the best was a typical journalist. Almost all his work shows the same characteristics. The ostensible theme is merely an occasion for the performance. There are the usual puns and witty metaphors; there are moralizing asides, pieces of incidental satire and 'pretty parentheses' on matters of topical interest; there is a good deal of miscellaneous information (the Elizabethans seem to have been particularly interested in popular etymology), and there are rhetorical declamations on set themes—such as the speech on travel by the English Earl and Cutwolfe's 'insulting oration' in *The Unfortunate Traveller*. Like the rest Nashe acts as showman to his own abilities: 'Prepare your eares and your teares, for never tyll this thrust I anie tragicall matter upon you'; 'To shewe how I can raile, thus would I begin to raile at him.' His attitude is indicated by the light-hearted abruptness with which he finishes an act as soon as he is tired of it: 'Whippet, turne to a new lesson, and strike wee up John for the King'. The Praise of the Red Herring makes the intention explicit: 'I may *Cum gratia et privilegio* pronounce it, that a red herring is wholesome in a frosty morning, and rake up some few scattered sillables together in the exornation and pollishing of it'.

Nashe exploited his medium in order to obtain a particular effect. But the important point is that he knew what he was doing, and his readers knew what they were getting for their money; there were no pseudo-profundities. It was, indeed, impossible that there should be. Neither, say, the end of *Tono Bungay* ('We make and pass, we are all

312

things that make and pass . . .') nor the paragraph from Mr Winston Churchill quoted at the beginning of this essay could have been written in Elizabethan English. To understand exactly why this is so is to understand the development of the language between the sixteenth and the twentieth centuries, and a great deal besides; it is to understand the Progress of Civilization. In the first place it is obvious that Elizabethan prose writings postulate a different audience from any of the modern audiences, with different attitudes and expectations and a different readiness to respond. The puns, metaphors and various forms of word play, the constant references to matters away from the main topic, the words rich in muscular content, read in much the same way as they were spoken, a system of punctuation not devised for the greatest ease of the greatest number—all demanded continuous activity on the part of the reader. Readers of 'lower grade' works were not, therefore, as now, conditioned into a state in which it was impossible for them to appreciate the highest contemporary achievement. In the second place, Elizabethan prose derives its virtue from a way of living, largely traditional, in which there was a satisfaction, equilibrium and certainty now destroyed; from, in short, the organic community. The popular art forms of such a society do not depend for their effect on the possibilities of substitute living (it is only modern critics who object to the ending of *All's Well*). Similarly, its language, which by its body and richness allows the poet to call 'the whole soul of man into activity' ('Soul' includes the nerves and the blood; we remember the seventeenth-century 'dissociation of sensibility'), cannot be used for exploiting shallow emotional responses, or for manipulating the semblance of ideas in a way that looks like 'thought'. Those Elizabethans who never got beyond Deloney, even those who remembered nothing of *King Lear* beyond the action and a couple of bawdy jokes, were not doomed to pass their lives in the emotional and intellectual muddledom of the readers of the *Daily Mail*.

I have said that Elizabethan prose was neither subtle nor intellectual; for subtlety we have to go to the later Elizabethan dramatists and the early Metaphysical poets. The remark could be illustrated in detail, but a reference to Donne should be sufficient. In Donne's best verse there is not only a finer emotional discrimination than in his sermons, there is an intellectual quality not found in his prose. To decide exactly why this is so would be an interesting problem. It would involve a consideration of the relation of 'thought' to 'feeling', and of the general relation of poetry and prose. It would help to explain some of the later developments of the novel—the work of D. H. Lawrence as well as of Virginia Woolf and James Joyce, about whose relation to Nashe some rather loose remarks have recently been made. There is all the difference in the world between Joyce's deliberate manipulations of the language and Nashe's spontaneous effusions, written, he explains, 'in my post-haste want of argent, as fast as my hand can trot'.

(1934)

SEVENTEENTH-CENTURY MELANCHOLY

THE last years of Queen Elizabeth and the reign of James I, towards the end of which Burton's *Anatomy* appeared, were marked by the prevalence of a particular kind of melancholy. All classes were affected by it, and it ranged from the deep-seated misery of Donne, a misery which 'crucifies the body and mind', to the affectation of Master Stephen. It gave the tone to a group of tragedies produced in the early years of the century and provided a background even for comedy. It was expressed in sermons, pamphlets and private letters. It was found in the court, the universities and the city, and contemporaries were sufficiently impressed by the pheno-menon to comment upon it at some length.[1]

Various theories have been put forward to explain its origin. It is perhaps commonest to attribute it to 'the swing of the pendulum' after the period of Renaissance exuberance; but the phrase means nothing unless it is care-fully analysed. Others have taken refuge in nescience and speak of 'the inexplicable apparition of unsought melan-choly which saddened the reign of James I'.[2] And one critic has suggested indigestion.[3] But, although the ex-planation may not be simple, it is possible to find some satisfying reasons for the melancholic humour of the age.

---

[1] One of the earliest books on the subject, *A Treatise of Melan-cholie*, by T. Bright, appeared in 1586.

[2] G. H. Mair, Introduction to Wilson's *Art of Rhetoric*, p. xxvii.

[3] Dr G. B. Harrison in his useful account of Elizabethan melan-choly included in his edition of Breton's *Melancholike Humours*, pp. 57-61.

In this note I wish to suggest first, that melancholy, for various reasons, was exaggerated by contemporary writers; secondly, that the undeniable residuum of misery and discontent was due partly to the prevailing attitude towards death, and partly to factors—hitherto insufficiently stressed —in the social and economic life of the time.

The age was not so melancholy as might at first sight be supposed. To start with, the evidence is largely, although not altogether, literary; it represents the working up of a mood for practical or aesthetic purposes. In the early years of the century the malcontent made his appearance on the stage; the theme proved popular and was exploited by Chapman, Marston, Shakespeare, Webster and Tourneur. This does not mean that the speeches put into the mouths of Hamlet, Malevole, Bosola and the rest did not represent a genuine mood of their creators; but before using them as social documents it is well to remember that they are not naïvely 'personal'.

There is no need to stress this point, but another semi-literary motive deserves to be considered. Even if melancholy had been no more prevalent in the early seventeenth century than at any other time, it is likely that it would have received considerable attention; for during this period psychology was becoming popular among a certain class, and the melancholy man presented an obvious case for analysis. 'Psychology', of course, was not called by that name, and the study was neither scientific nor systematic, but a lively interest in the workings of the mind and the combination of humours in the individual was fashionable amongst the intellectuals of the day. Even during the first half of Elizabeth's reign Ascham had devoted several pages of *The Schoolmaster* to a discussion of the different characteristics of 'quick wits' and 'hard wits',[1] and Lyly had made

[1] *The Schoolmaster* (1570, ed. Arber), pp. 32-36.

Euphues declaim on the theme that 'Education can have no show where the excellency of Nature doth bear sway'.[1] Each of these discussions finds a parallel in modern text-books of psychology. The debate on education versus nature proved of perennial interest, and fifty years later the subject was still being discussed.[2] Matters such as this were the object of considerable curiosity, and there were many who agreed with Bacon that 'The first article of this knowledge is to set down sound and true distributions and descriptions of the several characters and tempers of men's natures and dispositions; especially having regard to those differences which are most radical in being the fountains and causes of the rest, or most frequent in concurrence and commixture'.[3] The psychology which was used in this 'sound and true description' was of course based on the theory of humours, and the different characters of men were attributed to the various combinations of blood, phlegm, choler and melancholy.[4] The literature of humours is abundant, although one has to note that in the work of satirists such as Rowlands and Turner, who used the term frequently enough, there is little that shows any

[1] Lyly, *Euphues, Works* (ed. R. Warwick Bond), I, pp. 191 ff.

[2] Richard Brathwait devoted some twenty pages of *The English Gentleman* (1631) to the subject of 'Disposition', and concluded that 'Howsoever our dispositions may seem forced from what they naturally or originally were, it is but a deception, they remain still the same, though advice and assistance may sometimes prevail so much with them as for the time they seem to surcease and discontinue from their former bent; but returning afresh, they will Antaeus-like redouble their strength and become more furious' (p. 59). Brathwait does not seem too sure of himself; in the next section education is said to be able to change even a man's natural disposition. Cf. Peacham, *The Complete Gentleman* (1622, ed. G. S. Gordon), p. 221.

[3] *Advancement of Learning, Works* (ed. Ellis and Spedding), III, p. 434.

[4] An excellent account of the theory is given in Mr Percy Simpson's Introduction to his edition of *Every Man in his Humour*.

real knowledge of psychology. 'Humorous' characters such as Luke Frugal and Sir Giles Overreach, however, together with Jonson's knaves and fools, are psychological studies, simplified and distorted it is true, but nevertheless based on a subtle analysis of human impulses and emotions, and bearing witness to the pleasure taken by the age in what can only be called psychological analysis.

Similar evidence is provided by the numerous books of 'Characters' which appeared throughout the seventeenth century. Casaubon's edition of Theophrastus appeared in 1592 and the book seems to have been well known in England. Hall's *Characters of Virtues and Vices* was published in 1608, and was followed by Overbury's *Characters* (1614), Breton's *Characters* (1615) and Earle's *Microcosmography* (1628),[1] besides numerous essays in the same vein by other writers. The Character did not profess to be either realistic or exhaustive in its enumeration of traits, rather it was 'a picture (real or personal) quaintly drawn, in various colours, all of them heightened by one shadowing;'[2] it was, in short, the description of an individual in terms of his dominant mental features. It was pseudo-psychological, literary and 'conceited' rather than scientific, and it was remarked, 'This kind of observation wandereth in words, but is not fixed in inquiry'.[3] Nevertheless the interest was real and was well attested.

Naturally, therefore, the melancholy type received a good deal of attention. Melancholy had its picturesque features, it was easy to recognize, and at the same time it was important enough to justify serious study. Burton was far from being the only one who desired 'to anatomize

[1] All edited in *A Book of Characters*, by Richard Aldington (Broadway Translations).
[2] Overbury, *What a Character Is*.
[3] Bacon, *Advancement, Works* (ed. Ellis and Spedding), III, p. 435.

this humour of melancholy, through all his parts and species . . . to shew the causes, symptoms and several cures of it, that it may be the better avoided; moved thereunto for the generality of it, and to do good, it being a disease so frequent . . . as few there are that feel not the smart of it'.[1] It is significant that one of the most acute psychological observations is made in connexion with the same subject. John Earle describes 'A Discontented Man', in terms which Adler would probably approve, as 'one that is fallen out with the world, and will be revenged on himself. Fortune has denied him in something, and he now takes pet, and will be miserable in spite.'

Although many of the 'melancholy musings' of the reign of James I can be explained as due to a heightened consciousness of a common mode of feeling, seventeenth-century melancholy cannot be explained away. It is significant that the fact of death inspired many of the most eloquent passages in the literature of the time. The sermon which Donne preached on death in Lent 1622 is well known; so are the passages in Shakespeare which express the horror of the 'cold obstruction' of the grave; but even minor writers whose prose is normally quite undistinguished sometimes attain dignity when they consider the ultimate fate of men's bodies, 'cottages of corruption'. An ordinary moralist, unknown to the anthologies, is capable of writing:

> After all these things, what the Prophet hath threatened shall come upon you, and what shall then deliver you? not your beauty . . . nor honour, for that shall lie in the dust, and sleep in the bed of earth. Nor riches, for they shall not deliver you in the day of wrath. Perchance they may bring you, when you are dead, in a comely funeral sort to your grave, or bestow on you a few mourning garments, or erect

[1] *The Anatomy of Melancholy* (Bohn's Popular Library), I, pp. 137-138.

in your memory some gorgeous monument, to show your vain-glory in death, as well as in life; but this is all. Those riches which you got with such care, kept with such fear, lost with such grief, shall not afford you one comfortable hope in the hour of your passage hence; afflict they may, relieve they cannot. Nor friends, for all they can do is to attend you, and shed some friendly tears for you; but ere the rosemary lose her colour, which stickt the corse or one worm enter the shroud which covered the corpse, you are many times forgotten, your former glory extinguished, your eminent esteem obscured, your repute darkened, and with infamous aspersions often impeached.[1]

Prose of this kind, on such a subject and by such an author, could only have been written in the early seventeenth century.

The realization of death was one of the most important factors in producing melancholy. Men of the Middle Ages had also been fascinated by death, they too had expressed a macabre fancy in their religious symbols, and the inhabitants of fifteenth-century Paris had paraded for pleasure in the churchyard of the Innocents, in a cloister heaped with bones,[2] but they had not fallen victims to the kind of melancholy under discussion. The attitude of medieval men towards death was a mixture of pagan stoicism and Christian hope, and, although the delights of the world were as attractive then as at other times, it was a commonplace that

al nis but a fayre
This world, that passeth sone as floures fayre.

Death was accepted as a release from a world which with all its pleasures was only a testing place for the life to come. With the Renaissance this was changed. A humanistic scale of values was restored, and men justified their deeds in terms of this world rather than of the next. The world was

---

[1] R. Brathwait, *The English Gentleman* (1631), p. 21.
[2] See J. Huizinga, *The Waning of the Middle Ages*, chap. xi.

large and exciting, and Marlowe's aspiring heroes, Rabelais' Abbey of Theleme, Shakespeare's eulogy, 'What a piece of work is a man!...' (although it ends in disillusion), testify to a new belief in the powers of the human spirit.

In this world, when a humanistic philosophy was current, death appeared more terrible than in the past; and death continued to present itself with medieval horror and medieval frequency. On the Continent the sixteenth and seventeenth centuries were a period of almost continuous warfare, and both abroad and in England the plague continued to exact its enormous toll of human life. Those who are interested can find its visitations recorded in Creighton's *History of Epidemics*, but the accounts of eye-witnesses show far more vividly how contemporaries were impressed by the plague. The literary evidence is abundant but only two short accounts can be given. Nashe thus describes a town in which the plague was raging:

> All day and all night long car-men did nothing but go up and down the streets with their carts and cry, 'Have you any dead bodies to bury?' and had many times out of one house their whole lodging: one grave was the sepulchre of seven score, one bed was the altar whereon whole families were offered. The walls were hoared and furred with the moist scorching steam of their desolation. Even as before a gun is shot off, a stinking smoke funnels out and prepares the way for him, so before any gave up the ghost, death arrayed in a stinking smoke stopped his nostrils, and crammed itself full into his mouth that closed up his fellows eyes, to give him warning to prepare for his funeral. Some died sitting at their meat, others as they were asking counsel of the physician for their friends.[1]

[1] Nashe, *The Unfortunate Traveller* (1594), *Works* (ed. McKerrow, II, p. 286). Nashe is describing a plague which Jack Wilton encountered in Rome, but there is no doubt that he is drawing on his own experience in London during the bad plague year 1593. Compare his poem *In Time of Pestilence* (1593).

This is a restrained account: rhetoric could easily heighten the effect.

> He that durst, in the dead hour of gloomy midnight, have been so valiant as to have walked through the still and melancholy streets, what think you should have been his music? Surely the loud groans of raving sick men, the struggling pangs of souls departing; in every house grief striking up an alarum; servants crying out for masters, wives for husbands, parents for children, children for their mothers. Here he should have met some frantically running to knock up sextons, there, others fearfully sweating with coffins, to steal forth dead bodies, lest the fatal handwriting of death should seal up their doors. And to make this dismal concert more full, round about him bells heavily tolling in one place, and ringing out in another. The dreadfulness of such an hour is unutterable.[1]

When all allowance has been made for the exaggeration of the journalist, the fact remains that Elizabethan London was accustomed to horrors unknown to later ages. The family losses of Donne and Jonson were not exceptional, and the frequent death of children explains why, in spite of the number of births, the population of England increased so slowly.

Sudden death was too common for the Elizabethans to ignore it, and death was the end of humanistic aspirations.

> As the earth is compassed round with waters, so are we, the inhabitants thereof, compassed round with woes. We see great men die, strong men die, witty men die, fools die, rich merchants, poor artificers, ploughmen, gentlemen, high men, low men, gross men, and the fairest complexioned men die . . . King or Queen whatever, thou shalt die and be buried.[2]

[1] Dekker, *The Wonderful Year* (1603), *Non-Dramatic Works* (ed. Grosart), I, p. 105.

[2] Nashe, *Christ's Tears over Jerusalem*, *Works* (ed. McKerrow), II, pp. 90-91.

What a thing is the heart of man, that it should swell so big as the whole world.[1]

The frequent death of the young as well as the old served as a reminder that there was one barrier that could not be overcome. Men were forced to 'consider whereof they were made, and that the dust was their great grandmother',[2] and once more it appeared that

> The world to the circumference of Heaven
> Is as a small point in geometry,
> Whose greatness is so little, that a less
> Cannot be made.[3]

With the consciousness of his limitations Renaissance man became fully adult.

> Pour l'enfant amoureux de cartes et d'estampes,
> L'univers est égal a son vaste appétit.
> Ah! que le monde est grand à la clarté des lampes!
> Aux yeux du souvenir que le monde est petit!

The persistence of the plague and the consequent realization of man's impotence by a generation hitherto impressed by man's powers was undoubtedly one cause of early seventeenth-century melancholy; but it was not the sole or even the main cause. Man can adjust himself to the fact of death, he cannot adjust himself to a life disorganized and thwarted, and the root cause of melancholy and discontent is to be found in the social and economic conditions of the time. A study of these conditions suggests why melancholy entered on a new phase about the

---

[1] *Ibid.*, p. 83. Compare,
   And though mine arm should conquer twenty worlds
   There's a lean fellow beats all conquerors.
                                   (Dekker, *Old Fortunatus*, I, i.)
[2] Nashe, *ibid.*
[3] Dekker, *Old Fortunatus*, Act II, chorus.

year 1600. Even under Elizabeth the factors already noticed had helped to produce symptoms of melancholy in literature. By the 'nineties it had become an affectation:

> Young gentlemen would be as sad as night
> Only for wantonness.

But in the seventeenth century the note of melancholy suddenly deepened; and the reason for this, I believe, was that those social and economic factors then took their full effect.

Under James I, in each rank of society, there were men who by character and education were fitted, or considered themselves fitted, for a higher position than they were able to obtain. Under Elizabeth there had been a considerable increase of educational activity, with a consequent heightening of men's expectations. Even before the close of the sixteenth century there were more than a few who could find no definite place in the existing organization of the state, and with the coming of the Stuarts, and the ending of the war with Spain, many more felt themselves capable of undertaking tasks which they saw in the hands of favourites and jobbers.

In 1611 Bacon wrote to the King:

> Concerning the advancement of learning, I do subscribe to the opinion of one of the wisest and greatest of your Kingdom, that, for grammar schools, there are already too many, and therefore no providence to add where there is excess. For the great number of schools which are in your Highness's realm, doth cause a want, and likewise an overthrow: both of them inconvenient, and one of them dangerous; for by means thereof, they find want in the country and towns, both of servants for husbandry and apprentices for trade; and on the other side, *there being more scholars bred than the State can prefer and employ, and the active part of that life not bearing a proportion to the preparative, it must needs fall out that many persons will be bred unfit for other vocations, and unprofitable for that in which they were bred up, which fill the realm full of*

324

indigent, idle and wanton people, who are but materia rerum novarum.[1]

There is no need to stress the hardships of university men and the difficulty that they had in obtaining suitable employment. Apart from the fairly lucrative professions of medicine and the law, they might take orders and seek a benefice, become schoolmasters or private tutors, or become professional writers; if all else failed or if drawn by natural inclination they might remain at the university. None of these courses offered many opportunities of obtaining fame or riches. Headmasters of provincial schools rarely obtained more than £20 a year, and the normal salary for undermasters or ushers was £10. Private tutors fared even worse; Studioso in *The Return from Parnassus*, who is engaged to teach the son of a rich farmer, is treated as a menial and forced to wait at table and work in the fields all harvest time, besides having to endure the tyranny of a stupid pupil.[2] Preferment in the church was hard to obtain and was often dependent on the favour of a mercenary patron. In Elizabeth's reign Harrison had complained that men preferred to study physic and the law rather than the Scriptures, 'for fear lest they should in time not get their bread by the same',[3] and in 1621 Burton echoed the complaint against the ignorance and avarice of patrons.[4] The profession of letters offered no better opportunities. The days of generous patronage were over (if they ever existed), and not until the eighteenth century was it possible for a writer to expect a regular livelihood from his pen. From the time of the University Wits dramatists had led a precarious existence, and Jonson's poverty and Dekker's long imprisonment for debt show how little was to be

[1] Spedding, *Life of Bacon*, IV, pp. 252-253.
[2] Part I, Act II, lines 638-817.
[3] 'Description of England' (ed. Furnivall), p. 37.
[4] Burton, *Anatomy* (Bohn's Popular Library), I, pp. 361 ff.

expected from the stage. Poets of any social standing were not expected to sell their verses, and poets lower in the social scale—minor satirists, ballad makers, pamphleteers and hacks—were at the mercy of publishers and plagiarists. As for the scholar's last resource, the university, says Academico, 'The university is a melancholic life . . . but the point is, I know not how to better myself, and so I am fain to take it.'[1] The general conclusion was

> Let scholars be as thrifty as they may
> They will be poor ere their last dying day;
> Learning and poverty will ever kiss.[2]

> Mechanic arts may smile, their followers laugh,
> But liberal arts bewail their destiny,[3]

for, 'The world is bad, and scholars are ordained to be beggars'.[4] These quotations are from the pen of a satirist, but it does not appear that in bewailing the lot of scholars he was unduly exaggerating their fate. In consequence disappointed scholars turned malcontents and satirists. 'Most other trades and professions, after some seven years' prenticeship, are enabled by their craft to live of themselves. . . . Only scholars are most uncertain, unrespected, subject to all casualities, and hazard',[5] so, 'Their Rhetoric only serves them to curse their bad fortunes'.[6]

---

[1] *The Return from Parnassus*, Part II, v, iii. There is no evidence to show that conditions had improved since Harrison wrote, 'It is a hard matter for a poor man's child to come by a fellowship, though he be never so good a scholar, and worthy of that room' (*Description of England*, ed. Furnivall, p. 77).

[2] *The Pilgrimage to Parnassus*, I, lines 74-75.

[3] *The Return from Parnassus*, Part I, III, lines 1092-1093.

[4] *Ibid.*, I, line 382.

[5] Burton, *Anatomy* (Bohn), I, p. 354.

[6] *Ibid.*, p. 357. On the whole subject see the Parnassus Plays (1598-1602), Burton, *Anatomy of Melancholy* (1621), Part I, section II, mem. iii, subs. xv, 'Study a cause of Melancholy', and P. Sheavyn, *The Literary Profession in the Elizabethan Age*, Introduction and chaps. i, iii and v.

Scholars and writers were not the only discontented members of the commonwealth. Those who sought a public career were just as likely to have their hopes thwarted, or if they achieved success it was only after long years of disappointment and delay. 'The reign of Queen Elizabeth', says Sir Egerton Brydges, soberly, 'was a period of difficulty for the individuals whom it excited to fame and distinction, in which was cherished an emulation of great things with insufficient means'.[1] The remark applies equally to the reign of James I, except that the standard of luxury expected from courtiers and public men was raised, and there was less chance than formerly of merit obtaining its reward. It was a frequent complaint of satirists that at court desert went unrewarded, and that wealth and a flattering tongue were the first requisites of a courtier, and the 'advancement of unworthy persons' by James I is well known.

Apart from the army and the learned professions an administrative career was the only one open to men of education and social standing, and there was a far greater number of aspirants than there were places for them to fill. Sir John Harington was a godson of Queen Elizabeth, a wit, a poet, and a man of considerable ability, yet he spent his life in looking for the preferment which he considered his due and which never came. In his 'Brief Notes and Remembrances' (1594–1603) he writes, 'I have spent my time, my fortune, and almost my honesty, to buy false hopes, false friends and shallow praise'.[2] He tried all ways to obtain advancement, paraded his wit for Queen Elizabeth, flattered King James, and at the age of forty-five was prepared to take orders if the vacant archbishopric of Dublin could be obtained for him, but all was in vain.

---

[1] Preface to Breton's *Melancholic Humours* (ed. 1815), p. 4.
[2] *Nugae Antiquae* (ed. 1804), I, p. 168.

'Now what findeth he who loveth the pride of life, the Court's vanity, ambition's puff ball? In sooth, no more than empty words, grinning scoff, watching nights and fawning days'.[1]

The first forty years of Bacon's life show the same succession of promises and disappointments accompanied by poverty. It is impossible to read Bacon's letters during the period when he was seeking advancement without realizing that the small measure of success which followed the highest aspirations was a fundamental cause of melancholy and discontent. Indeed Bacon himself is explicit. When he was beginning to give up hope of the Solicitorship he wrote to Essex, 'I humbly pray your lordship to pardon me for troubling you with my melancholy';[2] and some time later, when the appointment was still unbestowed, he declared, 'This is a course to quench all good spirits, and to corrupt every man's nature'.[3] Political discontent was common; from the Earl of Essex downwards there were many who knew that their natural abilities were not being used as they might be by the state; unexercised they became restless, and unrewarded, melancholy. Donne's letters in the period between his marriage and his ordination show how mere poverty can distort the outlook and depress the spirit. There is no need to-day to emphasize the miseries of unemployment.[4]

Although the economic cause of seventeenth-century melancholy is rarely mentioned in modern accounts of the

[1] *Nugae Antiquae* (ed. 1804), I, p. 170. See also the Introduction to his *Letters and Epigrams*, ed. N. E. McClure.

[2] Spedding, *Letters and Life*, I, p. 291.

[3] *Ibid.*, p. 359.

[4] It should be remembered that men matured more quickly then than now, and that a man was expected to be 'settled in life' at an earlier age. When thirty-one years old Bacon wrote, 'I am now somewhat ancient', and at forty-five Harington considered himself 'old and infirm'.

subject, contemporaries were well aware of the danger of over-education and thwarted ambition. In chapter xxxvi of his *Positions* (1581) Mulcaster declared that it was dangerous for a commonwealth to have either too few learned or too many:

> Too many burdens any state too far, for want of provision. For the rooms which are to be supplied by learning being within number, if they that are to supply them grow on beyond number, how can it be but too great a burden for any state to bear? To have so many gaping for preferment, as no gulf hath store enough to suffice, and to let them roam helpless whom nothing else can help, how can it be but that such shifters must needs shake the very strongest pillar in that state where they live, and loiter without living? [1]

The danger was not confined to any one rank of society. If tradesmen's sons are allowed to learn Latin they will not be willing to follow their fathers' occupations:

> For all the fear is, though it be more than fear where it still falleth out so, lest having such benefits of school they will not be content with the state which is for them, but because they have some petty smack of their book, they will think any state, be it never so high, low enough for them.[2]

Thereupon they become dangerous members of the commonwealth: 'For youth being let go forward upon hope, and checked with despair while it roameth without purveyance, makes marvellous ado before it will die'.[3] Bacon's opinion has been quoted, and the *Essays* utter the same warning as the letter to the King. It is dangerous for the State 'when more are bred scholars than preferments can take off'.[4] 'Ambitious men, if they find the way open for their rising, and still get forward, they are rather busy than dangerous; but if they be checked in their desires, they

[1] *'Positions'* (ed. R. H. Quick), p. 135.   [2] *Ibid.*, p. 144.
[3] *Ibid.*, p. 166.   [4] *Essays*, 'Of Seditions'.

become secretly discontent, and look upon men and matters with an evil eye'.[1] Similarly Harington wrote concerning Essex, 'It resteth with me in opinion, that ambition thwarted in its career doth speedily lead to madness'.[2] Discontent with one's fortunes was generally regarded as a cause of melancholy or madness; the occasion, said Earle, is 'commonly one of these three, a hard father, a peevish wench, or ambition thwarted'.[3] The malcontents of the drama frequently owed their melancholy to the same causes. In *The White Devil* Flamineo is disgusted by his own poverty and dependence: 'O, 'tis a brave thing for a man to sit by himself (in the saddle)! he may stretch himself in the stirrups, look about, and see the whole compass of the hemisphere'.[4] In *The Revenger's Tragedy* Vendice speaks of 'discontent, the noble man's consumption';[5] and Jonson describes Macilente as, 'A man well parted, a sufficient scholar, and travelled; who, wanting that place in the world which he thinks his merit capable of, falls into an envious apoplexy'.[6]

This section may be closed by a quotation from *The Worth of a Penny, or a Caution to keep Money*, by Henry Peacham the Younger, which forms an interesting addition to the gallery of seventeenth-century 'Characters':

> He that wanteth money is for the most part extremely melancholy in every company or alone by himself, especially if the weather be foul, rainy or cloudy, Talk to him of what you will, he will hardly give you the hearing; ask him any questions, he answers you in monosyllables. . . . He walks with his arms folded, his belt without a sword or rapier, that

[1] *Essays*, 'Of Ambition'.
[2] *Nugae Antiquae* (ed. 1804), I, p. 179.
[3] Earle, *Microcosmography*, 'A Discontented Man'.
[4] *White Devil*, V, iv.   [5] *Revenger's Tragedy*, I, i.
[6] *Every Man out of his Humour*, Folio, 'The Characters of the Persons'.

perhaps being somewhere in trouble, hat without a band, hanging over his eyes, only it wears a weather-beaten fancy for fashion's sake. He cannot stand still, but like one of the Tower wild beasts is still walking from one end of his room to another, humming out some new Northern tune or other. If he meets with five or ten pieces, happily conferred upon him by the beneficence of some noble friend or other, he is become a new man, and so overjoyed with his fortune that not one drop of small drink will down with him all that day.[1]

By 1647 when this was written the connexion between poverty and the melancholic mood had become proverbial, —a sort of music-hall joke. Indeed the connexion is so obvious that it is difficult to understand why it has been so constantly overlooked. 'Augent animos fortunae saith the Mimist, and very truly, for nothing pulleth down a man's heart so much as adversity and lack.' [2]

In the economic and social organization of the state the early seventeenth century was a period of transition. The relatively stable medieval society had decayed, and the new economy was not yet understood. Throughout the six-teenth century the Tudors had followed a policy of encouraging the middle classes, but by 1600 neither the new aristocracy nor the new commercial classes had altogether adjusted themselves to the changed conditions. The beginnings of the Industrial Revolution can be traced to this period, but commerce and industry were not yet sufficiently developed (nor always sufficiently reputable) to provide attractive careers. 'They are happy men', said Bacon 'whose natures sort with their vocations.' Inevitably at this time there were many whose occupations were uncongenial, who were dependent upon precarious and ill-paid

[1] *The Worth of a Penny*, pp. 14-15.
[2] Puttenham, *Art of English Poesy*, Book I, chap. xx.

331

professions, or who were unemployed. And under James I non-material causes increased the general unrest. Until about 1599 there had been a constant threat of a Spanish invasion.[1] Under Charles I constitutional issues became important and once more, on one side or the other, men found occupation and—many of them—ideals. But between these periods no great national question focused the attention of all, and the court of James I was not an inspiring centre of the national life. The literary expression of melancholy was in part the result of this combination of circumstances.

(1933)

[1] At the time men were impressed by the dangers of peace rather than by its blessings, and many evils, economic and moral, were attributed to 'peaceful times . . . the nurse of pride and idleness, wherein people increase yet hardly get employment' (Peacham, *The Worth of a Penny*, p. 4). 'Peace draweth the very corruption of manners after it, and there is nothing that brings so sweet and easy a subjection to vice as the season and idleness of peace' (Rich, *Faults, Faults, and Nothing Else but Faults* (1606), p. 53). Turner, *Nosce Te (Humours)* (1607)—Sig. A 3—ends a description of riotous townsmen with

O had we never ended Spanish jars
Then these had never been our English wars.

Cf. also Bacon, *Essays*, 'Of the True Greatness of Kingdoms' ('A foreign war is like the heat of exercise, and serveth to keep the body in health', etc.); and Brathwait, *A Strappado for the Devil* (1615), p. 15.

BIBLIOGRAPHY

(I have not listed here historical or critical works that have not a direct bearing on the Elizabethan-Jacobean period, or the works of dramatists not discussed in Part II or the Appendices. (REF) following an entry means that the book has been used for reference.)

ECONOMIC AND GENERAL HISTORY

Ashley, W. J., *An Introduction to English Economic History and Theory*, Part I, The Middle Ages; Part II, The End of the Middle Ages.

Burgon, J. W., *The Life and Times of Sir Thomas Gresham*, 2 Vols.

Cheyney, E. P., *A History of England from the Defeat of the Armada to the Death of Elizabeth*, 2 Vols.

Social Changes in England in the Sixteenth Century, as Reflected in Contemporary Literature, Part I, Rural Changes. (No other part published.)

Cunningham, W., *The Growth of English Industry and Commerce, The Middle Ages* (4th edn., 1905).

The Growth of English Industry and Commerce, Modern Times, Part I, The Mercantile System (5th edn., 1912).

Dictionary of National Biography. (REF)

Dodd, A. H., 'The Story of an Elizabethan Monopoly, 1585–1823', *Economica*, Vol. IX, 1929.

Durham, F. H., *The Relations of the Crown to Trade under James I* (Transactions of the Royal Historical Society, New Series, XIII).

Ehrenberg, Richard, *Capital and Finance in the Age of the Renaissance*, translated by Mrs H. M. Lucas.

Febvre, Lucien, 'Les Nouveaux Riches et l'histoire', *Revue des cours et conférences*, 15 juin 1922.

Friis, Astrid, *Alderman Cockayne's Project and the Cloth Trade, The Commercial Policy of England in its Main Aspects, 1603–1625*.

Hall, Hubert, *Society in the Elizabethan Age*.

Hamilton, Earl J., 'American Treasure and the Rise of Capitalism', *Economica*, Vol. IX, Nov. 1929.

American Treasure and the Price Revolution in Spain, 1501–1650. (REF)

Harrison, G. B., *Elizabethan Journals, 1591–1603*, 3 Vols.   (REF)

Heckscher, Eli F., *Mercantilism*, trans. Mendel Shapiro, 2 Vols.

Holdsworth, W. S., *A History of English Law*, Vols. IV and V.   (REF)

Keynes, J. M., *A Treatise on Money*, Vol. II, Chap. 30, 'Spanish Treasure'.

Kovalevsky, M., *Originating Phases in the Development of a Capitalistic Economy* (Chap. I translated for me by Prof. Trofimov).

Levy, Hermann, *Monopolies, Cartels and Trusts in British Industry*.

Liljegren, S. B., *The Fall of the Monasteries and the Social Changes in England leading up to the Great Revolution*.

Lipson, E., *An Economic History of England*, Vols. II and III, *The Age of Mercantilism*.

Palgrave, *Dictionary of Political Economy*. (REF)

Price, W. H., *The English Patents of Monopoly*.

Robertson, H. M., *Aspects of the Rise of Economic Individualism, A Criticism of Max Weber and his School*.
'Sir Bevis Bulmer, A Large-Scale Speculator of Elizabethan and Jacobean Times', *Journal of Economic and Business History*, Vol. IV, Nov. 1931.

Sargent, Ralph M., *At the Court of Queen Elizabeth, The Life and Lyrics of Sir Edward Dyer*.

Scott, W. R., *The Constitution and Finance of English, Scottish and Irish Joint-Stock Companies to 1720*, 3 Vols.

Shakespeare's England, 2 Vols., especially 'Commerce and Coinage', by George Unwin, and 'Education', by Sir J. E. Sandys.

Sombart, Werner, *The Quintessence of Capitalism*, translated and edited by M. Epstein.

Tawney, R. H., *The Agrarian Problem in the Sixteenth Century*. *Religion and the Rise of Capitalism*.
See Wilson, Thomas, under 'Contemporary'.

Taylor, E. G. R., *Late Tudor and Early Stuart Geography, 1583–1650*. (REF)

Taylor, G. R. Stirling, *A Modern History of England, 1485–1932, A Study in Politics, Economics and Ethics*.

Traill, H. D., and Mann, J. S., *Social England* (Illustrated edn., 1901), 6 Vols. (REF)

Trevelyan, G. M., *England under the Stuarts*.

Unwin, George, *The Gilds and Companies of London*.
Industrial Organization in the Sixteenth and Seventeenth Centuries.
Introduction to *The Early English Cotton Industry*, by G. W. Daniels (Publications of the University of Manchester, Historical Series, no. XXXVI).

Verney, F. P., and Verney, M. M., *Memoirs of the Verney Family during the Seventeenth Century*.

Weber, Max, *The Protestant Ethic and the Spirit of Capitalism*, tr. Talcott Parsons.

BIBLIOGRAPHY

Wood, H. G., 'The Influence of the Reformation on Ideas Concerning Wealth and Property', in *Property, Its Duties and Rights*.

CONTEMPORARY

Acts of the Privy Council, ed. Dasent. (REF)

Ascham, R., *The Scholemaster* (1570) (Arber Reprint).

Aylett, Robert, *Peace with her foure gardens* (1622).

Bacon, *Collected Works*, with his Letters and Life, ed. Spedding, Ellis and Heath, 14 Vols.
  Advancement of Learning (Everyman edn.).
  Essays (Everyman edn.).
  New Atlantis, ed. Henry Morley, in *Ideal Commonwealths*.

Becon, Thomas, *Works* (Parker Society), 3 Vols. (REF)

Brathwait, Richard, *A Strappado for the Divell* (1615), ed. J. W. Ebsworth.
  (pseud., 'Musophilus'), *The Good Wife* (1618).
  (pseud, 'Clitus Alexandrinus'), *Whimzies, or a New Cast of Characters* (1631).
  The English Gentleman (1630), 2nd edn., 1633.
  The English Gentlewoman (1631).
  Art asleepe Husband? A Boulster Lecture (1640).
  The Card of Courtship, or The Language of Love (1653).

Breton, Nicholas, *Melancholike Humours* (1600), ed. Sir Egerton Brydges (1815), and G. B. Harrison (1929).

Bullinger, Henry, *Decades* (Parker Society). (REF)

Burton, *The Anatomy of Melancholy* (Bohn edn.), 3 Vols.

Calendar of State Papers, Domestic. (REF)

Carew, Richard, *The Survey of Cornwall* (1602).

Chamberlen, Peter, *The Poore Man's Advocate or England's Samaritan* (1649).

'*Characters*', *A Book of*, ed. Richard Aldington (contains Hall's *Characters of Virtues and Vices*, 1608, Overbury's *Characters*, 1614, Earle's *Microcosmography*, 1628, etc.).

Crowley, Robert, *Select Works*, ed. J. M. Cowper (E.E.T.S.).

Davies, Sir John, *Epigrams*, ed. C. Edmonds.

Davies, John, of Hereford, *Works*, ed. Grosart, 2 Vols.

Deloney, *Works*, ed. F. O. Mann.

D'Ewes, Sir Simonds, *Autobiography*, ed. Halliwell, 2 Vols.

Discourse of the Married and Single Life (1621).

Donne, John, *Fifty Sermons* (1649) (Sermons I, II, III, V, VIII).

Elizabethan Critical Essays, ed. Gregory Smith, 2 Vols.

English Critical Essays, XVI-XVIII Centuries, ed. E. D. Jones (World's Classics).

First Newspapers of England, Printed in Holland, 1620–21, ed. W. P. Van Stockum.

Fuller, Thomas, *The Holy and Profane State* (1642).

Greene, R., *A Quippe for an Upstart Courtier* (1592), *Works*, ed. Grosart, Vol. XI.

Greevous Grones for the Poore (1621).

H[eath], J[ohn], *The House of Correction* (1619).

H. T., *A Ha! Christmas. . . .* Here is proved the cause of Free-Will Offerings, and to be liberall to the poore . . . taken and proven out of Scripture (1647).

Hannay, Patrick, *A Happy Husband, or Directions for a Maid to Choose her Mate* (1618).

Harington, Sir John, *Letters and Epigrams*, ed. N. E. McClure. *Nugae Antiquae*, edn. of 1804, 2 Vols.

Harrison, William, *Description of England*, Books II and III (1577), ed. Furnivall, with the additions of 1587.

Herbert of Cherbury, Lord, *Autobiography*, ed. Sidney Lee.

Hooper, *Works* (Parker Society). (REF)

Latimer, *Works* (Parker Society), 2 Vols. (REF)

Lawe's Resolution of Womens Rights: or, The Lawe's Provision for Women (1632).

Lyly, *Euphues, The Anatomy of Wit* (1578), *Euphues and his England* (1580) (Arber Reprints).

Malynes, Gerard de, *Saint George for England* (1601). *A Treatise of the Canker of England's Commonwealth* (1601). *The Maintenance of Free Trade* (1622). *The Centre of the Circle of Commerce* (1623).

Milles, T., *The Custumer's Alphabet and Primer* (1608).

Misselden, E., *Free Trade, or The Means to Make Trade Flourish* (1622). *The Circle of Commerce, or the Ballance of Trade, in Defence of Free Trade* (1623). (REF)

Mulcaster, Richard, *Positions* (1581), ed. R. H. Quick. *The First Part of the Elementarie* (1582), ed. E. T. Campagnac.

'Munda, Constantia', *The Worming of a Mad Dogge: or, a Soppe for Cerberus* (1617).

Nashe, Thomas, *Works*, ed. McKerrow, 5 Vols.

Niccholes, Alex., *A Discourse of Marriage and Wiving* (1615), edn. of 1620.

Overbury, Sir Thomas, *The Wife* (1614).

Peacham, Henry (the younger), *The Compleat Gentleman* (1622), ed. G. S. Gordon. *The Worth of a Penny, or a Caution to Keep Money* (1647, probably = 1641).

BIBLIOGRAPHY

Percy, Henry, ninth Earl of Northumberland, *Advice to his Son* (1609), ed. with a biographical introduction by G. B. Harrison.

Perkins, William, *Christian Oeconomie: Or a Short Summary of the Right Manner of Erecting and Ordering a Family, according to the Scriptures*, trans. Thomas Pickering (*Works*, 1618, Vol. III).

Rich, Barnaby, *Faultes, Faultes, and nothing else but Faultes* (1606). *My Ladies Looking Glass* (1616) (partly a reprint of *Faultes, Faultes*, with additional matter).
The Excellency of Good Women (1613).

Rowlands, Samuel, *The Letting of Humours Blood in the Head-Vaine* (1600).

Saltonstall, Wye, *Picturae Loquentes* (1631).

Selden, *Table Talk* (Temple Classics).

Smith, Sir Thomas, *De Republica Anglorum* (1583), ed. L. Alston.

Smyth, John, of Nibley, *The Berkeley Manuscripts*, ed. Sir John Maclean (1883), 3 Vols. (Vols. I and II, *The Lives of the Berkeleys*, 1066–1618; Vol. III, *A Description of the Hundred of Berkeley and of its Inhabitants*).

'Sowerman, Ester' (pseud.), *Ester hath hang'd Haman* (1617).

Speght, Rachel, *A Mouzell for Melastomus* (1617).

Swetnam, Joseph (pseud., 'Thomas Teltroth'), *The Arraignment of Lewd, Idle, Froward, and Unconstant Women* (1615).

Swetnam, The Woman Hater, Arraigned by Women, A New Comedie, Acted at the Red Bull (1620), ed. Grosart (1880).

Swinburne, Henry, *A Treatise of Spousals or Matrimonial Contracts* (1686, written c. 1600).

Tudor Economic Documents, ed. R. H. Tawney and Eileen Power, 3 Vols.

Turner, Richard, *Nosce Te (Humors)*, 1607.

Tyndale, William, *Works* (Parker Society), 3 Vols. (REF)

Whateley, William, *A Bride Bush, or a Direction for Married Persons* (1623).

Wilson, Thomas, *A Discourse upon Usury* (1572), edited, with an Introduction by R. H. Tawney.

THE DRAMATISTS

Beaumont and Fletcher, *Works*, Variorum Edition (1904), 4 Vols. (not completed).

Beaumont, *The Knight of the Burning Pestle*, in *Six Plays by Contemporaries of Shakespeare*, ed. C. B. Wheeler (World's Classics).

Brome, *Dramatic Works* (Pearson Reprints), 3 Vols.

Dekker, *Dramatic Works*, ed. R. H. Shepherd (Pearson Reprints), 4 Vols.
Best Plays of, ed. Ernest Rhys (Mermaid Edition).
Non-Dramatic Works, ed. Grosart, 5 Vols.
Famous Victories of Henry the Fifth, The.
Greene, R., *George a Greene, The Pinner of Wakefield.*
Haughton, William, *Englishmen for my Money* (Dodsley, *Old Plays*, ed. Hazlitt, Vol. X).
Heywood, T., *Dramatic Works* (Pearson Reprints), 6 Vols.
Best Plays of, ed. A. W. Verity (Mermaid Edition).
A Curtaine Lecture (1637).
Gynaikeion, or Nine Bookes of Various History Concerning Women (1624).
Jonson, *Works*, ed. Gifford, Cunningham (1875), 9 Vols.
Every Man in his Humour, ed. P. Simpson.
Discoveries, ed. M. Castelain.
Jonson, Chapman, and Marston, *Eastward Ho!* ed. F. L. Schelling (Belles Lettres Dramatists).
Massinger, *Plays*, ed. Gifford (1805), 4 Vols.
Merry Devil of Edmonton, ed. Hugh Walker (Temple Dramatists).
Middleton, *Works*, ed. Bullen (1885), 8 Vols.
(Peele), *Locrine* (*Shakespeare Apocrypha*, ed. C. F. T. Brooke).
Pilgrimage to Parnassus, and *The Return from Parnassus*, ed. W. D. Macray.
Representative English Comedies, ed. C. M. Gayley, 3 Vols.
Shirley, *Best Plays of*, ed. Edmund Gosse (Mermaid Edition).
Thomas, Lord Cromwell (*Shakespeare Apocrypha*, ed. C. F. T. Brooke).
Wilkins, *The Miseries of Enforced Marriage* (Dodsley, *Old Plays*, ed. Hazlitt, Vol. IX).

CRITICISM AND LITERARY HISTORY

Bapst, G., *Essai sur l'histoire du théâtre*. (REF)
Barrett, W. P., *Chart of Plays, 1584–1623* (for the Shakespeare Association).
Beljame, Alexandre, *Le Public et les hommes de lettres en Angleterre au dix-huitième siècle, 1660–1744.*
Bradbrook, M. C., *Themes and Conventions of Elizabethan Tragedy.*
Cambridge History of English Literature, Vols. III, IV, V, VI. (REF)
Castelain, M., *Ben Jonson, l'homme et l'œuvre.*
Chambers, E. K., *The Elizabethan Stage*, 4 Vols.
Clark, A. M., *Thomas Hewyood, Playwright and Miscellanist.*
Coleridge, *Lectures and Notes on Shakespeare, etc.* (Bohn edn.).

BIBLIOGRAPHY

Cruickshank, A. H., *Philip Massinger.*

Deane, C. V., *Dramatic Theory and the Rhymed Heroic Play.*

Eliot, T. S., *The Sacred Wood* (2nd edn., 1928).
Selected Essays.
Elizabethan Essays.

Gregg, K. L., *Thomas Dekker, A Study in Economic and Social Backgrounds.*

Harrison, G. B., and Granville-Barker, H., *A Companion to Shakespeare Studies.*

Herford, C. H., and Simpson, Percy, *Ben Jonson*, Vols. I and II, *The Man and His Work.*

Leavis, Q. D., *Fiction and the Reading Public.*

Lynch, Kathleen M., *The Social Mode of Restoration Comedy.*

Owst, G. R., *Literature and Pulpit in Medieval England.*

Palmer, J., *Ben Jonson.*

Schelling, Felix E., *Elizabethan Drama*, 1558–1642, 2 Vols.
The English Chronicle Play.

Seccombe, Thomas, and Allen, J. W., *The Age of Shakespeare* (1579–1631), 2 Vols.   (REF)

Sheavyn, Phoebe, *The Literary Profession in the Elizabethan Age.*

Sisson, Charles J., *Le Goût public et le théâtre elisabéthain jusqu'à la mort de Shakespeare.*

Symmes, H. S., *Les Débuts de la critique dramatique en Angleterre.*

INDEX

INDEX

Smythe, Sir Thomas, 93-94
Social Theory, 140-168
Sombart, W., 49 n., 61 n., 121 n.
Southampton, Earl of, 52
Speirs, John, 192 n.
Spenser, Edmund, 171
Stoddard, George, 94
Stow, John, 237, 244
Strachey, John, 2
Swinburne, A. C., 259
Swinburne, Henry, 120
Symes, J. E., 131 n.

TASTE, Indications of Elizabethan and Jacobean, 10-11, 141-142, 228 ff., 243 ff., 312-313; changing in the seventeenth century, 292, 298-300
Tawney, R. H., 20, 41, 42 n., 45 n., 51 n., 98, 99, 100, 103, 107, 128 n., 130 n., 140 n., 142, 145, 151 n., 154 n., 155, 161 n., 162, 164, 165 n., 167, 171, 177, 230
Taylor, E. G. R., 50 n.
Taylor, G. R. Stirling, 32 n., 52 n.
Tin-Mining, 64-65, 89
Tourneur, Cyril, 10, 294, 316, 330
Trade Depressions, 130-139
Trade, Overseas, 47-58
Tradition, 6-7, 17, 20-21, 22, 27, 55-56, 111, 140-141, 160, 174, 177, 179 ff., 188, 202, 232, 241, 254, 280, 292, 313
Trevelyan, G. M., 145 n.
Trigge, Francis, 142 n.
Turner, Richard, 317, 332 n.

UNEMPLOYMENT, 98, 130-139, 324-325, 328
Unwin, G., 17 n., 18 n., 19 n., 23, 24 n., 25, 26 n., 27, 28, 72, 73, 75 n., 77 n., 78 n., 85 n., 88 n., 120, 131, 132 n., 137 n., 148 n., 160 n., 163, 212, 215
Usury, 127-130, 146, 151, 162, 164-168, 175, 176, 192, 254, 262, 263

VERNEY, SIR EDMUND, 80 n.
Verney Family, the, 107, 111 n., 126 n.
Vetus Comoedia, 188
Vocation, 146-148, 152

WAGES, 37; Regulation of, 162
War, 38-43, 62, 134, 172, 324, 332n.
Warner, William, 244
Watson, Foster, 247 n.
Wealth, Attitudes towards, 152-156, 232-236, 252, 254 n., 279-280, 288-291 (see Anti-Acquisitive Attitude)
Weber, Max, 108 n., 126 n.
Webster, John, 101 n., 233-234, 280 n., 316, 330
Wells, H. G., 312
Whateley, William, 141 n.
Wheeler, John, 48 n., 50 n., 56 n.
Whig View of History, 31
Wilkins, George, The Miseries of Enforced Marriage, 6, 127 n.
Wilson, Thomas, 51
Winchcombe, John, 59
'Wit', 197
Wolsey, Cardinal, 160 n.
Woolf, Virginia, 314
Woollen, Industry, 34, 58-63, 167, 174 (see Cloth Trade)

YEATS, W. B., 11